The Non-Modern Crisis
of the Modern University

The Non-Modern Crisis of the Modern University

✦

Willy Thayer

Translated from the Spanish by D. Bret Leraul

NORTHWESTERN UNIVERSITY PRESS

EVANSTON, ILLINOIS

Northwestern University Press
www.nupress.northwestern.edu

Cover art by Gonzalo Díaz, *The Non-Modern Crisis of Modern Art*, 2018,
Santiago. From a graphic series of eight plates created for this book in its 2019
Spanish-language edition. Courtesy of the artist.

An extension of this copyright page appears beginning on page 181.

Printed in the United States of America

10   9   8   7   6   5   4   3   2   1

Library of Congress Cataloging-in-Publication Data

Names: Thayer, Willy, author. | Leraul, D. Bret, translator.
Title: The non–modern crisis of the modern university / Willy Thayer ; translated
   from the Spanish by D. Bret Leraul.
Other titles: Crisis no moderna de la universidad moderna. English
Description: Evanston : Northwestern University Press, 2024. | Includes
   bibliographical references and index.
Identifiers: LCCN 2024031406 | ISBN 9780810146846 (paperback) | ISBN
   9780810146853 (cloth) | ISBN 9780810146860 (ebook)
Subjects: LCSH: Education, Higher—Philosophy. | Education, Higher—Social
   aspects.
Classification: LCC LB2322.2 .T4313 2024 | DDC 378.001—dc23/eng/20240703
LC record available at https://lccn.loc.gov/2024031406

CONTENTS

Translator's Introduction: Untimely, Uneven, Combined   *vii*

I. The Non-Modern Crisis of the Modern University

1. A Few Things That Must Be Stated   *3*

2. From the Epic to Kitsch, from Enthusiasm to Boredom   *33*

3. "Our" Actual Faculties of Philosophy   *43*

II. University, Universality, and Languages

4. *Transcendentia*, the Medieval University, and the Missionary Structure of the University (A Sketch)   *55*

5. The Modern Franco-Cartesian-Napoleonic-Comtean University   *61*

6. The University of Berlin: The Modern, Philosophical, German University   *77*

7. Kant's Architectonics   *83*

8. Nietzsche: From the Faculty of Philosophy to the Faculty of Genealogy   *89*

III. The Non-Modern Transition of the Modern University

9. Transition from State to Market   *105*

10. The Categorial Crisis of the University   *115*

IV. Pinochet's Signature

Afterword to the Second Edition   *137*

Notes   141

Bibliography   173

Credits   181

Index   183

Untimely, Uneven, Combined

Untimeliness

The modern university is untimely. It is an institution woven of competing and often contradictory visions of pasts and futures. As an educational institution entrusted with the reproduction of a culture through its youth, it bears hopes for the future. As a knowledge institution, it is entrusted with gathering and preserving traces of the past that are then woven into new knowledges and new narratives. Like the head of Janus—the Roman god of thresholds, frames, beginnings and ends—it looks in two directions at once. Or else, like Walter Benjamin's angel of history, it looks upon the past as an unending catastrophe even as it is pulled inexorably into the future.[1] The modern university's double face or double movement figures at once the seamless succession of generations, the forward march of chronological time and the disjuncture of a kairological time, a time just in time that feels somehow always out of joint, not yet or too late.[2]

Like the institution it addresses, Willy Thayer's *The Non-Modern Crisis of the Modern University* is an untimely text—a threshold, a frame, a beginning that is at once an end. The untimeliness of its object is announced in its title: the mismatch between the university's modern form and its non-modern crisis. This is not a postmodern crisis, as Jean-François Lyotard famously asserted. The "postmodern" implies a modern, historicist figuration of time as chronological succession of epochs and events. The untimeliness of the crisis of the university today is as much epistemological as it is historical—not *post*modern but *non*-modern.

> We are not dealing with a conceptual crisis in the face of the eruption of a new, substitute university categorization, the emergence and repositioning of one discourse upon the demise of another. Instead, we are dealing with the crisis of discourse, of the categorial full stop. . . . We lack the categories for analyzing the event of the crisis of the categories, including the category of "crisis" that runs throughout this text. (36)

For this reason, perhaps the text's untimeliness is more accurately captured by Thayer's more polysemic term *inactualidad*, or inactuality—that is, at once historically out of date, temporally out of joint, and virtual, unreal, or not yet actualized or instantiated.[3]

This second, more epistemological acceptation of untimeliness as inactuality is borne in the notion of crisis announced by the title and also throughout by the recurring question concerning critique. The word "crisis" entered vernacular European languages through the field of medicine, which had conserved the term in Galen's treatises, which governed medical practice in Europe for almost 1,500 years. Crisis in this medical sense is at once a physical state and the judgment about that physical state that decides whether a patient lives or dies. Crisis is the razor's edge, the moment of suspension before the decision, before the event, the space of the virtual, the interregnum.

We know that the terms "crisis" and "critique" share an etymology, a metaphorology, a conceptual history going back at least to the Ancient Greek verb *krino*, which signifies "to separate, choose, judge, decide, dispute."[4] Critique is also the watchword of modern philosophy in the wake of Kant's Copernican revolution and therefore a watchword of the modern university under its German aspect.[5] *The Non-Modern Crisis of the Modern University* tells us that the crisis of modern crisis is also the non-modern crisis of modern critique, the non-modern crisis of modern categories that once demarcated the conditions of possibility of critique as the condition of possibility of knowledge in general. But without falling into gross contradiction, Thayer cannot step back like a Descartes or a Kant in order to gain the critical distance needed for a discursive accounting of the university and its knowledges.[6] Thayer's text cannot be a critique of this or any other university, just as it cannot be the history of its idea. Instead, Thayer's text *performs* a crisis—with all the virtuality and artifice connoted by that term—but a crisis without a sovereign subject, a *minor* crisis,[7] which like the text never comes to a decision, instead making deferral, delay, hesitation into the non-modern form of *a* critique[8] that is also, seemingly, its only sense of a future. A perpetual present of unending crisis would seem the price for this untimely "critique."

Bearing in mind Thayer's emphasis on the epistemological inactuality of the book's untimely reading, it nonetheless intervenes into its contemporary context. This too is an untimely intervention, given that its contemporary context is at least double: at once the early years of Chile's transition to democracy following Augusto Pinochet's dictatorship (1973–90), when the first edition of the text was published with Cuarto Propio, and the years leading up to the insurrection of 2019, which shook Chile's neoliberal social order to its juridical foundations, the same year that the second edition of the book was published by Ediciones Mimesis.

Along with Tomás Moulián's *Chile actual: Anatomía de un mito* (Chile today: Anatomy of a myth; 1997) and Nelly Richard's *La insubordinación de los signos* (*The Insubordination of Signs* [1994; Duke 2004]), Thayer's *Non-Modern Crisis* represents one of the most significant works of theory to emerge from the early years of Chile's postdictatorship. When it was first published in 1996, *The Non-Modern Crisis* offered an early and trenchant critique of Chile's dictatorship and neoliberal development model in unabashedly philosophical terms.[9] Thayer's text proposes a genealogy of the idea of the university—its Cartesian, Kantian, and Nietzschean iterations—to tease out the theoretical and historiographical consequences of contemporary changes to the institution from a perspective at once at the margins and in the vanguard of late twentieth-century capitalist modernity.

This position is afforded Thayer because Chile has the sad distinction of being the social laboratory for neoliberalism, that concatenation of neoclassical economic theory, monetarist policy, and neo-imperialism. Before Margaret Thatcher and Ronald Reagan coupled deindustrialization and financialization in the class war against organized labor, before the accumulation by dispossession effected by IMF- and World Bank-enforced structural adjustment programs around the world, a set of Chilean economists trained under Friedrich von Hayek and Milton Friedman at the University of Chicago found a sympathetic ear for their radical economic proposals in Pinochet's brutal dictatorship. The global hegemony of neoliberalism into the present means that Chile is still seen by policy makers and grassroots movements around the world as either a model or a cautionary tale.

The country's higher education landscape bears the scars of this history. Pinochet's earliest decrees, enacted after the approval of the 1980 constitution, catastrophically reformed higher education, allowing for the creation of largely unregulated, unaccredited private universities. While the proliferation of marketized higher education dramatically increased the percentage of the population with a tertiary degree, it did so at the expense of deep student debt, abysmal quality verging on fraud, a precarious higher education workforce, and overall state disinvestment. By 2011, Chilean higher education was among the costliest in the world relative to household income, and the country's household indebtedness among the highest in the region. As Thayer has it, "In the neoliberal interface, financial profit represents the mission and quality criterion of the university . . . so that whatever yields the greatest profit at the least cost is deemed excellent."[10]

The year 2011 is significant because it represents the highwater mark of a flood of student protests against this unregulated, profiteering higher education system.[11] For the first time in mainstream public discourse, the protests openly indicted forty years of neoliberalism and its very real failures over and against its illusory successes. In the decade that followed, the salience of the university as a site of contestation prompted a flurry of debate about the nature of Chilean higher education. It also underlined the (untimely) relevance of Thayer's then out-of-print *La crisis no moderna de la universidad moderna. Epílogo al conflicto de las facultades* and laid the groundwork for its 2019 reedition.

The 2011 student protests invigorated Left politics and galvanized subsequent mobilizations against Chile's marketized pension system and environmentally destructive megaprojects and for women's rights and Indigenous Mapuche claims to sovereignty. These multitudinous movements culminated in the October 2019 insurrection, whose demands crystalized around the call for a constituent assembly to rewrite Chile's 1980 constitution, which has stymied efforts to change the market fundamentalist underpinnings of the social contract. The same cycle of protests can be credited with delivering the socialist former student leader Gabriel Boric to the presidency of the republic in December 2021. In short, the last decade of social mobilization has questioned the ruling orthodoxy and contested its iron grip on the country's social and political institutions. Much as Chile's elites pioneered neoliberal society, the hope is that its people can point the way out.[12]

The twenty-three years between 1996 and 2019 unfold space-time like the pages of the book itself. In that unfolding, a decidedly untimely book that seeks to unwork historical causality has itself become an historical palimpsest. This is thanks to the changes—indeed, actualizations—introduced by the author that bring the 2019 text closer to the proper names of social and historical events. Where the 1996 edition spoke of capitalism in general or market heteronomy, the 2019 edition more frequently cites finance capital and neoliberalism specifically. Where the 1996 text invoked "facticity" as a kind of capitalist solvent of every modern *doxa*, the 2019 text also speaks of subsumption and financialized volatilization.[13] Where in 1996 Thayer wrote about the coup in and to Chilean history, in 2019 he also names Pinochet, legal reforms to higher education, and the student and feminist movements of recent years.[14] The 2019 reedition is more firmly anchored in the everyday, in events, in that which "is" than its 1996 counterpart, which spoke through the veil of a present it seemed reticent to name. If this represents the text's giving in to the facticity of facts and events, to the "heteroclite identity, articulated pluralism that disguises the general equivalent of postnational capitalism,"[15] or if it represents an opening to the possibility of change beyond the medium of the market singularity that seems to foreclose any action against it,[16] it is undeniable that the text has become doubly historical. It is at once a documentary witness to Chile's long Transition and an engagement with its historical events—albeit an (un)timely one.

The text's historical quality is only accentuated in the present translation, which has corseted the fluid, essayistic scholarly apparatus of Latin American philosophy into a set of formal citations bristling with page numbers. Thayer carries his argument about the formatting of thinking by university discourse into his citational practice by creatively paraphrasing his source texts. In reconstructing Thayer's scholarly apparatus, I have tried to balance this practice and its significance for his argument with adherence to the norms of English-language academic citation. In the notes that accompany what Thayer calls his "glosses," I invite the reader to "compare" Thayer's text to its source, so that she may directly experience this practice and divine its logic. This transculturation of Thayer's citational practices and those of the anglophone academy redoubles the text's role as archive, as another instantiation of the gathering principle of an imperial, modern university, but one in the throes of crisis.[17]

Despite its changed historical context, most of Thayer's book remains the same, perhaps because Chile's Transition remains seemingly intransigent. Similar transitions from authoritarian to democratic regimes took place around the globe following the collapse of the Cold War order, giving rise to a veritable cottage industry among social scientists that became known as "transitology." From Thayer's perspective in Chile, "transition" is a misnomer, for it signifies not a period of change but one of continuity with the neoliberal order imposed by the dictatorship. This intransigence of the Transition allows Thayer to see it as coinciding with non-modernity, the negation of the modern social order and episteme. "In the transition understood as the end of history . . . capitalism will remain and difference, the unequal, will vanish."[18]

Such a statement resonates with the image of an enigmatic graffiti from the 2019 insurrection that was published on the cover of the reedition of *The Non-Modern Crisis* alongside drawings by Gonzalo Díaz Cuevas, commissioned by Thayer, that represent ways to achieve different gradations of light in a four-by-four square, one of which also graces the cover of this translation. The graffiti reads, "1973 = 2019." Like the Transition, this equating of the right-wing military coup against Allende's socialist regime with the civil repression of an insurrection against the subsequent neoliberal order negates difference, the unequal, the condition of history. It provokes the question to which Thayer's text continually returns in its untimely reading of the history of the university's idea: Can change be thought? That is: Can we think an event insofar as we think in terms anterior to its occurrence? And not only this question, but also its near inverse: Can we think from its unchanging facticity the heteroclite identity of the capitalist lifeworld?[19] Is thinking, like history, the work of difference? If there is cause for hope, perhaps one day the two editions of *The Non-Modern Crisis of the Modern University* will be seen as framing, Janus-like, the Transition's beginning and end.

Unevenness

Willy Thayer is one of Latin America's foremost contemporary philosophers. His thinking ranges over many disciplines: media and film theory (*Imagen exote* [Exoimage; Palinodía, 2020]), psychoanalytic theory (*El barniz del esqueleto* [Skeleton varnish; Palinodía, 2011]), political theory (the essays collected in *El fragmento repetido: Escritos en estado de excepción* (The fragment repeated: Writings in a state of exception [Metales Pesados, 2006]), and of course, the theory of knowledge (*Tecnologías de la crítica: Entre Walter Benjamin y Gilles Deleuze* [Metales Pesados, 2010], translated as

Technologies of Critique [Fordham University Press, 2020]). He writes in conversation with a similarly wide range of canonical figures in continental philosophy, including Gilles Deleuze, Jacques Derrida, Walter Benjamin, Martin Heidegger, Friedrich Nietzsche, Karl Marx, and many more.

Upon the publication of the 1996 edition of *The Non-Modern Crisis*, Thayer joined a vibrant group of Chilean theorists working in a broadly poststructuralist tradition that grew alongside Santiago's underground, avant-garde art scene in the 1980s, a group that includes Federico Galende, Olga Grau, Pablo Oyarzún, and the aforementioned Nelly Richard.[20] In the intervening years leading up to the 2019 publication of its reedition, *The Non-Modern Crisis* also engaged a younger generation of Chilean theorists, including Alejandra Castillo, Elizabeth Collingwood-Selby, Rodrigo Karmy, Francisca Pérez, Felipe Rivas, raúl rodriguez freire, Miguel Valderrama, and Sergio Villalobos-Ruminott. If in the anglophone world we have spent the last decades repeatedly declaring the death of theory, in Chile theory is very much alive thanks in no small part to Thayer.

Such a discrepancy points to the geopolitics of theory production that parallels the uneven development that is the geographical hallmark of the contradictions of capital.[21] The chauvinism of those who prognosticate the death of theory is to overlook the vibrant theoretical work coming from the Global South or merely from outside the disciplinary circuits running through North American literature and area studies departments, where "theory as such" became visible in the 1970s and '80s. *The Non-Modern Crisis* represents a sophisticated refraction of continental philosophy through the political realities of the Global South as well as an original contribution to it. It is not just a history of philosophy but philosophy itself.[22] Indeed, *The Non-Modern Crisis* cannot but address the uneven political economy of knowledge given its institutional genealogy of Western knowledge production and legitimation from a peripheral perspective. At the same time, Thayer's wide-ranging, radical thinking about the Western university implies the deconstruction of the identity formations and processes of racialization that silo knowledge production for its differential valorization.[23] Thanks to this oblique or uneven position, anglophone readers will find Thayer's objects and interlocutors at once familiar and strange insofar as they have been recontextualized on the vibrant, leading-edge peripheries of theory, testing its pretension to be as global as the value supply chains that bind the world to capital. Felicitously, the last decade has seen a turn away from the largely North Atlantic circuits of theory production and circulation and toward the reception of theory produced in and about the Global South.[24]

The first edition of *The Non-Modern Crisis* was published in the same year as Bill Readings's posthumous *The University in Ruins* (Harvard University Press, 1996). This coincidence marks a missed encounter. *The University in Ruins* is often cited among the founding documents of critical university studies. Despite the fact that the university is a social form that has circumnavigated the globe, this field's center of gravity remains in the United States and Canada despite recent contributions from other English-speaking academies. The present translation of *The Non-Modern Crisis of the Modern University* represents the restitution of one of the unrecognized founding texts of critical university studies, an act that would begin to redress the field's uneven development over the last three decades. In the intervening years, the lessons of Thayer's text have only become more pressing as his analysis has been borne out by the continued devaluation of philosophical reflection and humanistic inquiry, the standardization and commercialization of knowledge production, and the precaritization of academic work.

In addition to Readings, *The Non-Modern Crisis* will find fellow travelers in historical, genealogical, poetic, apocalyptic, and utopian texts by the likes of Marc Bousquet, Abbie Boggs, Roderick Ferguson, Sandy Grande, Jodi Melamed, Fred Moten and Stefano Harney, Eli Meyerhoff, Chris Newfield, David F. Noble, Conor Tomás Reed, Sheeva Sabati, Jeffrey Williams, and K. Wayne Yang (under the pen name la paperson), texts that advocate for free, public, quality higher education, for a parasitism on the university of unprofitable bodies and ideas in order to construct a fugitive commons, for a decolonization that would rematriate concrete lands and more-than-concrete territories conquered in part by imperial university modernity, for the abolition of the university form as such.[25] This incipient archive will recognize in *The Non-Modern Crisis* not only the Chilean lesson as laboratory of savage neoliberalism and the financialized university. It will also recognize a desire shared by many who think the university today: to choke every triumphalist metanarrative about the university at the moment of its enunciation.

That recognition may not be an easy one, for Thayer's text defies categorization and eschews simple communication, making its style into the bulwark of its inoperative politics. Often associated with the poststructuralist practice of *écriture*, the preoccupation with the aesthetics of philosophical discourse is endemic to continental philosophy at least since the Romantics, serving as a counterweight to Descartes's *mathesis universalis* and its successors in the natural and social sciences as well as analytic philosophy.[26] What Roland Barthes says about literature, in a text that Thayer cites, applies here too: "Because it *stages* language instead of simply using it," Thayer's philosophical discourse "feeds knowledge into the machinery of infinite reflexivity. Through writing, knowledge ceaselessly reflects on knowledge, in terms of a discourse which is no longer epistemological, but dramatic. . . . Writing makes knowledge festive."[27]

Thayer's emphasis on style is substantiated by his argument, for the non-modern crisis of the modern university is "a crisis of philosophy that cannot be controlled or regulated by discourse, at least not by a philosophical discourse that would be able to speak to the university."[28] This is the corollary of the text's framing questions, which gnaw at its necessarily discursive frame from the very start: "How to speak nonuniversitarily about the university? . . . How should we avoid adopting its style so that for once we might slip through its fingers and gain discursive autonomy from it? . . . How to be heard without allowing oneself to be assimilated?"[29] These questions at once typify and ground Thayer's style. On the one hand, his style is a syntaxis of accumulation and dissemination, of the fragment, the interrupting punctuation mark, the period elected instead of the comma, a writing that stammers "and, and, and, and . . ." before finally giving in to the legibility of the "is."[30] On the other hand, it is the unevenness of a text—unsettled, unsettling, disseminating, and mutating—written mostly in the present conditional. In an early review, Pablo Oyarzún claims, "The grammar of the present conditional . . . wants to mark the place where we are, an indecisive place . . . that excludes the apocalypse of the condition (its full and immediate appearance) and that also impedes all representation or image of it; that undermines . . . the possibility of critically reflecting on it."[31]

In translation I have tried to capture the text's hypnotic prosody of accumulation and dissemination even as I have modified punctuation to aid the reader's understanding. I have not always captured the present conditional, allowing a relatively undomesticated translation to unsettle the English-language reader instead.[32] Thayer's conceptual scope and idiomatic style will prove to be generatively uneven ground.

There are, of course, certain terms that become proving grounds for any translation. Some are so soaked in the subjectivity of an author's particular usage that they strain against the structures of any language. In the present text, one example among many is the term *universitariamente*, which I have rendered as "universitarily"—as in the section titled "Everything Speaks Universitarily; Nothing Speaks 'of' the University"—not only because the word is Thayer's invention but because its strangeness in English reflects its strangeness in the Spanish.

Other terms are so freighted with conceptual genealogies and histories of translation that they must adhere to the etymologies invoked by other authors and the work of other translators. An example is the term *facticidad* and its derivatives. While *facticidad* is sometimes translated according to the context as "mere existence," "contingency," or even "effectiveness," Thayer's sustained engagement with the thinking of Heidegger and his successors more often warrants the use of the philosophical term "facticity" to indicate the genealogy of the concept. While in existentialist philosophy "facticity" signifies the world that can be objectified from a third-person perspective, which is necessarily bound up with the transcendence or self-reflection that allows one's existence in that factic world to be experienced, in Heidegger's thought facticity (*Faktizität*) is the stuff of life itself, the thrownness (*Gewor-fenheit*) of being-in-the-world which discloses our being there (*Dasein*), first through our forgetfulness of ourselves in our practical absorption in the world.[33] While informed by these understandings, Thayer's usage is broader than either tradition while still pregnant with both.

Finally, there are still other terms that emerge from the missed encounters between languages. Such missed encounters enact translation's immanent theory of language and its poetic knowledge. This is the case for the term "non-modern" in the book's title, which attempts to express Thayer's usage of the phrase *no moderna*. Earlier I distinguished the non-modern from the postmodern, which Thayer almost certainly selected against, given that the first edition of book is coeval with the raucous Latin American postmodernism debates.[34] Neither the severing and distancing of "not modern" nor the inversion connoted by "unmodern" nor still the austere otherworldliness of "amodern," non-modern signifies a negation of modernity beholden of modernity. Recall that the crisis of the modern university is the crisis of modern categories of thought and the crisis of modern political forms. In this totalizing vision, *The Non-Modern Crisis of the Modern University* entirely negates modernity, but even so we remain bound by a hyphen to dwell in its ruins.

In the introduction to his translation of Thayer's *Technologies of Critique*, John Kraniauskas reminds us that "the materiality of language—its constitutive sociality—makes translation a practice of transculturation (rather than . . . of imperial acculturation or mere technical interculturation, however self-assured their administered equivalences may be)."[35] Into the era of its non-modern crisis, the university, as the gathering of knowledges, functions as a prosthesis of imperial acculturation, a process that is today sedimented but still active in certain sectors of academia. It has also served as an apparatus of imperial *accumulation*, as Thayer notes in the present book, representing "a silent outpost of conquest and colonization . . . by managing and naturalizing imperial unity through the incorporation, discrimination, and hierarchical segregation of languages, knowledges."[36] A transculturation that would not be acculturation or interculturation nor mere tool for accumulation is one whose prefix—"trans-"—would resist reduction to the multiform spectacle of contemporary capitalism. Such a transculturation is already implicit in Thayer's style. The work that unworks itself is constantly becoming another. In this case, it is becoming into another language.

The materiality of language is shaped by the work of many hands. The present work of transculturation would not have been possible without support and encouragement, at the start, from raúl rodriguez freire and Mary Luz Estupiñán at Ediciones Mimesis and, at the end, from Faith Wilson Stein and her team at Northwestern University Press as well as two anonymous reviewers. In the spaces and times in between, Katryn Evinson, Janet Hendrickson, Marc Kohlbry, and John Kraniauskas provided punctual help with translation and revision, and Bruno Bosteels, Suzanne Guiod, and Kerry Webb provided advice about the field of academic translation. From start to finish,

Willy Thayer generously gifted me his time, his criticism, and above all that ecstatic discourse that conveys an unflagging faith in the project of a philosophy to come, one that spirited this translation to its completion. Of course, any errors or infelicitous turns of phrase in translation are my own.

I

*The Non-Modern Crisis
of the Modern University*

When it comes to contemporary philosophical discourse, the university today has stipulated that the essay, the thesis, and critique are the only competent forms of writing, the only university writing, a style that ends up reducing philosophical writing to the writing of papers. Thus, freedom of thought becomes, in fact, the iron submission of professors and students to the most miserable form of repression: theoretical production governed by the norms of non-philosophical, technical production. For all that, the university today must willfully ignore the way its knowledge works, that is, its forces, desires, movements, and power relations, in a word, the scenes on which it is based. Modern and contemporary university philosophical discourse defines the philosophical idea as that which is essentially without a scene. Thus, if writing names theoretical work on those scenes that condition philosophical ideas, concrete opposition to university philosophical discourse begins when such writing is allowed to be produced.

—Patricio Marchant, "Sobre la creación de un centro de estudios de todas las formas de escritura que escapan al discurso universitario" (On the creation of an institute for all those forms of writing that escape university discourse), unpublished manuscript, 1983

1

✦

A Few Things That Must Be Stated

Context as University

To open a dialog about the university and to begin examining it requires that we attend to and question its surroundings,[1] especially today, when it appears that the context constitutes the university in its entirety, leaving no room for independent action. The question of whether the university has—if it is possible for the university today to "have" anything—autonomy, interiority, self-possession, authorship, agency, or responsibility relative to the missions, duties, and historical activities that (once) befitted it and that its modern framing [*verosimilitud*][2] commits it to, the question of whether the university is or can still constitute itself as a subject, the question of whether it was ever able to do so, and the question of whether it contests its context or gains distance from it and in what way it does so, whether it is still plausible for it to consummate the difference on which it is founded, as the walls and boundaries that often surround universities would seem to attest,[3] and present itself as an autonomous space beyond current events into which it could only intervene like some deus ex machina—questions like these seem the first we should ask and address.

Can we call the university a subject, that is, a subject of modern knowledge in its two principal activities, "basic research," or the truth of truth, and "applied research," or the professional application of knowledge? Is the university overseer and lookout, regulator and guarantor of knowledge in various fields and trades? Is the university responsible for the instrumentalization of knowledge as well as its reverberation across whole swaths of human activity? Is the university the accountant of last resort one must keep up with in order to stay up to date but also that one queries to demand an account of the universalization of an enlightened way of life, its expansion and otherworldly intensification along far western horizons? Is it responsible for the professionalization and gradual supplanting of local languages and customs by the codes and formats of the alma mater? Is it responsible for the gradual, worldwide modernization and updating of ways of life it deems backward or else still on the path toward development? Is it responsible for the emerging

mutation of the object system and environmental flows; for the demarcation, ranking, and power of disciplinary languages; for the balkanization of
knowledge and its canons of censure and discipline; for behaviors, competencies, and pertinences, in every instance [*en cada caso*]?[4] Or is the university
entirely heteronomy, milieu, exteriority, such that its name remains, out of
sheer inertia, on the directory of institutions that constitute the menu of the
present, regardless of the aforementioned boundaries and limits through
which the university continues to feign independence, inaccessibility, some
might say autarky relative to its surroundings?

It might also be that the university is little more than an on-ramp or an
inroad, a mere intersection in the workings of knowledge and power that
pass through it not even as a node, procedures that, lacking a recognizable
or locatable origin, let alone an intention, establish, regulate, and administer
the university and not the inverse, as one might assume were we thinking in
modern terms. In this case, the university would be but one more moment in
the market's casual processing of information, certification, and absorption
of habits, techniques, and protocols for conduct, care, and recognition.

University as Context

To double the line of questioning: What happens to the context when we
imagine it from inside the university? To what extent has the university constructed its context by realizing itself as metropole, as the university city
or professional planet where the performances, gestures, and autonomous
preuniversity regions have been engulfed in totalitarian fashion by higher
protocols and habits? Internalized by the social body since nursery school,
the university, with all of its linguistic and disciplinary variety and mobility, subjects both subject and object to its panopticism more exhaustively
and automatically than ever. Each professional, depending on the intensity
with which he has absorbed and allowed himself to be absorbed by his spe-
cialty, not only monitors the objects that fall into his professional purview.
He also monitors himself and the zones of desire that perturb his professional
efficacy and output. In a society determined by the university, we "sweat"
an enlightened, university style.[5] The totality of objects around us, objects
produced and manipulated by the professions and by technoscientific progress, behave universitarily. At a minimum we demand from them specificity,
efficiency and performance, visibility and mobility, openness, durability, and
serial reproducibility. Even advertisements promote universities by exagger-
ating the performance and normality that the historical episteme ascribes to
them. In each case [*en cada caso*], this apparatus is constructed, monitored,
and regulated by the university's professional divisions.

Our mannerisms and worldview are of the university not only because of
our educational system. One need not pass through a specific curriculum to

be formatted by the universality of the university. One need only have a pass-ing interest in or affinity for mass media to become universitarily alienated in one's ideas, symbols, and modes of conduct, which through repetition amplify or diminish the body according to its efficiency or inefficiency, desirability or undesirability, normality or abnormality, or which become routinized by needs and performances we do not seem to create but nonetheless incorpo-rate into ourselves, everything from our subjection and circulation to those standards that beckon to us from advertisements or through publicity "mas-sages" (McLuhan). Our worldview and mannerisms tend toward the given universality because we are committed to it since nursery school. The nursery school, like publicity and publicists, is a product of university universal-ity. In the nursery, the university conditions our sphincter systems (desire, emotion, fantasy) to conform and become sensitive to the coaxing, seduc-tive stimuli deployed most effectively not in the directly academic format (a conservative refuge) but in the mediatic matrix of screen and audio, in the velocity of electronic publicity and its translocal menu of options. There is not one advertisement that is not of the university or universitarily defined. Even the mistake, error, lapse, or unprofessional behavior of the publicist or producer—that is, their resistance—even a power cut or an attack on the (wireless) power grid is inscribed in the professional university network. The same goes for the business-savvy production of knowledge that occurs in nonuniversity spaces, insofar as such knowledge production responds to the university's method, style, and universal. Even if these institutes and think tanks are no longer monitored by the university-state—the regulatory axis of knowledge and professional activity—they remain inscribed in the university by a university subjectivity internalized as professionalism, a subjectivity that reproduces itself and grows wherever market competition commands with-out any state oversight.[6]

Disseminated every day as context, the university is a professional panop-ticon automatically activated by the university architecture of the eye and of the body in general.

To what extent is the university in this view the source of subjection that produces and is produced as context, that produces subjects and objects in general, professional subjects and objects? To what extent has the univer-sity, its style imperiously expanded beyond its walls? To what extent has it reformed the outside, eliminating with "insatiable greed"[7] the nonuniversity reality it opposes or that is opposed to it? To what extent has it resisted sub-ordination or supervision by that nonuniversity other? To what extent has the university achieved its full extension, demolishing the walls and eliminat-ing the distance, limit, difference that separate inside from outside?[8]

What kind of empire or totalitarianism, what form of subjection would the university represent? Perhaps a totality that does not need interior or closure because everything outside is already enclosed? Perhaps an elec-tronic enclosure[9] or a telematic one?[10] Perhaps a totality with neither subject nor autonomy, distributed in administrative, economic-commercial, public-publicity performances of credit and accreditation, a totality that operates unconditionally as demonstrated by its use, the hustle and bustle, the daily routine colonized by a mode of perception emanating from the professional faculties? Or is it even possible to think or to want a university that knows itself, its operations, and its context, a university that contains itself, critically administering the given through esoteric means that are neither articulated with nor exposed to reality games, through means, anasemic reserves by which the university would still constitute itself through a distance, a silence, a scriptural difference vis-à-vis its exoteric, pedagogical, professional per-formances and activities without being subjected to their instrumentality; a university that still conserves the division of labor, the "conflict of the fac-ulties," or "class struggle" between professional "manual labor" (*fusis*) and speculative "intellectual labor" (*meta-fusis*), the difference between under-standing and thinking?

The idea of the university as historico-critical, speculative, interrogative center of society and its knowledges [*conocimiento*] is superseded by the operations of present-day knowledge [*saber*].[11] The idea of a speculative, reflexive, critical university is consummated in its absolutization as instru-mental, productivist, techno-professional intellect. Such an idea coincides with the modern myth that has slowly taken root in the common sense of the university medium, that the university is the wellspring of science, tech-nology, and the professions as well as, eventually, the arts, literature, music, critique, theory, philosophy, and thought, too.

In effect, if one accepts the premises that science and the organization of knowledge and the professions and their division into many more or less specialized fields as well as the premise that critique, art, music, literature, thinking are properly and legitimately cultivated in the university, if we start from these premises, we will readily agree that the university is indeed called to assess and certify not only what is knowledge, understanding, thinking, art but also that the university is called to disciplinarily monitor society in all its orders and mutations by means of the specializations and languages that the university bestows, the worldviews it generates and through which it is suffused with the organigram of culture. For as we have been suggesting, whether they like it or not, professionals universitarily monitor each other by monitoring the objects and language allotted to them by their profes-sion. In general, debates about their objects—insofar as there "would be" any debate—are in the end restricted to university codes, languages, and pro-cesses: positivism, technocracy, late Platonism.

Starting from this premise and mapping the territories it irrigates, not only does science appear to be fruit of the university—the current university universality—but so too does the social "totality" appear as an enlightened "totality." According to this preconception, the university—that product of a society passing through modernity [*en su tránsito moderno*][12]—would become the principle of modern society, a principle that translates into a university society, a disciplinary panopticon (Foucault).

According to this preconception of the university as wellspring of science and technology, as assessing and correcting overseer of its technologies, languages, and products, we would also readily agree that all knowledge which outgrows university and professional society and aspires to commodity status in order to compete on the market would have to pass through university censorship, as it once had to pass through royal censorship, before entering into circulation. In keeping with the institution's exclusionary spirit, this would ensure that the sense, applicability, conduct, and appearance of the knowledge or objects elaborated on the university's periphery circulate according to the value and rank they are assigned by the university. Thus, the university also appears as the *spirit* of society much as it did in the context of modern, Enlightenment society.

University as Center

We are witnessing the decline of the idea of the university as hegemonic, national center for the oversight and direction of research, teaching, and the performance[13] of objects and their teleologies in use and exchange. What for Kant (1794) were the outer margins of the university (specialized academies and societies), whose knowledges neither threatened nor competed with university knowledge, have today become noteworthy centers for knowledges that in many cases cannot be taught, published, or administered by the university. Today, competition from those margins has made the university itself marginal and its knowledge propaedeutic, subordinate, and parasitic. The fact that there are powerful domains of knowledge not subject to university assessment is enough to threaten the modern university's basic architecture. That the idea of the university-center as regulator of knowledge no longer corresponds to today's university reality is apparent in the extramural question of those centers that grow just beyond the university's administrative reach, centers that the university not only does not control but has no right to control[14] and whose knowledges and information it often lacks the financial means to access.[15]

Judging by the nature and development of the technoscientific competencies possessed by these strategic, mercenary research hubs, it would appear they have gotten the better of the university, relegating it to the reproduction en masse of knowledges whose epistemic-commercial, geo-telematic secret has been devalued. The telematic commercialization of knowledge has slowly rendered obsolete the state university's centralization of knowledges, whether for educational, spiritual, historical, and national purposes (Humboldt) or for educational, technical, historical, and national ones (Napoleon-Comte). The relationship between knowledge providers and knowledge users tends to mimic the relationship between commodity producers and consumers.

Knowledge has been losing its historical "use value."[16] And instead of being disseminated from the university to civil society for the capitalization of the nation-state, the nation's "intellectual and moral education,"[17] it is gradually incorporated into the expanded circuit of abstract financial accumulation.

In the neoliberal interface, the Chilean university (1973–present) has slowly ceased to represent an industrial sector for the production and reproduction of use-value knowledges and instead represents an entrepreneurial circuit of financial accumulation. In Chile's neoliberal university interface, it is not that university use value is financed by capitals derived from different sectors but rather that all-encompassing finance capital selects for whatever will yield a hefty profit, including the university or education sectors, health, pensions, etc. In the neoliberal interface, financial profit represents the mission and quality criterion of the university (and of all things), so that whatever yields the greatest profit at the least cost is deemed excellent. In the heteronomy of financial accumulation, all qualities, all university consumer goods are converted from their academic value to a return on investment, from use value to exchange value. Modern subordination of state capital to the use value of national education has in short course become the non-modern entrepreneurial subordination of the nation-state and its institutions, the subordination in general of all use values to value useful for financial accumulation, a point to which we will return.

The fact that there are important areas of knowledge inaccessible to university education, assessment, and control;[18] the fact that the university has no right to access, not even by purchasing, relevant but forbidden knowledge; the fact that it does not decide what can be researched or taught—these facts indicate that its standing as the center of knowledge production and regulation is a mirage of modern philosophical discourse, seemingly the only discourse we have about the university, although not for that reason one that necessarily corresponds to the state of university affairs today.[19]

The Organic Unity and Gathering Principle of the University

Long ago, the university presented itself as the totality of knowledge and teachings, with all their geographic and linguistic fluctuations and annexations, as the outline of their transformations gathered under one principle, narrative, tradition or history. Since the Ancient Greek philosophers, the propensity and desire to gather and fully articulate multiplicity has served as the maxim of Western knowledges.[20] Since Plato, the good is that which gathers, the bad that which dissolves.[21] According to Seneca, good is the "primary genus on which other species depend and which is the source of every division and in which all things are included."[22]

Good is the category that assembles, assesses, and stabilizes the storm of multiplicities that otherwise never cohere. Good is the God who congregates, and good the theology and the sciences of gathering. Bad is the Nietzschean genealogy that transforms every towering canon into the provisional effect of colliding forces. Bad is the Epicurean who insists that neither death nor life gathers anything. Bad is the conjunction that in its undefined "and, and, and, and . . ." destabilizes the stabilizing intentionality of the "is."

> There has always been a struggle in language between the verb être (to be) and the conjunction et (and) between est and et (is and and [which in French are identical in pronunciation—Trans.]). It is only in appearance that these two terms are in accord and combine, for the first acts in language as a constant and forms the diatonic scale of language, while the second places everything in variation, constituting the lines of a generalized chromaticism.[23]

> AND is of course diversity, multiplicity, the destruction of identities. . . . Because multiplicity is never in the terms, however many, nor in all the terms together, the whole. Multiplicity is precisely in the "and," which is different in nature from elementary components and collections of them. Neither a component nor a collection, what is this AND? . . . AND is neither one thing nor the other, it's always in between . . . a line of flight or flow . . . 'power lies on the border.'[24]

> [One speaks of] "purity" only in connection with a people's highly developed sense of language, which, in a large society, establishes itself, above all, among the aristocracy and educated. Here it is decided what is to be considered as provincial, as dialect, and as normal; viz., "purity," then is positively the customary usage of the educated in society, which received its sanction through the usus, and the "impure" is everything else which attracts attention in it. Thus, the "not-striking" is that which is pure. There is neither a pure nor an impure speech in itself. A very important question arises of how the feeling for purity gradually is formed, and of how an educated society makes choices, to the point at which the whole range has been defined. It evidently acts according to unconscious laws and analogies here: a unity, a uniform expression is achieved. . . . Barbarisms, repeated frequently, finally transform the language; thus, the koinē glōssa . . . arose, later the Byzantine rōmaikē glōssa . . . and finally the completely barbarized new Greek. Who knows how many barbarisms have worked in this way to develop the Roman language out of Latin? And, it was through these barbarisms and solecisms, that good rule-bound French came about![25]

Long ago, in the twelfth century, if universitas signified the administrative gathering of persons of the same profession and not a gathering of knowledges and techniques, there was nonetheless a desire to unite the disciplines, the utopia of a total encyclopedia of scholarship and scholars.[26] This has always been one of the university's teleological principles, its metanarrative of unity and totality. One could even say, the university has always claimed to be a totalitarian system tasked with absorbing, assimilating, distributing, ranking, instituting as knowledge or nonknowledge, as university or nonuniversity, according to a general criterion that assigns status, gestures, mannerisms, tastes and smells, hues and tones, languages, rhythms, practices, experiences, and moods; speculations, points of view, inventions, products, discourses and melodies; codes, methods and techniques. The university graded and arranged this multitude of shifting, unstable activities above and below, inside and outside the academic institution.

The university has presented itself to us as a living, malleable machine that digests, expels, stimulates, locates, and dislocates knowledges and activities dispersed across various traditions, knowledges, and practices that, before having been examined and judged by the university, wandered among languages and across territories, scattered, barbarian, pagan, left to their own devices without a universal, public status or rank.

The university brought together "other" languages and experiences that, lacking a shared tradition or history, are irreducible to each other. It assimilated them to a singular logic of knowing, it transformed them into the same type, or else it proscribed them.

The identity and logic of the university, its unity and familiarity, the might, prestige, presence, and public power of its knowledges and endeavors derived from a process of articulation, gathering, and assimilation of dissimilar and disjointed experiences and activities, activities that in many cases were persecuted and condemned by the university. Consider the medieval university's disdain, condemnation, and at the same time "fear" of the monstrosities authored by Bruno, Galileo, and Descartes. Upon their appearance, the strangeness of these monstrosities and names threatened and repulsed the university subject of the age. Shortly after stepping beyond the law, the universal, the current paradigm, these phenomena stealthily and imperceptibly became the very heart of the classic modern university, its statute and principle of command and control, the subject, law, and new universality of the university regime.

More than strangeness to or unfamiliarity with the university, this nascent body of work proved unfamiliar because, with respect to the "medieval" universality, hegemony, and purpose that historically and effectively governed the university, it constituted a limit to medieval governance, purpose, and hegemony, a limit to its imperiality when faced with the eruption of these monstrosities and signatures in its very heart. These new monstrosities kept coming to inhabit and graze upon the same pastures, the same encyclopedias, catalogs, dictionaries, the same territories long since inhabited by and divvied up among naturalized medieval monstrosities, simulacra, and beasts. Above all, their arrival contested the governance, purpose, and user hegemony of those pastures and their distribution of places, positions, and ranks—the dominant script that leads to the university—sparking a conflict, a land war for university pastures now finally modernized below a new firmament of names, writings, monstrosities.

A total war between medieval purpose, universality, script, and theological simulacrum, on the one hand, and modern purpose, universality, simulacrum, and teleological-anthropological script, on the other; a clash, a conflict of wills, each with its heraldry, flags, gestures, and slogans that are welcomed, housed, placed beneath the same categorical roof, whatever the nature of their rivalry. What else would the university be but the conflict of wills, positionalities, universalities, imperialities under the hegemony of one cat- egorical, grammatical articulation, one structure of recognition, one style: a kind of history painting in which the most diverse factions battle in all-out war that does nothing more than contribute to the canvas onto which they are painted. The warring parties at once supply the style and elaborate that style through its variation.

A conflict among monsters that, however powerful they may be relative to one another and to their modes of representation, do not threaten in any case [en cada caso] to weaken the grammar, language, style, and relations of pro- duction in which they are immersed and which they support and transform. Thus, if these modern anthropological monsters at all threaten or displace the government of the medieval theological monster of the university they are threatened and persecuted by, they do not in fact threaten but instead feed, nourish, and enable, at least in part, the hegemony, the dialectic, the rich uni- versity synthesis that subsumes them and disseminates itself through them.

Nothing, not the old monsters, the new monsters, or their warring, seems to weaken the grammar of the university. Instead, they seem to feed, reaffirm, fortify, and enable, at least in part, the very conditions of the university, its meager hospitality, its closure in every instance [en cada caso].

The University as a Gathering of the Strange

How is it that something illegitimate, strange, lacking, threatening even, an object of derision that elicits foreboding, becomes over time the distinguish- ing and organizing criterion of legitimacy? How is it that points of view like those of Copernicus, Galileo, Descartes, Lavoisier, etc., come to represent a significant part of the university's subjectivity and common sense? And how is it that non-knowledge, non-understanding, even the superstitions of the Other are incorporated by the university apparatus and put to work producing, advancing, and making profitable the business that expropriates and assimilates them and to which they conform as they shed their outsider perspective? What happens in the transition whereby the strange becomes so familiar as to become an academic subject, a bibliographic cliché, before finally becoming customary, common, classic? How is it that the *lapsus* comes to govern, inscribing itself as the law or hegemony of a specific academic circuit? How is it that the exception, that which falls outside the norm, becomes the norm that reassigns positions and ranks?

It appears that the university cannot tolerate any creative process without a law of laws, a politics of politics, in short, it cannot tolerate the "methodological error" inherent in creative activity. It is readily apparent that the university stands against any activity that destroys its dialectic, its entertainment,[27] its willful accumulation of capital. In contrast to the process of academic research—which in each case [*en cada caso*] ensures its own development, conditioning legitimated knowledges upon the methodologies and rankings of "normal"[28] university research today—in the "genial" (Kant) or genealogical (Nietzsche) process, rules are not simply given or preordained by tradition. Instead, tradition is read and rewritten from a perspective beyond its horizon, where there is no a priori that would articulate or pacify poetry: "I do not know what the relation of my disasters will be."[29] If research is genial, it remains an implacable outsider in its reception, outside current objectives, for it is precisely these codes that its writing retraces. And so, it will demand new codes, new rules that are always immanent to and singularly valid in each and every writing, in the play of their refraction through others. We are not referring here to inventions or discoveries that one expects within the current university frame [*verosímil*], compatible "novelties" that complete and consolidate what is already known, illuminating and polishing those opaque zones of the familiar and the everyday. We are referring instead to events and eruptions that are *incompossible* with the university series in *conatus* [*en conato*];[30] events outside the series, noise irreducible to ready and available meanings, whose series would only be ideologically advantageous in some perverse world in which the excrement of this one would furnish a royal banquet in the other; events from another series, another university context that erupt into this university context only to convey that the university, the world could be entirely different (Leibniz); a differential university series misaligned with and deviating from the current university series.

If we can say, in each case [*en cada caso*], that poetry is the unpresentable *conatus* of another world already in *conatus* [*en conato*], an "out-of-the-series" that appears like the anticipation of an experience incompatible with the series of possible experiences today, one would expect that every particular university would shun poetry and the poet (writing). At the same time, this indicates that the truth of every university is but an effect of its framing [*verosimilitud*] relative to its universality, its reigning objectives. It follows that neither this nor any other particular university fulfills or has fulfilled the promise of its name to take on the role of uni-version or university of universities, the totality of knowledges. And in order to fit the teleology that "the University" (as metauniversity) demands, it should open hospitably to truths that prove to be *incompossible*, something that any university, any empirical universality resists. The university of universities, which from the outset prefigured modernity's avarice, can never coincide with the project of any particular university. They are but hollow metaphors of the totality [*universitas*] that they promise.

In its "idea" the university has imagined itself not only as the totality of any one possible world but as the *universitas* of them all. In its "idea" it has always wanted to be the total library with no outside. However, during the modern era, it always and in each case [*en cada caso*] constituted an economy for the capture and capitalization of any possible world on behalf of a particular interest, class, race, point of view, on behalf of a particular body, no matter how much it publicizes itself as universal understanding, that is, knowledge without a body. This "all-consuming desire"[31] is the economic principle that empirically drives the modern university. In modernity, the university has always revolved around an economy of gathering and accumulation.

The university wants to be the system of heterogeneity, the collection of diversity, the version of versions or "knowledge of knowledges" expressed in the "uni-" of the university. The modern university imagined itself "God's mind" or "monad of monads" (Leibniz), as the "absolute idea" (Hegel), as capital immersed in infinite self-valorization (Marx). Its principle would articulate infinite series of compossibility—series incompossible with respect to one another. In the university, "all things conspire" as in "the mind of God," the "absolute idea" or "capital": σύμπνοια πάντα.[32]

In this sense, the university appears baroque. In and through the university, diverse knowledges, languages, and temporalities have been mixed and confused (Greek, Arab, Judeo-Christian, Roman, Visigothic, Indian, German, French, English, and in today's multicultural neoliberal university, Mapuche, Quechua, etc.). In spite of its sterile policy of collecting through judgment, the university is a promiscuous institution that slowly aspires to the logic of the "trans," but a neoliberal "trans" that fetishizes a rainbow logic of homogeneity and equivalence.

That the university integrates and absorbs with pageantry those small, nonuniversity knowledges that it once feared and fought, that in this way it goes about constructing its experience and its archive does not mean, however, that it incorporates them intact, just as they arose in the course of their nonuniversity life. By what means was Marx's writing transformed into the canon of the Stalinist university? The same goes for Nietzsche and the Nazi university or Descartes and Comte and the Napoleonic state-technical university. Consider how it proved impossible to institute Humboldt and Schleiermacher's philosophical university, which was instead translated into the humanist-technical university—strictly separating "first-rate minds" (philologists, encyclopedists) from "second-rate minds" (bureaucrats and professionals)—and finally into the positivist-humanist university, negligent and wholly complicit with the goals of the state, for example, during the rise of Nazism.[33]

The transplanting and recontextualizing of nonuniversity knowledges and strategies into an institution whose methods and rankings are gradually becoming planetary and homogeneous (as they always have been given its imperial universality)[34] presupposes the formatting and framing of those knowledges—as information or knowledge, as university universality—and the reduction of their experiential density, their body, their singular exception. It presupposes their subordination to university assimilationism, in which differences diverge among themselves but never differ from the university, an assimilationism that, from time to time, expands its protocols to appropriate barbarous experience, those corporeal nonuniversity forces.

It demands that all knowledges produced outside the university that would be strategic to incorporate be made presentable within the university. The constant reshaping of these "reception aesthetics" constitutes the rhetorical principle of university collection and inclusion. The university is no refuge for knowledges in pre- or parauniversity states. It absorbs them once they have been translated into the university's objectives and imperial designs, once the university has digested them without harming itself. It is as if the university were waiting for this stammering writing to express itself and grow accustomed to the no-man's-land beyond the university's dominion or to a state of nature before the state before such writing can be included in its canons.[35]

Refracting the crisis of its law, the university waits for the exception to conform to its norms or for the norm or concept of strangeness to become imminent to it. Its barrage of protocols, its system of limits, its control over orifices become more effective the more invisible they become. They dampen and domesticate the onslaught of uncustomary forces [*fuerzas inverosímiles*], instructing that the monsters become urbane just beyond the university's walls, so that they will attenuate the innervation, the threat to educational universality that the encroachment of their foreign bodies poses. Shortly after their domestication, one of the university's key strategies for capture is to let them enter and give them shelter as it converts them into one of its points of view, canons, curricular grids, fleeting bibliographies—into one of its innovative products.

The morality, economy, temporality, and paradise of genius are, as a rule, the perversion of the university's politics, economy, temporality, its theater of representation. They are also the raw material for the university's development strategy, its baroque modernization.

Thus we must consider that the many original and surprising things that appear in the university have their humble origins in an earlier writing process, a process followed by another, similarly humble process that is not therefore any less exciting or contentious, a process of reception and canonization, a process that posthumously institutes the monster wrapping it in a long chain of protocols that reduce it to one function with many uses, because it is this same process of reception and canonization of the strange that ultimately makes the strange familiar enough that it disappears into the insignificance of inference. Every writing that disappears into the utility [*usuariedad*] of university exchange awaits a helping hand, a sympathetic ear that, cutting through the layer of conventions that normalize its use, counteracts the inertia and releases its virtuality in reserve, its inexpedient body.

Such a helping hand reminds us that Freud had no idea about psychoanalysis as he was writing those texts that later became the documentary sources that founded the university psychoanalytic institution. He could not know anything about psychoanalysis because there was no psychoanalysis to know anything about. The same could be said of Plato. He knew nothing about philosophy.

If Freud knew anything, it was about neurology. And he knew about neurology (like Plato knew about mythology) not only because he had dedicated himself to studying it, becoming a professional neurologist and coming to understand the world through the code of this professional (de)formation. More than having absorbed it to the point of becoming a neurological subject, he knew about neurology because, after neurology had transformed his vision, those very eyes through which Freud the neurologist viewed the world, he slowly began to distance himself, changing his neurological eyes for analytical ones, letting his neurological eyes fall from the position of the seeing subject to the position of the object seen, the position of the analysand.

For example—and there are many—in the fourth chapter of *Beyond the Pleasure Principle*, we read, "What follows now is speculation, speculation often far-fetched, which each will, according to his particular attitude, acknowledge or neglect. Or one may call it the exploitation of an idea of curiosity to see whither it will lead."[36] From these stammering and speculative beginnings, the nodal categories of the institution of Freudian psychoanalysis were born.

Kant: The Faculty of Philosophy as Principle of Gathering

It was Kant who clearly expressed that the question concerning the conditions of knowledge [*conocimiento*], and not knowledge itself, must constitute the center of the university, its principle, its autonomy. Kant proposed displacing knowledge, understood as the higher faculties or dogmatic principle of the university, in favor of research, understood as the critical question concerning the conditions of possibility or the limits of knowledge. With Kant, the university, which had once housed study and knowledge arranged according to various canons, becomes a restless critical performance that, in each case [*en cada caso*], interrogates its conditions, its possibility, and the possibility of its knowledges, its language, its audibility. The university ceases to be the center for gathering and accumulating knowledge that positively advances across the rich diversity of given phenomena and becomes, above all, the question concerning the possibility of these very phenomena and our knowledge about them. Kant proposed that the critical need to investigate both the conditions of knowledge and the university as the location of its enactment—a demand proper to the lower faculty of philosophy—should be raised to the highest faculty, which would rule over the university.[37] We must emphasize that the university would no longer be a place for study or for the development of canons of knowledges, but would be itself the performance of the questioning and critique, in every instance [*en cada caso*], of what "is understood as" or "acts as" knowledge. In no way would it be simply the place where different books and schools, doctrines and knowledges would be criticized, but instead it would be the center for investigating the conditions of knowledges that positive research must necessarily ignore, regardless of its field of application.

Dogmatism is less the intransigent affirmation of an opinion or doctrine than the incautious application of unforeseen conditions. Thus, it often takes on a liberal and flexible disposition. One can be flexible, pluralist, and tolerant with respect to doctrines and judgments and at the same time reckless and dogmatic with regard to the conditions that underpin such a pluralism. Dogmatism is less about a relation with the figurative content of rights than it is about ignorance of the conditions that enable and govern them, forcing them to appear one way while recklessly presuming that they represent freedom. The true source of dogmatism is the athematic, inertial application of these conditions in all contexts, conditions that involuntarily and performatively instruct that which makes them possible. Often, the more unconscious the conditions of a right to action, the greater dogmatism's impact and violence. Any mode of appearance that ignores the terms and conditions by which it appears is dogmatic, reckless. By disavowing its conditions and limits, it forfeits its autonomy from them only to redound upon them. It replaces a sovereign relation to its limits, its frame, with a consular one.

After Kant, the university's gathering imperative can only be carried out by the lower faculty of philosophy, not as a canon of knowledge but as knowledge about the conditions of every knowledge and pursuit. The faculty of philosophy not only is not a faculty or a canon of university knowledge but also indisposes itself to all knowledge by querying its condition and the condition of that condition. The question concerning the condition and the condition of the condition illuminates the limit, the structure of intent, the dogmatic imperiousness of that knowledge, which has been naturalized as universal, unconditioned knowledge. Making visible the conditions of the universality of the university and its knowledge weakens the technical, interested, skewed closure of the imperial interests of the state as leader of the people.

With Kant, the university became the conflict of the faculties, and it remained in conflict until the *big bang*[38] of the non-modern university, which revealed that the conflict of the faculties, the question concerning the condition of really possible knowledges, the lower faculty of philosophy's paradigm of critique were but expressions of the technical higher faculties' positive knowledges. Today it would be impossible to distinguish the affairs of the two faculties, so that their conflict, the central conflict of the modern university, appears as the uninterrupted hegemony of the technical faculties. What becomes apparent posthumously, non-modernly is that the modern critical university was but a modulation of the technical university, that the speculative critical paradigm was just another cog in the technical paradigm of applied research.[39]

Breakup of the Unity of the University

On this point it will be important to note the current state of affairs regarding the primary unity contained in the word "university," the diversity of knowledge that it supposedly systematizes, and the modality of this gathering.

Today, not only is the organic unity of knowledge—a unity that Husserl attempted to reestablish—bankrupt. What must be declared bankrupt is also the very inquiry into the paradigm or foundation. Knowledge today is essentially disparate. Here, "disparate" does not mean lacking any preordained harmony that would guarantee its communicability, as, for example, when it is said that different specializations have no contact with one another, that they are atomized and cloistered without windows or doors. "Disparate" here points to the fact that the speculative ideal of the systematic unity of knowledge under one principle has programmatically failed;[40] nor do we find a principle of reflection that is not entrenched in one particular discipline but would questioningly encompass them all, representing a knowledge of knowledge[41] and a knowledge of nonknowledge.[42] It is no long possible to think the unity of the university as a knowledge of knowledges, as the question concerning the condition of the condition. There can be no unitary metaknowledge that, freed from facticity,[43] would gather and orient the university amid the events in which it finds itself immersed, a metaknowledge that would grant it temporary freedom of movement amid contingency. The crisis of the university would be its inability to think itself and its context in a single thought not beholden to facticity, leaving it at the mercy of events.

> If the modern university is defined by the capacity it has for reflecting on the unitary foundations and conditions of the technical diversity it contains, we would have to conclude that the contemporary state of the university is marked by the growing impossibility of this kind of reflection. This would amount to asserting the university's end.[44]

In this same vein, the call for papers for the international colloquium "The Possible University" [La universidad posible], a call included in the resulting book, titled *La universidad (im)posible* [The (im)possible university; 2018],[45] noted the following:

> The question about the possibility of the university returns with some frequency over the course of its history. In that line of questioning, the university event appears compromised, as if its very existence depended on the question of its possibility. If this question comes from somewhere, it is from the university's customary vacillation between, on the one hand, the condition and contingencies that enable, equip, and enclose it and, on the other hand, the desire, forces, events, and contingencies that unconditionally dislocate it. Without this vacillation, the university event is eclipsed.
>
> There is nothing new in this statement. We only reiterate in broad strokes the themes of key texts published and debated in the last three decades of the twentieth century and the start of this one, texts that in turn reread and translate historically more distant and more seminal ones. What these texts methodically advance is that the university event only becomes viable when, in the midst of the facticity and conditionality that frame its possible being, an unconditional, impossible breath makes it happen. . . . [T]he memory of this questioning touches and interpellates us in those moments when the university seems to plunge into a facticity that not only blocks its relation to the unconditional but also begins to suggest that it no longer needs relation of this kind, as if the university were already not the subject of the university.
>
> At the same time, the genealogy of the university teaches us in its documented existence that the historical frequency with which the university does ask after its possibility is similar to the frequency with which it is eclipsed as pure facticity. For example, in exceptional times—when are they not, especially if we admit that "normal" times are usually just exceptional times become the rule—when the university militated in Europe's imperial vanguard as the third of its three pillars (*sacerdotium, regnum, studium*) representing, one might say, a silent outpost of conquest and colonization, evangelization, propaganda, and imperial advance, becoming itself European by managing and naturalizing imperial unity through the incorporation, discrimination, and hierarchical segregation of languages, knowledges, and bodies into the Roman-Christian vernacular (*vulgata*) of the faculties of theology, law, and medicine (its criteria) through the *ius ubique docendi*, and the *Doctor universalis ecclesiare*, the *ratione fundatorum, ratione privillegiorum*, through its monolingualism, monotheism, and monosexualism, its monopoly of the temporal and the eternal that

disciplines bodies and populations with every act of institution. Or when the medieval university became worldly, it became the weapon of choice for the European conquest and colonization of Mexico and Peru and all non-European worlds, collapsing them into the facticity of fear, hate, extermination of the other, their exclusionary inclusion as heritage and ruins, economy and slave labor, or as a *blank page* or a *page possessed* by superstition and idolatry ready to be written upon and thus purified. Or when, later, the university performed in its modern vernacular as an apparatus of nation-state sovereignties, ruling over languages, knowledges and bodies. Or when it set sail around the world as the postsovereign rentier university, the university for the transnational accreditation and ranking of programs, persons, and writings too singular to be translated into the proficiencies prescribed by globalization. Lastly, as the apparatus that simultaneously includes and excludes the university *factum*, in which—in each case [*en cada caso*] and according to different historical modes of production of its universality—the possibility, the unconditionality of the university event either draws breath or does not.

The Collapse of Disciplinary Organization

The fracture of the guiding principle of gathering stamped upon the word "university," the breakup of the university as uni-version of possible worlds would also mark the crisis of its systemic-disciplinary organization.

With regard to this disciplinary crisis of the university, one must point out that for "us," if I may say so, the disciplinary distribution of knowledge is its natural state. Whatever the degree of separation between specializations, whatever the hierarchical prestige of certain areas or the possibilities for investing in such prestige, whatever the rigidity or permeability of its generic frontiers, this state of the institution represents the only point of departure for its historical analysis in every instance [*en cada caso*].

It is impossible to fully account for how such a distribution came about, which areas were the first to consolidate and which came later; how disciplinary powers have become fixed; what disputes, reversals, and combinations have taken place; etc. Such an account would be impossible not for lack of exhaustive recounting and interpretation, but on account of events which themselves have always been in excess and inexact (Nietzsche)[46] and on account of the fact that we always arrive late to history, "after the party"— *post festum* (Marx)—so that *any* knowledge of what has happened is constituted *a posteriori—après coup* (Lacan). We must endlessly question the conditions of the "emergence" and "origin" of any itinerary that we propose for the genealogy of this disciplinary institution, if it is to help us form an image or general concept of that institution. For example, according to a

Christian conception of the world, the totality of the real is divided into three regions: God (creator), nature (creature), and man (privileged creature). Fields of research were dedicated to each, making up the concentric disciplinary organization of the medieval university: rational theology or the study of the supreme being; rational cosmology or the study of the created being; and rational psychology or the study of the privileged creature (the soul).[47] Constituting a "special metaphysics," these same disciplines set the course of the faculties of law, medicine, and theology. Furthermore, modernity's intensification of the spirit of fragmentation dismembered entire fields into "simple things" with the goal of controlling the totality through its elements.[48] The goal of a perfect medicine that would enable technical control over life and death through the mechanical transplantation of bits and pieces presupposed a "discrete" vision of the human body. The desire for an indestructible state unscathed by civil wars led to the detailed study of the passions of the spirit, the elaboration of a calculus of affect and morality that assumed methodical knowledges of the world-machine or machine-state where liberty would make its habitat.[49]

Through various narratives and famous authors, modernity conjugated its eagerness to divide and classify the real with the will to systematize everything under one heading (*ratio*), illuminating objects with equal clarity just as "the sun gives us light."[50] Modern categorical tables (tables of the elements for every possible, thinkable, buildable, appropriable world) would reach their physical-chemical zenith in the nineteenth century with Mendeleev's periodic table of the elements, exemplary evidence of the modern zeal for inventorying and observing all "there is" (Descartes) through the zoo-logic of its parts.

In the modern will and drive to divide and systematize the real into fields of objects, we begin to see the fragmentary specialization of knowledge and labor into so many fields and codes and the explosion of the four faculties of the medieval university into the fifteen or twenty faculties of the modern university.

The gradual segmentation of knowledge until it is dissolved into inorganic points of view that cannot be gathered into one territory or under one metanarrative proves that the logic of fragmentation and regionalization combined with the will to systematization underlies the whole history of the university, from the Middle Ages to its current crisis, a crisis that dissolves the teleological-theological ideal of a total gathering into today's proliferation of nomadic microknowledges and microlanguages that respect no boundary, no tradition and that, since they do not gather among themselves, are even less likely to do so under some general principle other than the unprincipled but nonetheless equivalent facticity of financial accumulation.

At the same time, knowledge is not exhausted by its sedentary, institutional state, as we can see in the continual crises of the boundaries of the university. These occur with such frequency that it would be logical to think that crisis constituted the norm of the modern university, for crisis always entails institutional redistribution.

Characteristic of the current crisis is the impossibility of a "new" university event that might move us beyond today's neoliberal degradation of the right to the university as the right to financial accumulation. In this sense we would have to call the current crisis the "crisis" of modern crisis, just as we have done until this point—that is, a non-modern crisis.

Informatics as University

Now more than ever, under the sway of telematics, heterogeneity appears bundled into the luminescent flow of a virtual nomenclature. Telematics satisfies the desire to computationally collect, archive, and organize everything there is. Telematics fashions itself as the technological realization of the teleological, encyclopedic project of the modern university by synthesizing in the continuum of media equivalencies the distribution of knowledge, the division of activity, the dream of an absolute in which things and their mediation coincide—in other words, telematic computationalization as university, university as the electrical gathering of heterogeneity. But what do we mean by "gathering" here? What type of unity does the amplified flow of electricity bestow? Why might that circulation, which defies every being to find its place within, end up dissolving that which its articulation includes through the conjunctive logic of the "and"?

André Lalande, in the second edition of his *Vocabulaire technique et critique de la philosophie* (1968), notes that the concept of organic structure designates, "in opposition to a simple combination of elements, a whole formed by phenomena in solidarity, such that each phenomenon depends on the others and can be what it is only in and through its relation with them."[51] In various texts but especially toward the end of Book VII of *The Metaphysics*, Aristotle outlines the metaphor of structure through the aporias that shape it. "'Structure' designates sometimes the prime and irreducible element of the object in question . . . that is, something more than the sum of its parts . . . an ensemble that is not a mere aggregate (σωρός)."[52] But where does this "something more" come from that transcends the simple conjunction of parts, that allows the aggregate to unify into a tense, living, organic totality? This "something more" that unifies the conjunction and gathers it into an organism must be "something other" (ἕτερόυ τι) than mere part, something other than the inorganic sum of parts. Otherwise, there would be no organicity to the organism, no structurality to the structure.

> For Aristotle, the "something else" that causes the whole to be more than the sum of its parts had to be something radically other, that is, not an element that existed in the same way as the other seven if

it were a prime, more universal element—but something that could
be found only by abandoning the terrain of division *ad infinitum* to
enter a more essential dimension. Aristotle designates this dimension
as the αἰτία τοῦ εἶναι, the "cause of being," and the οὐσία, the principle that gives origin and maintains everything in presence: not a
material element but Form (μορφὴ καὶ εἶδος).[53]

This "other thing" (ἕτερόν τι) is for Aristotle the form (μορφὴ καὶ εἶδος) in
which organic unity resides and which manifests in form by unifying and
gathering the multiplicity of its parts into an organism: the radically other
"other thing" that can only be found upon abandoning the conjunctive terrain of multiplicity that does not achieve unity; which only by transcending
it rises to the level of the cause of being, that indivisible unity that maintains
the unity of any thing through its self-presence.

Regarding the metaphor of the organism as a structure composed of
parts—as opposed to the aggregate (σωρός), elemental matter, unformed,
unarticulated, irreducible substrate deprived of rhythm; deprived of its ability to transform and copy itself, increasing the number of its parts or their
sizes; deprived of the relation among parts and of parts to whole; deprived
of the ability to adapt to the environment, to absorb energy to maintain a
constant, homeostatic internal environment, to regenerate its elements, to
manage the wear and tear of its parts, its immunity; deprived of the ability to
move one or all of its components, its internally networked processes, tropes
and translations; to maintain their unity, the functionality of the whole, the
soul or anima, the motor; deprived of their processes, whether centralized
or not, of its center, their center, its living principle, their living principles,
their autonomy, their separation; deprived of the crisis of or break from
the apparatus of which it is part, its purpose, the mode of its composition
or decomposition, of its generation or corruption, its creation or annihilation, its provenance and metamorphosis, of its rhythm, harmony, dynamics,
health, "truth," its critique and its crisis—one must distinguish mechanist
from organicist technology, whose exposition we have here exhausted. This is
the metaphor of the organism, of the living and centered structure, of the unified and structured whole that in ordinary times has played the muse, model,
and rule of the university.

If *in* telematics there appears to be no metanarrative doubling that transcendentally articulates the totality of the active reflections of the world into
one unified world—since a metareader is but one telematic data point—then
telematics serves as the factic medium in which heteroclite things are dispersed, one next to the other, conjoined by an "and"—the "and" as the final,
factic site of metanarrative.

This telematic surface would be a liberal medium. But we should not
confuse telematic liberalism with political liberalism. The latter was discre-
tionary and exclusionary of ideological totalitarianisms. Telematics is not. Its

liberality is apositional. And it is this apositionality that allows it to house every ideological position or user value [*valor usuario*]. Telematic liberal pluralism stretches to fit the morality it contains, as opposed to modern liberal pluralism, which is the polar opposite of totalitarianism. The telematic surface, blindly limitless in its capacity for absorption, offers itself as a "site" where the diversity of things comes together. In this sense it offers itself as uni-versity. Instead of the medieval-Enlightenment ideal of the university as total encyclopedia or mind of God that knows the state of things according to a principle of organic hierarchy, the informationalization of society gives way to a technological form of the university whose identity resides not in the reflexive meta-unity or metanarrative of diversity but rather in the unstable oscillation between diversity and plurality, like waves on a sea of electrons in which all things go astray.

Telematics still binds us to the nonplace, the nonground of Borges's Chinese encyclopedia. In the Chinese encyclopedia things are placed in no "place," arranged among sites so different from one another that, from the moment the encyclopedia itself becomes one of the elements it classifies, it would be impossible to find a place that would embrace them all. The Chinese encyclopedia makes us suspect that "there is no universe in the . . . unifying sense of that ambitious word."[54] In such an encyclopedia nothing floats, nothing sinks, nothing surfaces. The surface has disappeared. Telematics still steadies us when faced with the encyclopedia's vertigo, unless the actuality of telematics turns out to be but one more element of telematic virtuality.

University and Electric Mediation

The university as the pedagogical mediation between state and people, as the mechanism for inculcating young spirits,[55] as the state's "means of securing . . . influence" over the people,[56] of advancing or retarding reforms,[57] as the principle of spiritual emancipation (Humboldt), as an ideological state apparatus[58]—such a university has been displaced and disseminated across circuits of sound and screen. Such a displacement tends to weaken the theater of the teaching cloister, that prototypical gesture of the modern university, whether it is a colorless course lecture[59] with its narrative logic of beginning, middle, and end or the seminar's supposedly more polyphonic and dialogical scene. Any pedagogical theater is radicalized or undermined by the photonic performance of the clip, the spot, television's frenzied miscellany, such that the "schematism"[60] of the television-watching masses is slowly reformatted and aroused more by the logical allusions of the "spectacle" captured on the screen (Debord) than by the Aristotelian "fable" of an oral pedagogy that adheres to a script.[61] Basic educational activities traditionally found under the syllabus subheading of "General Course Objectives," such as the capacity to reason, argue, associate, conceptualize, rank, select, match, causally connect, etc., are slowly eliminated by the "frenzy" of screens, by the dispersed, heteroclite, proliferating symbolic of clip and spot, by the contiguity and simultaneity of programs, themes, and images whose rhetoric and impact are flattened and leveled.

Thus displaced and disseminated, the modern state's proclivity for central oversight of the ideological and methodological directives of the professoriat slowly wanes. And if in many localities, as in Chile, there is still a basic ideological conflict over the censorship and restriction of teaching—to which not only educational institutions adhere, private and public alike, but also the media, political parties, national networks, etc.—if such a displacement and dissemination occurs, one cannot but imagine the imminent overpowering of the professoriat by the open market and its satellite networks of information and culture, networks that, mediated by the "universal satellite," extinguish every "dark place," dissolve the principle of limits, and lead local legal systems either to destruction or to subordination to a de facto, "performative" (Lyotard), multiform, and unsettled transnational law. The modern university as the conflict between nation-state, people, language, technique, economy, truth, knowledge, and power "melts into thin air" as it is subsumed first by the expansion then by the implosion of photonic planetarity. With this expansion, local differences disappear into national differences, national differences into transnational differences. Today, if one were to try to create a synchronic cartography of knowledges, languages, traditions, styles, etc., by marking "identities" with tiny flags, we would find that the influences, colonizations, implantations, absorptions, transactions, injections, imports and exports, translations, and receptions in the academic realm, and in general, have reached such a point that we would find flags from everywhere all over the map. We would note that on such a map points and places of gathering have dissolved into transitory sites or "passages."[62] We would note that, with the ascendence of telematics, cultures no longer move from one place to another, for there are only passages. The flags have procreated. They cannot be identified as representative identities. Each flag is as variable as the map on which it is inscribed and vice versa. It does not matter if you look at a part of the map or the whole. The distinction between the whole map and one region on it has disappeared into the plurality of equivalence, the emergent secularization of the point of view.

Globalization Seen from the Year 1848

When only a few roads had scratched the surface of the planet, and means of transportation and communication still had a local reach and relied on artisanal rhythms like the rotation of the earth, it was more likely that each locality preserved its cultural and linguistic niche and the local tempo of its particular history. Viewed from Europe's sleepy villages, the discovery of the Americas and the circumnavigation of Africa gave rise to new fields of knowledge and incentives for exchange. The Indian and Chinese markets and trade with the American colonies multiplied goods and means of exchange and gave commerce, industry, and communication new motivations. Demand increased steadily. Steam power and machinery replaced small-scale manufacture with industrial production. Local markets had to seek outlets across vast swaths of the earth. Big industry also drove the creation of the universal market, which has slowly endowed production, consumption, education, and communication with a cosmopolitan character, first, by subordinating localities to the norms of the nation-state—the modern national language and university—only to later detonate the national foundations of education, the market, history, production, language and transition them toward the multi- or transnational hypermarket. The old national industries are perpetually destroyed and replaced by new ones that no longer use domestic raw materials but source from anywhere in the world, whose products are consumed both domestically and in the most distant corners of the globe. Instead of the old isolation and peripheralization of places, a communicative exchange and universal economic and spiritual interdependence have taken root, breaking down every barrier and subjugating even the most hostile and alien barbarians, who most fanatically insist upon their difference. And just as literatures become cosmopolitan, so too do sexualities, ethnicities, and their points of view from different traditions. Under penalty of being consumed as the raw materials for valorization, globalization slowly directs the peripheries to adopt modern styles of production, education, sensory perception. A planetary civilization arises that forges the world in its likeness and its image.[63]

Globalization Today

If Marx believed that a schoolteacher was a productive laborer insofar as she prepared the labor force for the labor market, today that kind of schoolteacher has multiplied infinitely under "integrated world capitalism"[64] and its performative networks for discipline, surveillance, and productivity expanding at microsocial and planetary scales, networks that generate a conglomeration of systems, environments, processes, agents, stimulations, vacuums, etc., without any necessary continuity or stability, a conglomeration of circuits that seems impossible to critique without reiterating and thus strengthening its configuration.

According to Guattari's analysis, this is no longer a network of repressive and ideological apparatuses as in Althusser[65] but rather a discontinuous megamachine composed of a shifting multitude of disparate elements not only tied to male, waged labor but organizing production everywhere at various levels: women, children, the elderly, the unemployed, professionals, etc. Through the family, television, day care, social services, etc., infancy is put to work from inception, given over to an educational process through which its various semiotic modes will be molded to awaiting productive and relational assemblages, the "equipment networks of capital."[66] It is the polymorphous and unstable nature of these assemblages that solidifies the regulatory means of regulation.

This is not the imperial expansion of a specific world, as Marx described, which makes other cultures unworldly as it becomes planetary. It is not the simple subsumption *in extenso* of whole territories by the capitalist economy but rather the intensive subsumption of the living populations of the planet. Telematic globalization would end up "really subsuming" modern subjectivity to the "process of capital valorization," such that even the nightly orgasms of anyone immersed in the expanded reproduction of capital are entirely captured by the valorization process.[67]

Since the onslaught of wireless communication, the disciplining of populations is no longer a peremptory concern about access to educational curricula but about whether or not one has coverage from the telematic satellite. As was optimistically foreseen in Hegelian times long ago, the speed and means by which putting-into-form or in-formation is electrically distributed means that the planet has become one cloister, one classroom in which each and every one is engaged in the same life lesson.[68] The potential of electricity for the educative-communicative apparatus seems limitless in a double sense. On the one hand, the communications network spreads across geographies—indefinite, planetary, interstellar.[69] On the other hand, every message can be incorporated, developed, translated, and wired into the electrical circuit. Wireless communications cast themselves as the imminent possibility of total differentiation, indefinite archive, language translocalization, the electric articulation of lifestyles, the instantaneity and simultaneity of the informatic nomenclature and luminescent flow.[70] That nomenclature or code acts as the university, and it figures the university as informatics.

If in the beginning electronic communication created a dense layer of information mediating between subject and object, today it has grown to entirely absorb subject and object, leaving nothing behind.

University in the Prospective Fiction of the Implant

According to Paul Feyerabend, scientific education "today" is tasked with carrying out a technical simplification of the "scientific process" by deadening those who participate in it—that is, everyone. Scientific and professional education proceeds in the following manner: (1) It defines an area of investigation. (2) This area is separated from the rest of knowledge and endowed with its own logic. (3) Training in this logic reconditions those working in the area. This type of training ensures that specialists do not involuntarily muddy the disciplinary asepsis that has been achieved. (4) Training inhibits and expropriates an essential part of the embodied peculiarities that would blur the boundaries the discipline defines and that define it. Thus, religious sentiment, humor, moods, sexuality, and ultimately the body must not come into contact with scientific activity. Imagination and language must restrict themselves to peculiar codes. This type of education compresses like a lotus shoe all the edges of the human physique that, as they protrude, also shape habits that are markedly different from the rationalist ideals currently in fashion among education theorists. In this sense, a specialist is someone who has chosen to excel in a narrow field at the cost of an open, polyphonic development. He has chosen to submit himself to codes and standards that stylize his behaviors, and he feels called to live a routine in every waking moment in utmost harmony with them, although it is probable that the same standards govern his dreams too. The consequences of this separation of spheres are unfortunate. Specialist subjects are seemingly bereft of contact with affective-embodied contents whose critical potential remains unclear. Such fields work with academic memory or informatics, whose potential meaning is exhausted by the subject of an enunciation that seeks to replace the speaking subject as much as possible. In this educational process, the decrease in zones of resistance is proportional to the growth of determining literalness.[71]

Analogously, "feminist criticism begins by denouncing the alibis of a philosophy of knowledge that obscures how an apparatus of hegemonic representation—occidental masculinity—captures and controls a [class, race, gender, species?] monopoly of absolute truth based on the false pretense of the transparency of its codes, the neutrality of its knowledges, its indifference to any difference."[72] Through its critique of heterosexual androcentrism, feminist theory makes visible the masculinity of university knowledges that pose as asexual, universal, disembodied. Feminist critique subverts one of the most mystified foundations of university knowledge, a presumably pure neutral knowledge, the product of a "dry intelligence without history, capable of . . . reading the truth of any text, from any time, at any time."[73]

Feyerabend also states in laymen's terms what in the language of technological speculators in education is known as the "implantation model" of habits, behaviors, structures of perception, memories, attitudes. For example, the "mechanical educator" that records in a few short seconds knowledges and skills that would take an entire university a lifetime to acquire, or the "auxiliary transducer" capable of converting light and sound waves, molecular chemistry, etc., into impressions the brain can synchronize so we can absorb animal and even vegetal subjectivity.

This implantation technique, however, has long been performed in the classic, modern educational format of the university, whose constructive (Humboldt) and panoptical (Foucault) mission internalizes habits, disciplines, specialized perspectives. Considering what therapeutic hypnosis can achieve with the implanting of false memories, one might well believe that modern education entailed performing a mass hypnosis that introjected and naturalized behaviors, codes, perspectives, and meanings.

Informatic Censorship

In *The Postmodern Condition*, Jean-François Lyotard makes the following claim: "Along with the hegemony of computers comes a certain logic, and therefore a certain set of prescriptions determining which statements are accepted as 'knowledge' statements. . . . The 'producers' and users of knowledge must now, and will have to, possess the means of translating into these [computer] languages whatever they want to invent or learn. . . . We can predict that anything in the constituted body of knowledge that is not translated in this way will be abandoned," will die.[74]

The Platonic warning about the challenges and dangers that face the stranger who chooses to reenter the "cave" after having exiled his inquiry to the outside is essentially about the linguistic-experiential transformations suffered by the traveler, mismatches and translations between the inert language of the cave and the language of whoever has spent the night outside, challenges and dangers framed by the political questions of familiarity/unfamiliarity, common language/critical language, difference, censorship, and death: the case of Socrates. Lyotard asserts that all knowledge incapable of being translated into bytes "will be abandoned." Plato suggests that linguistic difference carries the risk of death. I would like to underscore the difference in emphasis in "will be abandoned" (Lyotard) and "risk of death" (Plato). Socrates's censure is forever recorded as a philosophical, ethical, and political intervention in history, as self-martyrdom, the necessary gesture to transform the "Socrates" signature into a historical symbol and for that signature to make history. Censorship and death allow a proper name to tower over anonymity and the life of its bearer as the universal and universalizing name, a proper name immortalized as signature of the dead.[75]

What becomes evident in Lyotard is that censorship in the context of the informatization of society is singularly pursued not by an ideological, deliberating agent but by a blind process with no clear source of its will; a process without a signature that does not harbor or absorb that which its conditions do not allow it to register and digest, and that leaves no trace and will remain unmarked by the names it erases. The phrase "will be abandoned" (Lyotard) can be read, "will pass unawares," "will not enter into the flows of electric circulation," "will be utterly forgotten, like the opaque residues of a paradigm no one uses," or a crypt in a cemetery no one will visit. Censorship, oblivion, and death that make no history.

Thanks to its unlimited capacity for data entry, its ability to absorb without censorship, informatics would make for a (data) society much more open and democratic than any actually existing society. Statements like this promote the illusion that informatics and telematics will deliver on the modern encyclopedic dreams of the total archive and an absolutely representative democracy. The boundlessness of informatic memory nonetheless finds its limit in experience. Informatics can inform everything except experience.

Experience is the foundation of all information; information erases all experience. There is then an incompatibility, an untranslatability between experience and information. The informatization or total modernization of reality would bring about the amnesia of experience, an amnesia doubled by the consumption of experience as informatic "experience."

If the two linguistic moves proper to modern university knowledge consist, on the one hand, in guaranteeing its disciplinary and instrumental code and, on the other, in developing a reflexive, metacritical language for research, then the preeminence of informatics would dissolve the difference that once established and distinguished these two pillars of the modern university.

> We have only to mention telecommunications and data processing to assess the extent of the phenomenon: the end-orientation of research is limitless; everything in these areas proceeds "in view" of technical and instrumental security. At the service of war, of national and international security, research programs have to encompass the entire field of information, the stockpiling of knowledge, the working and thus also the essence of language and of all semiotic systems, translation, coding and decoding, the play of presence and absence, hermeneutics, semantics, structural and generative linguistics, pragmatics, rhetoric. I am accumulating all these disciplines in a haphazard way, on purpose, but I will end with literature, poetry, the arts and fiction in general: the theory that has these disciplines as its object can be just as useful in ideological warfare as it is in experimentation with variables in all-too-familiar perversions of the referential function. Such a theory may always be put to work in communications strategy, the theory of commands, the most refined military pragmatics of jussive utterances.[76]

The informatization of society forces us to consider that the university city is no longer a metaphor referring to the separation of the university campus from its context by barriers and walls. That campus has become a metropolis and the ordinariness of civic life. It has literally become a city university, a professional informatics planet.

The growth of telematics into its current interface often appears pathetically as a medium that unilaterally subsumes, disciplines, and controls other mediations, which it seeks to subordinate entirely. The homogenizing record of this uniform, planetary subsumption, the transcendental *factum* so often spoken about, can be described as the record of a planned, productivist, calculating, utilitarian thinking that subjects, organizes, and regulates everything it touches, the whole of society. A mediating *factum* that embraces all zones of existence, outfitting it in the flow of an intelligent automaton that arranges all that exists into vectors of certainty, functionality, automatization, bureaucratization, information, communication, administration, cognitive capitalism.[77]

But this understanding of telematics as university medium in the conjunctive metanarrative of the "and" seems to reanimate a recurrent fetishization.

Would there not be in the subsumption of a present in which multiple modes of production, technologies, heterogeneous media bodies coexist, in which coexisting languages clash, refract, and translate each another, subordinate and resubordinate one another in their disagreements and deflections and at different tempos—according to this understanding of telematics would there not be a one-sided hypertrophy of a mediality that emulates in its homogeneity other media and bodies without containing even a bit of them but instead poses as their encyclopedia, as the metamediality of mediation, as the university of universities? Would this not once more reinscribe in the fetish of subsumption the ongoing homogenization that precedes the eruption of this overpowering mediality capable of emulating with its succinct mediality other coexisting medialities, suggesting by the immediacy of its eruption that it had supplanted them, as film and photography once did? Film, which like many technologies is in fact transmedial, also gave the illusion of subsuming precinematographic technologies and temporalities to its plane of immanence. For example, "When Abel Gance fervently proclaimed in 1927, 'Shakespeare, Rembrandt, Beethoven will make films. . . . All legends, all mythologies, and all myths, all the founders of religions, indeed, all religions, . . . await their celluloid resurrection, and the heroes are pressing at the gates.' "[78] Do not Shakespeare, Rembrandt, and Beethoven, legends and myths, prophets and heroes, literature, theater, music, dance, painting, and poetry—to which we might add cinema, Ricciotto Canudo's seventh art[79]—crowd together onto the screen awaiting their resurrection, as Gance suggested? According to Benjamin, they crowd together to the point of "comprehensive liquidation," that is, to the point of replacing the auras of their literary and historiographical positions.[80] In film, in photography, in digital publicity, in photomontage, electrical fusion, and in general in the workings of citation materially realized in the same mode of production, there is no collision of modes of production but instead the inbreeding of the producibility and emulating power of the same medium. The supposed collision of media is nothing but the reiteration of the same technology in the guise [fetiche] of presenting another. When photography photographically treats painting, it does not collide with painting; it simply unfolds, regarding only itself and its image-producing capacity. When film treats painting, the spoken story, Greek mythology, the history of the Roman Empire's expansion or the extermination of Indigenous peoples in the United States or in Argentina, when it promotes the cultural fundamentalism of exemplary lives in Hollywood megaproductions, it only tautologically regards its own potential for fabricating images and cinematographic narratives. The only revival, the only resurrection is of film itself and its possibilities.

Were Pixar to digitally produce an analog *Pinocchio*, and not digital technology or Collodi's Italian literary work, it would exhibit endogenously its own medium in the illusion of presenting an artisanal handicraft through postindustrial cinematography's frame. Painting is only about painting. Film is only about film. The digital is only about the digital. The digital circulation of an image of someone disappeared does not represent the disappeared person. And if we aestheticize the image with the aura of the disappeared, that is, when the spectator materializes in the belief that he has discovered his "magic cloak," disappearance is only further interred in the appearance of digital circulation. Thus, telematics is only about telematics and its impacts on a society that began its planetarization long before its arrival, regardless of how arrogant and imperialist the capitalist use of this medium may be.

At the same time, we must mention that there simply are no pure media. There are no pure media in a world where *"truth begins at two."*[81] There is no pure quantity of mediality, except as a referential illusion and as an attempt to ground a specific mode of production. Where there is a medium, there are already media, just as where there is color there are already colors. Each medium is constituted like a Bororo myth, a patchwork or citationality of many myths, a translation or refraction that says and does in one medium what the other medium cannot say or do.[82]

The mode of production, that unilateral mediality, no longer works. There was never a single mode of production, except as an illusion or myth created by a singular technology whose comprehensive framework endogenously organizes the multiplicity, fetishizing it through one general, homogenous mediation.

2

✦

From the Epic to Kitsch, from Enthusiasm to Boredom

But before adopting the perspective of the context, perhaps we should begin with the crucial question of affect, the state of mind in classrooms and on university campuses, as well as the feeling that our topic, the university, arouses in us.

Nowadays just speaking about the university, setting out to write about it, or beginning a reading that takes it as a topic leads only to weariness. For starters, the university seems unable to generate intellectual "enthusiasm" (Kant) or even "entertainment" (Hume). When we get even a whiff of it, we look to flee the state of mind and the heaviness that it threatens.[1] Weariness and heaviness imbue the presidential addresses that inaugurate and conclude each academic year; they imbue the committees of administrators, rectors, and ministers; they imbue the calculating sociology of higher education, its accreditations and rankings, its up-to-date commercial mission and vision statements.

For us, such heaviness is not, however, merely accidental or purely circumstantial in relation to the university. In many places, it is an evental affect, and not only when it comes to the university object but for society in general. The university is no longer an epic institution not because of the rector's pronouncements or the sociologists' measurements but because the context has brought about the end of epic, that of the university and of global society, the end of the "enthusiasm"[2] that imbues all epic, of every self-conscious act that stages its own occurrence in the utopian teleology of progress and emancipation.

For the university and society, this context signifies a weakening of politics, science, and those modern practices that bear an ideology or philosophy of history. First and foremost, it signifies a weakening of the ideology of progress. This context signifies the bankruptcy of the progressive teleological ideal of emancipation, the bankruptcy of the illusion that struggle can achieve something new and better. It signifies the sinking into the immanence of routine tasks, dispossessed of any narrative expression that would assign ranks and places, bestowing on them a future dense with meaning. It signifies the weakening of exhilaration in the face of crisis because, strictly speaking, crisis will no longer signify progress. This context signifies the end of crisis as the crisis of progress.

There was a time when the word "university" channeled this epic affect into the *house of intellect*.[3] The scholar, the academic was the hero and priest of history. Without question, the importance of everything brought under that heading earned it the most exclusive privileges: autonomy from the state and society; archive and center of universal knowledge; education and construction of the spirit of a people; qualification of the labor force; source of national learning; "knowledge" of knowledge, that is, reflection and questioning of the truth of science, justice, and law; guardian and regulator of progress and emancipation; surpassing individual human figures through the construction of the universal human figure; integrating native dialects and local poetics into the national language; the gradual integration of the national language into "trans-" or multinational relations, protocols, and formats; and so on—an endless stream of words about the "mission" of the university, of the missionary university and thus the imperialist university.

The current atmosphere surrounding knowledge, the state, the people, language, spirit, truth, nature, history, the human race—if these do not stand in the way of the higher education industry and the expanded circulation of knowledge in the marketplace or the generalized imperative to professionalize—has at least dulled the university's shine, its epic brilliance as hero of history, leader of nations and of humanity as a whole.[4]

The emblems of its epic now constitute its kitsch, the kitsch of the university, knowledge, history, its neoliberal public face in the philosophies of the history of value in motion. It cannot be otherwise in a context in which the heroism of science and creativity—organically linked to teleological narratives, utopian transcendence, dogmatic vanguardism—has been slowly unveiled by the functionalism immanent to our curricular regimens and methodical means for appropriating professional intelligence in installments,[5] credentializing curricula that are as easily exchanged [*transitable*] as goods in a supermarket or items in a buffet where anyone can order from a menu of specializations and codes and, on the condition that one adapts to current customs, create one's own techno-professional smorgasbord for surviving the already discredited daily routines devoid of any philosophy of history. The humanist and progressive emblems and impulses of the modern university—emblems that indiscriminately populate today's presidential addresses—have no other function than to adorn and veil the university's commercial ties and public relations. Such emblems, in any case, do not tell us either the meaning or the direction of the university administration. On the contrary, the administration determines and deploys the reach and impact of the university's meaning.

The university no longer resides in the meaning and temporal density that generated these emblems and promises long ago. The corrosion of the speculative principle (the internal and organic unity of knowledge) and the immanentization of the practical, teleological principle of progress, these principles that once legitimated knowledge practices (research and teaching) by endowing them with metafunctional meaning have now been emptied by the *performativity* of functionality, technological productivist effectiveness, and the mere communicative contiguity of knowledges and practices.[6] Due to this delegitimation—or legitimation through performance alone—the university is no longer oriented toward training an elite capable of leading the nation to emancipation or professionalizing the workforce according to the teleology education → production → income → freedom → happiness.[7] It instead appears oriented toward supplying the agents needed to fill the practical positions that businesses require,[8] what Parsons and Platt defined as "instrumental activism."[9] The university does not project itself beyond the translation of curricular routine into professional routine, effective and accurate management, the self-referential process of technical work and the improved reproduction of "itself." It admits no future beyond deadlines and student debt, and it harbors no expectations beyond the acquisition of the codes, keys, and cosmetics for entering and exiting the hegemonic market.

Rather than light the university's way against the tide of capital, philosophies of history reveal themselves as the outcomes of a process that, lacking any philosophy of history, produces philosophies of history that fetishize this process as emancipatory conflict.

Immersed in the mediocrity of reproductive maturity, far from its teleological protagonism, the university goes unnoticed as one process among many everyday processes, more productivist and commercial than ever, and as vigorous and stable as the financialized market. On occasion it garners attention when a service breakdown occurs or when it goes off script. Only the lack of university, the threat of its scarcity or inaccessibility—due to a lack of capacity, high tuition costs, academic deficiency, etc.—only when faced with the imminent possibility of losing or lacking the university utility and university credentials indispensable for earning a living in a society committed to professionalism, only then are we interpellated by the university. It makes itself felt and it opens up to us as it breaks down, when it fails us, exposing us to the insecurity of being discredited and incompetent on the national or transnational labor market and in everyday *marketing*, vulnerable to the demerit of being unable to guarantee the introjection (psychological incorporation) of a diet of university-professional habits and competencies even in small doses, vulnerable to the threat of that which is "out of context." To be of the university is to be equipped with a set of habits that authorizes and grants access to a decent salary, although this is not always ensured. To be of the university means having the means to live. But even before that, it means meeting the necessary conditions to embed oneself in the context. That is its only privilege.

The Crisis of University Representation

If we accept the hypothesis that Kant's *Conflict of the Faculties* (1798) and the series of German philosophical writings surrounding the creation of the University of Berlin in 1810 (Schelling, Fichte, Schleiermacher) outline the system of categories, limits, and relations that constitute the "transcendental architectonics" of the modern university vis-à-vis the medieval university's system of limits, if we abide by this hypothesis, we must consider that when we talk about the crisis of the modern university, we are also talking about the total or partial inapplicability of Kant's table of categories. We are talking about the empirical university's displacement beyond the limits of modern categories, and the limits not only of the modern code but of any code.[10] We are pointing out the impossibility of mapping the current state of university affairs. Modern categories (state, people, language, autonomy, reflection, truth, technique, history, progress, etc.) have lost their representative and referential power.

We are not dealing with a conceptual crisis in the face of the eruption of a new, substitute university categorization, the emergence and repositioning of one discourse upon the demise of another. Instead, we are dealing with the crisis of discourse, of the categorial full stop. For the same reason, this is a crisis of philosophy that cannot be controlled or regulated by discourse, at least not by a philosophical discourse that would be able to speak to the university. We lack the categories for analyzing the event of the crisis of the categories, including the category of "crisis" that recurs throughout this text.

The Disempowerment and Transparency of the University

Even speaking about the modern university, its structure and its code, likely indicates its collapse. It may well be that one can only speak about that which is in decline, that which has been dislodged from its "subject" position and now finds itself degraded to the status of an object. It may well be that we can only speak about that which has begun to deteriorate. Thus, when we speak of the modern university, we do so because the power that sustained it is in decline. Disempowered, it becomes visible and is readied for its discursive disruption, which, in a certain sense, it already is.

The modern university's structure no longer operates invisibly, as its full strength once allowed. Everyone talks about the modern university, the state and its crisis, as well as the crisis of the people, progress, epic, and history. Its essence is to be seen and spoken about often, an object ready for use and commentary. That said, when we talk about the collapse of one power or force, we assume the emergence of another that causes it. Such an "other," emergent power would remain hidden, discursively unrepresentable. Unseen, it becomes the eyes we use to see it, the invisible condition of visibility. We cannot define or situate this new force or its imaginary, given that the reverse is true. Behind our backs, it is this force that defines and situates us.

We cannot define it, but we understand it. Indirectly we can sense it, and we must presuppose its existence upon realizing that we ordinarily see, speak, and refer to the modern university's imaginary, its code and architectonics. Indeed, the act of handling and deciphering the "entrails" of the modern university would be impossible from within its cleft body.[11] As stipulated by the analytic procedure, every reading requires distinct sites for that which reads and that which is read, a site that opens to reading. Without this spatial difference, there can be no reading.

Making use of a contemporary formulation, we might call this emergent power the "non-modern university." At the same time, we admit that our words and concepts are powerless to refer to this power that would today determine us. Even the word "university" would be an example. Our attempt to theorize the current state of the university, in the sense of making visible its invisible conditions of possibility, would be characterized by linguistic-categorial impotence.

Information and Theory of the University

Neither novel nor urgent, examining and talking about the university appears common and even redundant considering its inflation and trivialization as a "topic" of study, measurement, historical scrutiny, and book-length interpretation. The publishing market, with its many niches, is flooded with innumerable books and papers on the university. Its name has been reduced to common currency, and everyone is informed and qualified to make claims about the university. Why, then, should we focus on the university or pause to reflect on it?

At the same time, this overabundance of measurements, information, monographs, and claims about the university could be a sign that the word "university" has become meaningless, a modern-day fossil. This swollen bibliography-by-the-bundle "about" the university is more likely [*verosímil*] data redundancy than a theory of the university, especially if we presuppose that both this bibliography and the process of informatization are professional-university in nature, that is, produced, legitimated, stylized, and directed by the university function. It is the university that speaks in every utterance that takes the university as its topic. Sociology and history speak topically about the university, and in this they easily perform their enlightening task. For such utterances to be enlightening, they must cloister themselves on university grounds, couch themselves in its style and its method of analysis and exposition. Thus, it is the university itself that is replete with these topical analyses, descriptions, chronologies, classifications, and comparisons. These works are university events, *empirie*, more than a theory of the university. And rather than speaking "about" the university, the university speaks through them. Whatever their value may be, these sociologies are still controlled by the same programmatic spaces they presume to analyze. If, as we have suggested, the form of the university in general is in crisis, so too is this copious bibliography dedicated to explicating the university—a bibliography that will one day become part of the history of a university that once was, a history (up)rooted in a present that has outgrown it.

We have a surfeit of information about the university and some comprehension of it, at least in certain corners of discourse. And although that understanding may not have a theoretical relation to the university, it nonetheless sustains our daily relationships and references to it.

The common sense of those who have passed through the university disseminates an understanding of it. Technical professional labor, research of many kinds, decentralized bureaucracy all move with university ease, all breathe university air. The university has formed them and informed them. The university is reiterated in every technically qualified or professional practice.

Everything Speaks Universitarily; Nothing Speaks "of" the University

Without necessarily taking it as our topic, we all speak of the university insofar as we speak like it. Every object speaks of the university; the university speaks through objects. Who would be able to speak "about" it, since it increasingly appears that any discursivity, any utterance endowed with status or authority, any serious professional talk presupposes the university as its backer and guarantee? Who or what could speak persuasively "of" the university, through its professionals or its logic, except the university itself? Moreover, it has long been thought problematic that one should try to account for or explain oneself. So how might an explanation escape incorporation into the explaining body as another limb that would itself require explanation, and so on and so forth?

How to speak nonuniversitarily about the university? How do we take precautions against its style so that, once we have gotten around it, we can claim theoretical autonomy from it? And were we to achieve this, how would we make it listen to us? If someone were to speak nonuniversitarily about the university, would that speech even be taken into consideration? And if it were, would it not be appropriated immediately by the university, turned into its medium, its guru of the day?

This is a poetic challenge for the language of critique, which risks reiterating in what it "says" that which it wants to recant. How and in what language can one not speak contextually about the context? How and in what language can one read the language of the university? How and in what language can one not speak the university's language yet still be heard by it? How can one not speak and ultimately still be heard? How can one be heard without being assimilated, not even by oneself?

Not Speaking Universitarily, the Faculty of Philosophy Gathers the University (Kant)

With regard to the modern university and its critical distance, the language of that distance can only be the language of its critique, its writing, phrasing, and philosophy—a writing, phrasing, and philosophy that did not exist until they occurred in the vicissitudes of Kant's writing. Just as with Freud and psychoanalysis, we cannot overlook that at the moment of writing the texts that would later become the documentary source of *critical philosophy*, Kant knew nothing of *critical philosophy*. He could not know critical philosophy because there was no critical philosophy to know. If Kant knew about anything, it was about metaphysics or dogmatic, precritical philosophy. He knew about metaphysics or precritical philosophy not because he had formally dedicated himself to studying it for many years. Rather, he knew metaphysics because he had internalized it to the point of constituting himself as a metaphysical subject, for after having internalized it, after metaphysics became his hands, the hands with which Kant the metaphysician worked and worried the world that he handled metaphysically, little by little he left that dogmatic comprehending handwork behind for a critical comprehending handwork instead.

Architectonically and universitarily, Kant entrusted critical performance to the faculty of philosophy. The faculty of philosophy withdraws questioningly from the limits that sovereignty outlines for the university, understood as teachable and publishable knowledges. Insofar as the university is a natural vehicle reproducing the law, the king, sovereignty—understood as teachable and publishable knowledges—it owes allegiance to that law and that sovereignty. Its ability to teach and to speculate in public, to transfer knowledges and habits to "civil society" is subject to the actuality [*actualidad*] of sovereignty.[12] In this sense, the reality of sovereignty and the reality of the university are coextensive. But the Kantian faculty of philosophy questions the limits of sovereignty, the limits of reality. It does not coincide with the reality of sovereignty, it is untimely. It withdraws questioningly from that actuality, its limits, its conditions of possibility. This withdrawal presupposes the crisis and critique of the limits and actuality within which sovereignty is exercised. It sets itself to setting the effective limits of what can be thought and said in public. It sets itself to setting the limits of the university's remit. By not simply adhering to those limits, not simply conforming to them, the faculty of philosophy enters into a state of exception, so to speak, with regard to sovereign language, its present, its communicability, responsibility, stability, and given historical actuality. The language of the faculty of philosophy, as critique of sovereign linguistic dispositions, is not for that reason simply actual, it is not simply communicative, not simply public. For that very reason Kant could assert that publishing need not make public. It falls on the margins of the public, of communicability and comprehensibility, on the margins of sovereignty, its tympanum,[13] its agency, its actuality. This inactuality [*inactualidad*], this misalignment between sovereign actuality and the faculty of philosophy's temporality or untimeliness is the essential, evental conflict of the modern university as critical university.

Above all, the walls of the university allude to this reflexive, untimely withdrawal of the faculty of philosophy from the system of sovereignty, actuality, and the university's remit. The crumbling of that wall, that boundary, that difference or dispute between critique and reality would mark the end of the Kantian architectonics of the modern university, the end of its possibilities. This impossible Kantian architectonics in the heart of precritical sovereignty inscribes and sustains its impossibility only so long as the boundary, the wall, the difference, the vacillation between reality and critique lives and breathes. More than anything—more than judgment, tribunal, or concept—this breathing, this difference, is what we call critique, critical philosophy, the critical university, *the conflict of the faculties*. (We will return to this point later on.)

As stated above, the documentary genealogy of the university also teaches us that the university fulfills its role as the historical questioning of its own possibility just as frequently as it is eclipsed as pure facticity. Today, it is eclipsed by the governmental facticity of the accrediting and ranking of programs, persons, and writings whose goal is to exhaust the time of critique, the untimely time of the modern university, by means of commercial accountability. They aim to exhaust the time of the conflict of the faculties with a conflict of universities without time, without untimeliness, universities rendered coextensive with financial facticity.

According to the Kantian blueprint, the task of the faculty of philosophy is not to pedagogically influence the people through disciplinary curricular means. The faculty of philosophy is not educational or edifying. It cannot be so if the specificity of its event is to question the hidden judgments of common sense, a questioning that exceeds the performative limits of actuality.

Instead of speaking in or from the organized and instituted possibilities of language, the faculty of philosophy is only interested in delving into the conditions of these possibilities. Instead of making itself heard in the actuality of language, it wants to make the limits of actual language audible, those linguistic limits in which the truth and meaning of the professional faculties and government management are inscribed. The linguistic atopia of the faculty of philosophy is to think and write actuality, power, organized and organizing possibility. The faculty of philosophy's task is only viable at the expense of the (im)possible: to think power without power; to speak of

language in language. This (im)possible turning [*peripecia*][14] of events constitutes the internal movement of the modern faculty of philosophy. Its reflexive
potential does not allow it to be determined by some linguistic canon. It is
autonomous. Obeying the motives of its own autonomy, it surpasses organized codes and speech. Its linguistic contorsions and incommunicability
derive from this.

If we call this (non)place or outside of power "esoteric," the esotericism
of the faculty of philosophy is such that it does not publish, as Kant points
out, but it does circulate its writings in the public square. It does not publish, because its idiolect is unintelligible and undecipherable to both common
speech and the language of the king.[15]

Moving queryingly among the conditions of possibility of actuality, Kant
conceives the modern faculty of philosophy as the possibility of historical
intervention. Therein lies its power—not an executive or constructive power
but a reflexive and critical one.

The Kantian inversion of the faculties and their conflict—the lower faculty (philosophy) displaces the higher faculties (theology, law, medicine) to
become the center of the university—marks the transition from the medieval
to the modern university: a secularized university as the critique of established
knowledge and power, as concern for autonomy, the history of emancipation,
and the historical transcendental conditions of truth.

If the faculty of philosophy withdraws from the present [*actualidad*] by
questioning the limits of its meaning, it does not withdraw from history.
Rather it gives rise to history through its power to read and withdraw.

3

✦

"Our" Actual Faculties of Philosophy

Our actual faculties of philosophy do not follow the Kantian design. The professional constitution of the faculty of philosophy as a disciplinary curriculum for teaching and learning the canon (with varying degrees of eclecticism or specialization) structurally forecloses the untimely difference, *the conflict of the faculties* between actuality, a canon's fetishistic power, and critique. It encloses concern for the conditions of knowledge in the professional will to form a nineteenth-century canon of knowledges.[1] The modern Kantian functions of the faculty of philosophy—(1) the knowledge of knowledge, (2) the questioning and critical gathering of instituted knowledge, (3) the condition of autonomy of university and state—are abdicated by the disciplinary linguistic institution of the faculty of philosophy understood as the repetition of a canon. The historical curricular inscription of the faculty of philosophy into the university-technical division of knowledge carries philosophical language from the critical zone into one of the flawlessly equipped, instituted, communicative districts of sovereignty and actual university governmentality. The disciplinary constitution of philosophy forecloses the faculty of philosophy's critical possibility in the act of canon formation. Reflection on the conditions of language in general—that question directed beyond language—is professionally redirected toward those conditions most expedient for generating a canon. In other words, it abandons philosophy as writing "in," "with," and "against" language[2] and recomposes philosophical production in the "organized poverty of papers . . . the technical interpretation of thinking as the defining philosophy of western universities . . . philosophy that, as conception of theoretical production and culture, need not be officially recognized in order to act as official philosophy."[3]

More than questioning actuality or the linguistic and disciplinary state of knowledge, our current faculties of philosophy align with the erstwhile technical or higher faculties (theology, law, medicine) by limiting themselves to a canon of authors and subjects. The content of this canon returns, in various modulations, to the history of philosophy and its systematic organization of philosophical disciplines: ethics, aesthetics, metaphysics, epistemology, philosophy of language, etc.

The faculty of philosophy has not been strengthened by replacing its reflexive function with a professional academic inscription. Contrary to the experience of other disciplines, which have become stronger to the extent they transgress the specificity of their field, professionalized philosophy has been losing its relevancy and necessity for the university, the state, and society. The modern university and society needed a faculty that reflected on history, science, language more than a department specialized in the history of philosophy. The faculty's surrender of its search without method for a metacriterion increasingly undermines it. Increasingly, its existence is no longer necessary. This void in the wake of its surrender is filled by the language of the social sciences, a language that methodologically abandons the "fundamental zone" only to performatively resolve the issue of the criterion. The secularization of meaning carried out by the social sciences' positivism has further weakened the transcendental critical focus that the modern faculty of philosophy once championed and that made it the "hero" of knowledge and history. The productive forces that still support the faculty of philosophy in the professional market of university languages represent the kitsch of a "knowledge of knowledges" that the faculty once (when?) epically monopolized as a guide by antonomasia. The faculty of philosophy survives out of inertia thanks to a middling culture that reproduces the idea of a "higher" knowledge (the knowledge of knowledges).

If one could point to motives for why this has happened, one would have to analyze the undifferentiation of philosophy's pedagogical task and its task in general. Indeed, in a modernized environment in which no one directly cites any philosophy other than curricular philosophy, the practice of the specialist, the professor of philosophy becomes associated with the practice of the philosopher. A practice bound up with a language and a society it has historically abraded, that categorically and metaphorically charts a line of questioning through the historical and technical conditions of knowledge and power—this practice comes to be identified with that of the specialist in philosophical texts. The practice of the specialist in Plato or Kant becomes confused with the practice that produced the work that bears those signatures. On this confused basis, when one points out the difference between a professor of philosophy and the "great" names of philosophical production, the difference between their activities is not underscored as it should be, but is instead treated only as a difference in intensity, ability, or genius among colleagues. One would have to strictly differentiate these practices in order to then specify their points of encounter and relation, following Schopenhauer's lead, for example:

> The teaching of philosophy at universities certainly benefits it in various ways. Thus it obtains an official existence and its standard is raised before the eyes of men whereby its existence is constantly brought to mind and men are made aware of it. But the main

advantage from this will be that many a young and capable mind is
made acquainted with it and is encouraged to study it. Yet it must be
admitted that, whoever is capable and thus in need of it, would also
come across it and make its acquaintance in other ways. For those
who cherish one another, and are born for one another, readily come
together. . . . But, in general, I have gradually formed the opinion
that the above-mentioned use of the chair-philosophy is burdened
with the disadvantage which philosophy as a profession imposes on
philosophy as the free investigation of truth, or which philosophy by
government order imposes on philosophy in the name of nature and
mankind. In the first place, a government will not pay people to con-
tradict directly, or even only indirectly, what it has had promulgated
from all the pulpits by thousands of its appointed priests or religious
teachers. . . . But through this circumstance university philosophers
land themselves in a very curious position whose open secret may
here receive a few words. In all the other branches of knowledge the
professors are obliged only to teach as far as possible and to the best
of their ability what is true and correct. But only in the case of professors of philosophy are we to understand the matter *cum grano salis.*
Thus we have here a curious state of affairs due to the fact that the
problem of their science is the same as that about which religion also
in its way gives us information. I have, therefore, described religion as
the metaphysics of the people. Accordingly, the professors of philosophy are also, of course, supposed to teach what is true and correct;
but this must be fundamentally and essentially the same as that which
is also taught by the established religion that is likewise true and
correct. . . . From this we see that in philosophy at the universities
truth occupies only a secondary place and, if called upon, she must
get up and make room for another attribute. . . . In consequence of
this, university authorities will always permit only such a philosophy
to be taught . . . [that] runs essentially parallel thereto [established
religion]; and so . . . it is always at bottom and in the main nothing
but a paraphrase and apology of the established religion.[4]

If in its Kantian design, the faculty of philosophy was an untimely center for reading the present and for that reason capable of intervening into
the present by asking after its truth, today's faculties of philosophy are pure
actuality and zero potentiality when it comes to reading their conditions. Into
oblivion with questioning the conditions of the present. Into oblivion with
the question of being.

II

University, Universality, and Languages

As is their nature, they camp under the open sky, for they abominate dwelling houses. They busy themselves sharpening swords, whittling arrows, and practicing horsemanship. This peaceful square, which was always kept so scrupulously clean, they have made literally into a stable. . . . Speech with the nomads is impossible. They do not know our language, indeed they hardly have a language of their own. They communicate with each other much as jackdaws do. A screeching as of jackdaws is always in our ears. Our way of living and our institutions they neither understand nor care to understand. And so they are unwilling to make sense even out of our sign language. You can gesture at them till you dislocate your jaws and your wrists and still they will not have understood you and will never understand. They often make grimaces; then the whites of their eyes turn up and foam gathers on their lips, but they do not mean anything by that, not even a threat; they do it because it is their nature to do it. Whatever they need, they take. You cannot call it taking by force. They grab at something and you simply stand aside and leave them to it. . . . The Emperor's palace has drawn the nomads here but does not know how to drive them away again. . . . This is a misunderstanding of some kind; and it will be the ruin of us.

—Kafka, "An Old Manuscript"

University, Universality

We hear from many disciplines about the collapse of the modern university, its consummation, its end, although not unequivocally. The preaching about the university's exhaustion applies just as much to politics. The collapse of the modern university and modern politics are inseparable so long as the modern categorial architectonics of the university coincides with that of politics.[1] The collapse of the modern national university and the collapse of the state and ideology are inseparable.

I want to emphasize that the crisis of the university also heralds the crisis of universality and the crisis of philosophy, if philosophy constitutes the *habitat* of the universal. The crisis of the university as crisis of universality gives greater import to universality than to the university. The crisis of the university is a dividend of the crisis of universality. On this account, the university would be the skin of universality, its mise-en-scène in every instance [*en cada caso*]. Philosophical universality would hypothetically serve as the university's pre-universitarily determined, pre-university foundation. From its Socratic establishment and Roman and Christian expansion, through its modern explosion[2] and contemporary implosion, philosophical universality has been translated as: (1) the monotheistic imperial university controlled by the heteronomy of a regressive teleological, theological universal; (2) the modern, technical, national university guided by the autonomy of the subject-knowledge that, supported by the sovereignty of its "internal jurisdiction," chooses the subjections over which to establish propriety in the teleological, progressive act of its self-production; (3) the telematic, transnational university, whose dispersed *factum* cannot be gathered under one discourse or representational cartography—a technological university that knows nothing of its knowledge, knows nothing of itself, and forgets its origins in the facticity of effects and influences; (4) the non-modern entrepreneurial university whose evental horizon is no longer the production and reproduction of knowledges, the professional and spiritual formation of the productive forces of the nation, the conflict of the faculties over the meaning of the university and the nation-state in an imperialist, neocolonial context, but rather the accumulation of postcolonial, non–state finance capital that, lacking any particular sector or usership [*usuariedad*], uses them all for capitalist growth—including education and the university—while also capturing bodies and actions by subsuming them financially.

When today one speaks of the crisis of the university, one also speaks of the crisis of modern universality. If that universality is the Eurocentric universality of the philosophy of freedom (Hegel) and progress (Comte), the crisis of the modern university corresponds to the crisis of freedom and progress. The crisis of universal progress and the universal progress of freedom stand at the core of today's crisis of the university.

When one speaks of the collapse of the university, one also speaks of the exhaustion of a meaning presupposed by the modern university and in which it was inscribed, an open-ended meaning in the modern university's categorial architectonics. Here we return again to Kant's *Conflict of the Faculties* and the series of philosophical texts produced in the context of the founding of the University of Berlin[3] and Germany's "spiritual resistance" to Napoleonic politics.[4] It was in this discursive context that the modern university's system of limits was worked out: the boundaries that enclose the university and the nonuniversity, the law or framework of obligations, the law or possibility that regulates the university's autonomy, censure, and remit. In the present, the university event cannot be captured by such an architectonics.

This entails an expansive argument—one that far exceeds this text—but that can be broadly organized in the following subsections: (a) a metaphysical conception of universality as origin or anteriority in Plato and Aristotle and its later Roman and Christian translation as the medieval university; (b) a metaphysical conception of the university as the progress of an instrumental utopia and its translation as the Cartesian-Napoleonic university, on the one hand, and the Kantian-Humboldtian critical university, on the other; (c) a metaphysical conception of universality as a statist, imperialist, expansionist position obeying the concepts of "interest," "struggle," "dominion," "world hegemony," etc., and its translation as the class university (Marx); (d) the factic realization of universality as the planetary movement of capital (telematics and market) that detranscendentalizes the performance of enlightened universality with micro-, panoptic, commercial disciplinary events; (e) the genealogical dissolution of universality (Nietzsche) and of the teleological and theological university (gathered) in the (unclaimed) atheist university; (f) the Spanish American university as (1) the formal subsumption of "Indigenous knowledge" to the grid of a Latin inventory or university catalog by teaching the Other to read and write in Spanish, in other words, the gesture of Bartolomé de las Casas in his *Historia*;[5] (2) the Spanish American creole reception of modern universality following Larra's motto, "Let us translate and weep"; (3) Bello, Sarmiento, Martí, Letelier, Darío, and the translation of other languages and the promotion of their study under the sovereignty of Latin American Spanish; (4) the formulation of the concept of translation starting from the Latin American university in a non-modern context in which some Europeans (many of them Latin American) conceive Latin American Spanish as a reservoir of meaning; (5) the idea of the Latin American university as a nonimperial, intranscendent, atranscendental general store filled with unintentional refractions of meaning that go against the grain of the modern, imperialist, creole university.[6]

University, Universality, and Philosophical Project

Contrary to its foundation and the ground of particularities that inhabit it, in every instance [*en cada caso*], albeit not universitarily, the university invests with universality those knowledges that it gathers, produces, and develops, drawing away from the solecism, idiocy, and particularity of life worlds. By this predication, the university claims that its knowledge hovers above linguistic geography unperturbed by the interest or finitude that articulates, comprehends, and translates it all at once.

A statement such as this thinks that truth and science are ultimately extra-linguistic. The fiction that truth lies beyond language had been necessary to guarantee a space for the univocity, universality, and communion that cannot be governed on the babelic terrain of languages. Every truth "reduced" to language is particularized and adjusted to the multivocal and polysemic.

A supralinguistic truth, the notion that truth cannot be fully restored through language, had to apply discretion in regulating the empirical inter-communication among languages and histories, prefiguring the community's common sense [*verosímil*]. The supralinguistic ideal of university truth managed to cancel out the noise, the experiential difference borne in every dialect, through an instrumental conception of language as a means of communicating and expressing a truth higher than and prior to dialect. In every instance [*en cada caso*], this supralinguistic university ideal denies dialect and experience as elements or environments suitable for truth.

Even in the origins of philosophy's project (Plato, Aristotle), the characteristics of universality, univocity,[7] communicability, and transparency clung to the idea of truth. The original motive of the philosophical project became confused with the motives of community and unity. According to this line of thinking, philosophy emerges in reaction to the dispersion and transhumance of truth and law as represented in the myth of Babel and the dissemination of languages. The philosophical project is rooted in the motive of universality, gathering, community, as the institution of the university institution will later reflect.

If we admit that every location or demarcation of the origin of philosophy is constitutively a philosophy about that origin—there being no "singular" origin—it is no less certain that the dominant philosophy about the origin of philosophy holds that it emerges "when the might of union vanishes from the life of men and the antitheses lose their living connection and reciprocity and gain independence."[8] According to this philosophy, philosophy originates in the need for unity and the will to shore up the eroded community, its gathering. Our need for philosophy springs from schism and dissent. "Philosophy is born from the mourning for unity."[9]

In the *Seventh Letter*, Plato voices his unease about the *istoria* of the polis, for it empirically evidences the unstoppable vortex of contrasting currents, the fractious spirit fostered by competing interests, the lack of law and universality. Thus, in *The Republic* it becomes imperative to put an end to the polis's historical linguistic dissolution and to return to its principle with a view toward the universality and unity of the suprasensible. Aristotle makes us aware that Platonic philosophy was driven beyond the sensible by its concern for the universal in moral affairs, "since it is impossible for there to be a common definition of any perceptibles, as they at any rate are always changing. He, then, called beings of this other sort 'Ideas,' and the perceptible ones are beyond these and are all called after these."[10]

With the universal disposed in the suprasensible, in the pure states of the soul,[11] every dialect or linguistic localism could make a claim to the community of universal truth by elevating itself above its particularities, transcending its idiomatic or particular linguistic exile, cutting out its tongue [*deslenguándose*].[12]

In this scenario [*verosímil*], the universal does not touch cultural and ethnic phenomena, nor is it contaminated by historical possibility. Only prelinguistic universality guarantees the idiomatic and episodic diversity of its complete dispersion. In this way, each language's empirical deferral of itself and others unfolds, in harmony with the Platonic scene [*verosímil*], as the possibility of finally being reunited with, rescued from, and abolished by the universal.

More than an epistemological project, the philosophical program that emphasizes universality and gathering can be considered a teleological, political, imperial project for the sedentary confluence of the *ethos*, where that which preserves (*sõxon*) and prospers (*õfeloun*) grows, and that which dissolves (*apollioun*) and destroys (*diaftheiron*) is eradicated.[13] In other words, this is a project in which the uni-versal gathers and capitalizes into the principle of the uni-version and stabilization of the di-version and per-version of dif-ferences.

The Platonic choice in favor of an ontology of the *idea* as well as the Aristotelian choice in favor of an ontology of substance (*ousia*) are understood here as teleological and economic choices against babel and transhumance. Thales's "All is water"—meaning everything is one and the same substance—is an exergue to philosophy that confirms its activity as the epic of unity and the gathering of diversity. Without these last three categories the university would be unthinkable.

Access to the universal, however, would not be complete, homogenous, or instantaneous. It would be declined in terms of the linguistic particularity of those who are inclined toward it and sheltered by it. In the Platonic scene [*verosímil*], writing and everyday speech, in all their phonetic and experiential diversity, had to constantly attempt the translation/appropriation of universal, ahistorical, and tongueless [*deslenguadas*] truths into each language. Through this translation and movement, the prelinguistic universal suffered a linguistic reduction or degradation of its ineffable "plenitude." Conversely, languages and idioms ascended toward the universal through their obedience and approximation to it.

Like Socrates, those terrestrial languages closest to the universal would be agraphemic if not altogether aglossic, refusing to write (to fix) the universal in one finite language, instead remaining ephemeral in that voice that constantly erases what it says, revealing the erratic exteriority of language and its abiding attraction to the *idea* and constant need to be reformulated relative to it.

Hence the priority of speakers over scribes, for if both were to share the dispersing exteriority of a language—the noise, intonation, rhythm of the dialect (body)—orality would be conjugated, evincing its provisional and contingent nature when faced with the living presence of a thinking that forever corrects and redirects it. Writing, on the other hand, becomes rigid, independent of living thought, feigning if not pretending to be as eternal and unchanging as truth and threatening to supplant it.

From the metaphysical and political ground of truth as guide or determination (Plato), it follows that the wise should lead. Modes of speech and dialects would gather close together under the universality of a supralinguistic language administered by the king. They would gather beyond language in the grammar that undergirds historical languages.

The idea of the philosopher-king reveals its inconsistency and its historical unviability. So long as the universal (philosophy) does not fit into the particular, it could not be otherwise. The universal cannot govern without negating itself through its empirical reduction. In fact, the universal would end up becoming an inconvenience for the king, who, fully installed in universality and removed from all contingency, would lose his grasp on the administrative present. Moreover, the universal would be incomprehensible to the needs and interests of the people. Although philosophers have never ruled over action, one cannot say the same about philosophy, at least when we pause to reflect on the *performative* impact of its canon, which orders and ranks anthropological diversity according to the categories true/false, mind/body, good/bad, state/people, masculine/feminine, etc.

4

✦

Transcendentia, the Medieval University, and the Missionary Structure of the University (A Sketch)

> It is therefore manifest, that the instruction of the people, dependeth wholly, on the right teaching of youth in the universities. But are not . . . the universities of England learned enough already to do that? or is it you, will undertake to teach the universities? Hard questions. Yet to the first, I doubt not to answer; that till towards the latter end of Henry the Eighth, the power of the Pope, was always upheld against the power of the commonwealth, principally by the universities; and that the doctrines maintained by so many preachers, against the sovereign power of the king, and by so many lawyers, and others, that had their education there, is a sufficient argument, that though the universities were not authors of those false doctrines, yet they knew not how to plant the true.
>
> —Hobbes, *Leviathan*

Oriented as it is toward a translinguistic universal—which maintains its imperial univocity through languages in so far as it is speculatively conceived as the nonlinguistic, transcendental ground of what is said, of immanent meaning, of linguistic essence—the university approaches pure incorporeal universality facing backward, forgetfully. The university of the *transcendens* directs the performance of the medieval university toward the utopian present of the universal that preceded it. As in Plato's cave allegory, the university event unfolds in a theater of locations and distances, frontiers and thresholds, movement [*tránsitos*] and traffic, entrances and exits, centers and peripheries, in light, shadow, and darkness, different focal lengths and orientations, captive and captivating bodily dispositions, dynamic movements, sudden or slow mood swings, gradual variations and shifts in posture (of heads, of bodies), visual inversions charged with life-and-death legal consequences, saving or damning theological consequences, true and false moral and epistemological consequences. In this dynamic theater, it is crucial to establish a center, a soul that tightens, orders, ranks, and gives meaning to movements and places. This is the *orthótes*—the correct orientation of the gaze, the recognition of the origin (*arkhé*)—of the prince who must be followed and obeyed. It is a theater for governing bodies, one of constant agitation or vibration between bound and unbound, audible and inaudible, but always according to one invariant: the theater is structurally staged every day as classroom, however precarious it may be.

Something like the Platonic *orthótes* is activated in the Christian pastoral too. "Every individual, whatever his age or his status . . . ought to be governed and ought to let himself be governed . . . be directed toward his salvation . . . in a relation of obedience . . . to truth," a truth specified by written word, dogma, or pastor.[1] Pastoral power also puts into motion an art of governing bodies. This regression does not imply neglect of the university's worldly and administrative tasks. In terms of the medieval university, it means directing the Christian Roman Empire from its dispersion across dialects toward its gathering under the universality of the *transcendentia*. The medieval university acts as a pedagogical apparatus that will define the empire's law (faculty of law), health (faculty of medicine), and meaning (faculty of theology) through the professional functionaries it produces: lawyers, legal scholars, physicians, clerics, professors, doctors, who, by internalizing the use of pagan languages and their many unstable forms, provide linguistic and juridical stability by the Christian subordination of those languages' gesture.

The identity of the university machine is ensured in this territorial advance by means of the linguistic and discursive univocity of its canon: the official and professional language of Latin, the reiterated written codes of each [*en cada caso*] subject matter, the protocols of the classroom setting, methodologies of teaching, etc. The monophone, monotheist university positions itself pedagogically and not reflexively in relation to polytheistic barbarism. Medieval scholasticism constitutes a sprawling, primordial watershed moment in the political theology of gathering, capitalization, economic production, and the banking of souls that spreads over continents and into non-Christian peripheries still dispersed in maternal babel, falling upon the young spirit and inculcating it with the views of the school in its missionary form.

The medieval *universitas* is built by cutting out the patient's tongue [*deslenguando*]—the mother tongue—and replacing that idolatrous emotional language with the university's academic and imperial one. We see this in the university's colonial constitution, its will to make missionary forays into human heterogeneity, subordinating barbarism, first, to the *transcendentia* and, later, to Enlightenment ideals.

Consider the fact that the conquest of godless languages required the university to teach barbarian languages and the cultural disposition to learn them in order to evangelize in them. Learning "savage" languages for evangelizing the world dates back to the thirteenth century. In 1276, the beatified

R. Llull founded a missionary college on the island of Mallorca at the behest of Pope John XXI, where they studied oriental languages with the hope of spreading Christianity from North Africa to Central Asia. The power of Christian universality to expand beyond its territorial limits gained juridical support at the Council of Vienne (1311), where council members approved the teaching of Arabic, Hebrew, and Chaldean for missionary purposes at the Universities of Paris, Oxford, Bologna, and Salamanca. The goal of learning Indigenous languages was not the propagation of difference but its eradication through the capture and production of Christian subjects,[2] for example, the conquest of the Americas understood as "spiritual conquest" (Bartolomé de las Casas). The medieval university makes explicit every university's missionary character, regardless of the form it takes.

Having regressed to the ineffable universal, the medieval university strengthens its empirical impact. Although it may be inclined toward the universality of the *transcendentia* above any generic universality, its empirical mission subordinates the heterogeneity of pagan languages and their accompanying animisms and witchcrafts to this orientation, thus alienating them in the sense of the alma mater cast as *vulgata*, the singular version. The university must not disperse into each person's particular interests but rather gather itself through the disinterest peculiar to universal truth as the subject matter of universalization. In this way, the University of Paris or any other university should appear naturally as the organon not of any one society but of Christian society as a whole. For Pope Innocent III just as much as Pope Gregory XI, the University of Paris was neither Parisian nor French but a "spiritual and moral power . . . Christian and ecclesiastic . . . with the same status and significance as Church and Empire."[3] As a consequence, it was essential that its control of identity and meaning be tied directly to the supreme, central power of the Christian universe and not to local power. Only the papacy was elevated enough to be able to perceive the relative value of things and put each one in its proper place while maintaining the hierarchy of local interests, whether of bishop or chapter, and imposing the univocal, universal interest, one of whose bureaucratic instruments was the university. Only the papacy, the highest commissioner of the *transcendentia*, could mark the limits of what was teachable. For example, Innocent III prohibited in 1215 the teaching of physics and Aristotelian metaphysics at the University of Paris. In 1231, Gregory IX exhorted theologians to limit their teaching to questions "whose solutions can be found in theology books and the writings of the holy fathers."[4] Only the pope, as imperial representative of timeless universality, could authorize the founding of a universal school or *studium generale* empowered to grant diplomas for teaching anywhere (*ius docendi ubique*). For the same reason, a doctor from any university was considered a *Doctor Universalis Ecclesiae*. The only other power that claimed and exercised this right was imperial power.[5] Thus Frederick Barbarossa backed the creation of the University of Bologna with the primary goal of combatting juridical regionalism. In any case, if the emperor could assume that prerogative, it was because he was considered Christianity's earthly leader.

From a genealogical perspective, the *transcendentia* technology involves the babelic event of the real history of languages, their nomadic or sedentary conditions, the sanction of the "proprietary," its identity, and the demarcation in language of pure from impure, with all the challenges that come with determining how the feeling of linguistic purity is formed and how it is that society makes choices to the point that it comes to constitute and fix the whole range of its language "according to unconscious laws and analogies."[6] It also involves the clash of languages, their destruction, dialogue, *mestizaje*, colonization, discrimination, the will to power in language that Antonio de Nebrija advanced in the introduction to his *Grammar of the Castilian Language* (1492) by conjoining "grammar and sword," "empire and language" in the context of Castille's conquest of the Iberian Peninsula and the Americas, of the national language and imperial language, of regional dialects and native languages.

Autonomy and Heteronomy in the Medieval University

Mayz Vallenilla's *El ocaso de las universidades* (Twilight of the universities) reads the medieval university through the categories of "monad" (Leibniz) and "substance" (Aristotle) in order to highlight the autonomy of these small, more or less independent republics.[7]

> Medieval universities conceived themselves as individualities, authentic monads endowed with the properties that Aristotle had given the name of *prima substantia* (οὐσία πρώτη). . . . Each university objectified itself as an autarchic entity, self-sufficient, subsistent, surrounded by a "here" (*hic*) and "now" (*nunc*), unique and unrepeatable. . . . Thus each university not only considered as natural and legitimate its claim to occupy a space closed off by its own *limits—compound, campus, walls, barriers*—it also considered itself inviolable and invulnerable. . . . Moreover, regarding teaching, each institution aspired to a particular, individual, incomparable, and irreplaceable *pensum* (point of view) . . . to the possession of full liberty and autonomy in the development of its teachings without any kind of constraint . . . and in setting the requirements to enter, graduate, and obtain titles that reflected its particular orientation. . . . [T]hey were also monadic and substantialist kingdoms, fiefdoms, and cities. Their craft mode of production and economic relations were likewise substantialist and monadic.[8]

Not everything in these institutions was autonomy. Just like Leibniz's monad and Aristotle's substance, their autonomy rested on heteronomy

derived from another origin.[9] This was an autonomy amid heteronomy. So
to the extent that these centers formed the functionaries that the universal
church needed to fortify itself ideologically and factically, the popes established a policy that, without openly contradicting the autonomous charter
of the university, still allowed the exercise of their unquestioned authority.[10]
They were also epistemically heteronomous in that the universality of the
university made them into attendants of the revealed truth and not the privileged subject of autonomous knowledge heeding its own experience.

> The Middle Ages bore witness to . . . the omnipotent authority of the
> Pope, and even some bishops and clerics, backed by the intellectual
> supremacy they were provided by the universities, by the dogmatic
> character of the theological pronouncements that prevailed in their
> teachings, and by the obedient subordination of the sciences to
> Church dictates. The universities, as instruments of the Holy Mother,
> were obliged to offer their unconditional support and to defend as
> commanded in order to safeguard dogma. In this way, as they multi-
> plied across the European landscape, universities increasingly became
> an intellectual reservoir of the clerical hierarchy.[11]

By the middle of the fifteenth century, there were more than one hundred
universities across Europe. Only in Spain were there more than fifty. They
were international in many respects: students and professors moved freely
from one to the other, and the teaching method and subjects taught were
international.

In this way the medieval university linguistically,[12] methodologically, and
ideologically gathered itself under theological universality and the papal and
imperial center while also subordinating from that position of subordination.

5

✦

The Modern Franco-Cartesian-Napoleonic-Comtean University

Let us beware of thinking that the world eternally creates new things.

—Nietzsche, *Gay Science*

"Despite its varying content, the term 'modern' again and again expresses the consciousness of an epoch that relates itself to the past of antiquity in order to view itself as the result of a transition from the old to the new."[1] We are particularly interested in working out the transition from the Latin university and universality to the modern national university and universality. That transition was realized by Descartes.

In modernity, the universal was positioned as a goal. It passed [*transitó*] from an earlier substantial state—a regressive and heteronomous regime for knowledge, the university project, and professional activity—to the promised universality that inaugurates the university's teleological regime of self-emancipation. The subject/object of that emancipatory process is humanity, a subject/object that understands and proposes itself as the finitude of judgment able to neutralize and "rebalance" to the point of indifference the inclinations and prejudices that condition and encumber its liberty and universality.

Descartes considers the critique of anthropological finitude, instituted as an apparatus of power and domination, to be the *conditio sine qua non* for the universalization of the modern subject, an apparatus that can be proprietarily projected as an endless, autonomous, self-produced, self-progressing knowledge project, only by understanding the prejudices and physiologies that confine it.

More or less reflexively, the modern Cartesian university emerges, analogous to the project of the medieval philosophical university in its promise of a supraterritorial and translinguistic universal. The priority of universality persists, only now cast as a promise to be fulfilled.

The "infinite" education of the universal community no longer must follow a Latin or French grammar but a pure grammar-logic, neither maternal nor phonetic, in which the order of the world will be constructed, without seeing it, without feeling it, without mercy.

The need for such a language puts the modern university on guard with regard to the regional languages and dialects in which it is empirically situated, languages grown and governed by a matrix of domestic, emotional, affective, babbling details; languages that resist, whether intentionally or not, the universal project of the "lettered city"[2] or "transparent society."[3] The language that will outline the university in its modern, Cartesian transition[4] is not Latin or French, not phonological but algebraic.

As we know, Descartes confronts and tries to escape from Latin, from its knowledge and universality, by writing in French.[5] He joins the modernizing battle of his mother tongue against Latin, a battle that won its first victory in 1539 under François I with the royal decree of Villers-Cotterêts, which imposed French as the language of administration and law throughout the land.[6] So Descartes writes in French, the mother language of nonknowledge "free from prejudice."[7] But he does not remain there. He writes in French as he enters into *mathesis universalis*, universal mathematics, into the language of simple categories and universal principles with which he will prepare the "order" of any possible state or interregnum.

Doubt as Condition of the Modern University

In modernity, erasing (*effacer*) the old is the condition of the new. No modern university, speech, or law can be established that is subjected to the past. Were that the case, the new would be translated into the old, as when a novice learner of a new language always understands it in terms of the language of his birth and only assimilates to the new language when he speaks without recalling the first language or when he entirely adapts the old language to the possibilities of the new one.[8] This is a shedding of language. As we have already mentioned, this shedding moves from Latin to French, and from French to algebra. It erases Latin memory, the language of that memory and that which was recognizable in it. The destruction of memory, freedom from heteronomy and subjection to the past, pulls down "the house where one is living."[9] The production of modern universality and the modern university requires removing "from the roots,"[10] making the ancient universality, university, and city a "plain"[11] or a "*tabula rasa*"[12] on which the blueprint for a new universality and new university city will be neatly drawn.

Indifference and Autonomy

That plain is textually produced in the first of the *Meditations on First Philosophy* (1636). The "First Meditation" is not only about nullifying the heteronomy of a series of "ill-founded" principles that enthrone an origin but also about subtracting the will, its freedom and autonomy, from all alienating heteronomy. The modern subject—understood as the will to grasp itself and others without also being subjected or captive to its own organization—that university spirit must constantly produce and secure the conditions of its autonomy, neutralizing to the point of apathy or indifference its inclinations and motives, prejudices and clauses, as the only way to decide the law without law, like a God who makes worlds on a whim, uncompelled by principles or interests, completely indifferent.[13]

Indifference, neutrality, deferral of inclination will be the condition of modern university autonomy: the utopian condition of the modern subject and modern university to the extent that topically the subject knows it has been plundered by extrauniversity forces and interests, particularities and contingencies that exercise capricious control. The Cartesian academic subject wants to be neutral, impersonal, unsexed. It aspires to erase, or at the very least dissimulate, the enunciating subject in the subject of the enunciation.

Don't Reform, Raze

Descartes proposes not the reformation but the razing of the old university. Metaphors of destruction are scattered throughout his work: "I had to raze everything to the ground and begin again from the original foundations";[14] "rebuild the house where one is living";[15] "peoples who, having once been half-savages and having been civilized only little by little, have made their laws only to the extent that the inconvenience due to crimes and quarrels have forced them to do so";[16] "start the painting all over again, by sponging out all its features";[17] uprooting the tree of Greco-Latin philosophy; razing the city of Paris, "buildings. . . . which many architects have tried to patch up by using old walls that had been built for other purposes . . . ancient cities that were once mere villages and in the course of time have become large towns are usually so poorly laid out,"[18] "the school"[19] and "philosophy . . . that has been cultivated for many centuries."[20]

By producing the tabula rasa so that the new painter or architect may draw or build according to one plan "rather than losing his time in correcting"[21] and without being perturbed by "proportions badly observed,"[22] the "new world,"[23] new painting, the theater of the subject and the modern particular organizes itself through autonomous decisions and practical technical applications. We are talking about producing the "zero degree" of knowledge and of the old "customs" whose coddling makes me not a "lord and master," making a tabula rasa of any decision that depends on another—for example, an innate principle or "some faculty . . . as yet unknown,"[24] a propensity, an interest, a prejudice, a habit.

In the first part of *The Discourse on Method*, Descartes diagnoses the calamitous state of science, ethics, and technology. The "First Meditation" announces itself as the dismantling of the universe of human representations—sense, memory, imagination, dreams, images, emotions, concepts—down to the unchanging principle and structural elements that make up and organize any representation or conceivable possible world, however fictitious or obvious it may be. Later in the hyperbole of the "evil genius," he acts as destroyer of those categories and principles that box in understanding, principles that understanding could never go beyond, even though "desire" may constantly push in that direction in its quest to liberate the representable (the possible) from the frames that bind and automate it, the desire to increasingly free representation from the table of categories and the rules that sap its strength.[25]

The fourth part of *The Discourse on Method* as well as the first paragraphs of *The Principles of Philosophy* also evoke the critical hyperbole amply performed in the "First Meditation."

So it is less about correcting than "suppressing" and "replacing" the old (heteronomous) institution with the new (autonomous) institution. "For I do not wish to be placed among the number of these insignificant artisans who apply themselves only to the restoration of old works, because they feel themselves incapable of achieving new ones. We can, however . . . while we are busy destroying this edifice, at the same time form the foundations which may serve our purpose,"[26] new conditions for decision-making, knowledge, and life, a life founded on autonomous principles or original motives. This devastating enterprise cannot be realized, however, by "survey[ing] each opinion individually, a task that would be endless."[27] Rather it must target the foundation of old knowledge, the source of sense and meaning of every Greco-Latin word.[28] This experience shows that "undermining the foundations will cause whatever has been built upon them to crumble of its own accord."[29] For Descartes, that foundation is metaphysical universality, the horizon of meaning chosen at the metaphysical base or root of the method,[30] which accompanies the method in its application to "nature" (Physics) and bears fruit in "medicine, mechanics, and morals,"[31] the established surface of the social. It is not about destroying the old *universitas* starting from "the branches," pursuing over the surface of the institution the empirical effects of the voices that metaphysically sustain it, a surface on which those choices emerge in an infinity of diverse, dispersed, and antagonistic opinions, performances, acts.

The Ruin of the City in Subjectivity

The ruinous replacement of the (heteronomous) old with the (autonomous) new does not go after Descartes but against the institutional materiality of the old metaphysics: the state, the university, the city, and medieval establishments generally, institutions that once fallen "are too difficult to raise up."[32] At least in principle, this is not a "practical revolution."[33]

It is certainly indispensable to suppress the state, university, and city that "taught from . . . youth"[34] prejudice and that mark the limits of subjectivity. One must extricate oneself from "inculcated" school commands that automatize subjectivity and prevent one from acting of one's own accord. Demolish the state and the university insofar as they represent an alien subjectivity that regiments one's range of choices and meanings. It is about exercising "methodical doubt" as the conscious revocation of heteronomous consciousness. In principle, this is a theoretical revolution, a changing of basic maxims that rob consciousness and the world alike, where the principle of objectivity now serves as subjectivity.[35]

When undertaken by an individual, that change has an individual character. Although universal in scope, the Cartesian revolution is particular in principle: a particular, albeit necessary, "foothold" or point or view promises to take the *universitas* off its hinges and reattach it according to its particularity become universal law.

This entails two things: (a) the liberation of subjectivity through "methodical doubt," and (b) the full extension of this subjectivity as objectivity and external order.

In this sense, internally determined subject-knowledge is not contemplative and reflexive but active and possessive. We are no longer dealing with "speculative philosophy" but with a "useful" philosophy that facilitates the domination of everything, installing humanity as "lord and master" over nature and history.

Cartesianism promises a medicine and a politics that will professionally control the physical and moral automaton. It empowers competencies that ensure a "firm and constant,"[36] "clear and distinct"[37] regimen for the social and individual body. That promise is elaborated in the "Letter to Picot," where he makes explicit a program of philosophy that will bear fruit in medicine, mechanics, and morality, in opposition to the speculative, regressive theology that predominates in the medieval university.

Cartesianism also determines the method for manufacturing this new regime, as opposed to the old method made of "sand and mud,"[38] old but still present, dominant, and concentrated in the Latin institutionality that Descartes drains out.

Descartes's rhetoric about destroying the old order and constructing a new one is governed from behind the scenes by two crisscrossing antagonistic "fables" that have weighed on us since the beginning of time: (a) the fable of the universe as clock or universal automaton, circumscribed by the law of noncontradiction; and (b) the hypothesis of a magical universe with neither rules nor motives, the fable of an omnipotent and indifferent, unpredictable and incalculable god who capriciously produces effects on a whim "as a King establishes laws in his Kingdom."[39]

The fable of the universe as clock, the fable of the rational god, plates the surface of the Cartesian text—philosophical discourse's strategies for political circumnavigation. On the other hand, the hyperbole of the magical world is academically construed as an esoteric trope, more feminine and better suited to the *Correspondence*. The two hypotheses join forces in strict administration. The identical force of their mutual gravitational pull will go on to articulate the text's cinematic play of reciprocal demands, rejections, and reflections.

This pair of tropes continuously transforms into other antagonistic pairs, such as understanding and desire, finite and infinite, intention and indifference, prejudice and freedom, female automaton and male automaton, machine and magic, etc. At the same time, these metaphors refer to the essential antagonism or conflict of the modern university: speculative knowledge (the knowledge of knowledge) and applied (professional) knowledge; reflection (critique) and definition (position); institution and revolution; higher faculties and lower faculty; right and left, etc.

Descartes had in sight the promise of a principle of free order infinitely unfolding from center to periphery: the *universitas* of things ordered by one believer. He also had in sight "indifference" and the possibility of desire without law or gathering, "malignant" and dissolving like the "genius" of the "First Meditation" or the God of the *Correspondence*. He desired order and definition whenever he (Descartes, the modern subject) was the subject that exceeded it. He wanted unrestraint to ground every consolidation: a university that restrains without being itself restrained, a critical-philosophical university that gathers from the forum of doubt, a university that only responds to decisions from the position of critical hyperbole.

The Step Back

The Cartesian procedure imposes on the visual field a method that pulls back to the invisible conditions of possibility of all vision and every field. This is also the method of the modern, Cartesian university that indiscriminately desires to understand everything fully. Whoever commits to Descartes's epistemic, political project is immediately tasked with desecrating the field by partitioning and boring into its physical puppets (the natural landscape).[40] This method reveals "little by little" the hidden scene, the inarticulate mechanics, the opaque conditions of possibility of all that is visible. Positive anatomical knowledge of the world's mechanics forms the basis of a praxis "by means of which, knowing the force and the actions of fire, water, air, the stars, the heavens, and all the other bodies that surround us, just as distinctly as we understand the various skills of our craftsmen, we might be able, in the same way, to use them for all the purposes for which they are appropriate, and thus render ourselves, as it were, masters and possessors of nature."[41] But this is "principally for the maintenance of health, which unquestionably is the first good and the foundation of all the other goods of this life; for even the mind depends so greatly on the temperament and on the disposition of the organs of the body that, if it is possible to find some means to render men generally more wise and more adroit than they have been up until now, I believe that one should look for it in medicine."[42]

Dividing fields into as many pieces as possible until one reaches indivisible elements, making exhaustive enumerations and detailed revisions to ensure that nothing has been omitted, this in short is the gradual path of the Cartesian method described in the *Rules for the Direction of the Mind* and the *Discourse on Method*: "I judged there to be no better remedy against these two obstacles [the brevity of life and lack of experiments] than to communicate faithfully to the public the entirety of what little I had found and to urge good minds to try to advance beyond this by contributing, each according to his inclination and ability, to the experiments that must be performed and also by communicating to the public everything they might learn, in order that, with subsequent inquirers beginning where their predecessors had left off, and thus, joining together the lives and labors of many, we might all advance together much further than a single individual could do on his own" except as a promise.[43]

Maintained by remembrance of the ongoing work of young and old, this chain of positive knowledge and its optimism are interrupted by basic research, "metaphysical meditation," or hyperbolic doubt, which question the conditions of the scientific method, defetishizing the "truth" value surrounding the results of the method in action and ascribing to them the value of the free and arbitrary.

For Descartes and the classical modern university he designed, questioning the limits of the method constitutes a "theory of knowledge." The question is no longer about the object known but about the eye that knows: What is its mechanism? What are its filters? What are its limits and influences? What are its mediations? What is its ultimate ground? This question asks about the subject of the object, the enunciation of the statement, resulting in the emergence of the human sciences, which disperse, little by little, classical Cartesian humanism.

It is not only about physiology—the dilation of the pupil that in the diagrams is objectively projected as the horizon or internal surface of a light blue curve, making the eye a point that bundles vectors and that, opening lines of sight, also hides the eye in them, concealing as it goes the blindness on which it relies. Physiology is not the only influencing limit. Language, memory, education, environment, common sense, money, or some "unknown faculty" may also entangle the gaze.

The suspicion that the very subjectivity on which ownership of knowledge and the methodological undertaking depend could be at once opening and bias, medium and support, such a suspicion makes the analysis of the subject indispensable.[44] The belief that the subject represents a bias that mediates and disrupts the present world with the "representation of the world"—that belief, along with the desire for an absolute truth or unimpeded vision, reoriented the positive, methodical investigation of the object-world toward the investigation of the subject of the world: a step back.

Excursus on the "First Meditation," the "Zero Degree" of Meaning

Let us return, then, to the "First Meditation." The form of the meditation follows its stated content: "Concerning Those Things That Can be Called into Doubt." It only ends when everything that can be doubted has been proscribed. Doubtful is any "conception" of that which "is" which entails "prejudice," clauses seen and unseen, every "word" of the understanding, whether pure or involved in other layers of representation—"sensation," "memory," "imagination"—since the possibility of a word is the clause from which it issues, clauses that are indispensable and proper to that message but not necessarily proper to that which "is." We presume to "write," "speak," and "conceive" that which "is" through our "conceptions" of thinking. To be sure, we take shelter under those "conceptions." The "First Meditation" slowly fabricates the distance between reality and those "conceptions"—the "objective ingeniousness"[45] of the word. It slowly turns signifieds into a floating world and that which "is" into a wasteland (*plaine*).

This removing of names in accord with the wasteland is only the surface of another movement, an earlier drive: the desire to revolutionize life, "to conduct it" by a new word that is "clear and distinct," and "to preserve it" there, "firm and constant," through the technical application and reinforcement of the innovative word "freedom" (indifference) and "immortality" (medicine). For Descartes this is not the "speculative" substitution of a few phrases ("old opinions"[46]) with new ones—"clear and distinct" modern concepts. If the immediate intention is not to "raze [a state] to the ground and begin again from the original foundations,"[47] "nor even also to reform the body of the sciences or the order established in the schools for teaching them,"[48] the "root" of the state and the university as well as "medicine," "mechanics," "morality," and "business" is for Descartes the word: a few words, a metaphysics materialized in those institutions (theoretical primacy).

"Erasing" these basic "opinions," erasing the clauses and determinations of the old metaphysics, will cause the institutions built on them to fall.[49] For Descartes, to raze the metaphysics one inhabits is a sufficient means to radically change "life." The life instituted by the state, the schools, prejudice will be revolutionized by the critique of metaphysics. It is about exchanging the "old" city that surrenders to heteronomy or "trust" in the "unknown"—obscure things, supernatural light that is taken to be familiar through "conjecture" and the usual terms—for a city planned by the applied certainty of an artificial knowledge, autonomously determined and produced,[50] a city, a knowledge that imagines itself to be the enclosure (capitalization) of that which "is" by means of that knowledge's complete "control" through its gradual technical consummation. Such a shift necessarily presupposes pulling down "the house where one is living,"[51] subtracting oneself from the old metaphysics, leaving the shelter at least "once in . . . life"[52] and entering into the wasteland (*plaine*) of that which "is." Without passing through the wasteland, there can be no revolution, no transition, no autonomous "rebuilding" of the new "dwelling," of that definitive "code of morals."[53]

Either one must pass through the wasteland toward the new that is housed in an instrumental humanity or in the promise of a project, or else one will sink into the quagmire. For this reason, we need a "provisional code of morals"[54] such as the maxims in *The Discourse on Method* or Odysseus's decision to have himself lashed to the mast of his boat. For this same reason, "methodical doubt" and the production of the wasteland is at the core of any project, its gale wind controlled in advance. It is not about giving up on life, losing oneself in the quagmire, but about "conducting [one's] life much better,"[55] restraining and forming oneself into an author (subject), "lord and master" over "nature" and never its "automaton." It is about conquering (subduing) oneself and maintaining (conserving) oneself through conquest.

The "First Meditation" lays waste. It asserts that mathematics is the underlying grammar of every possible conception. It also warns that the possibility or limits of that which "is" are not obliged to coincide with the possibility or limits of the concept. This warning distinguishes and separates the possibilities of "conceptualizing" from the possibilities of what "is." This separation is the necessary preparation for the journey into the open pit of the concept, which will expose institutions and the human to the elements, since, for Descartes, the human is always the institutional consolidation of a concept. This separation turns our attention to that which "is" without the signifying clutter. "Methodical doubt" marches backward into the barrens by confining words. Increasingly crippled by doubt, words hover above the wasteland like a ghostly *conatus* [*conatos*] toward objectivization.

In contrast, doubt is not a concept but a "performance" against the concept, the "revoking" of every word in the hopes of a "firm," "certain," "definitive" (irrevocable) word. But this "performance" gives rise to elements of a project still complicit with words, words not "yet" spoken, future modern words.

Methodical doubt, or the derogation of the words it inhabits, labors against the ancient Greco-Latin word on behalf of the modern, algebraic, Cartesian word, which had been institutionally impeded with the backing of the Latin institution. At the heart of its Latin, feudal dwelling, methodical doubt produces "the plain" where the Cartesian utterance erupts as "principle" of a "new" life, the "order and measure" of the modern *universitas*. Methodical doubt contains an utterance and a dwelling that are not yet institutionalized and can only unfold when they can do so on their own, without so much as a memory of the old world.

Methodical doubt is consummated in the derogation of every proposed, uttered, conceived, instituted word, of every signified and Latin metaphysics. Methodical doubt is consummated in the meaningless dead letter, the zero degree of every utterance or the "material existence" of thinking.[56] This materiality is located outside meaning, outside the institution of the signified. It is neither concept nor praxis of a concept. It escapes the command and is put into doubt. Only the signified can be doubted, as well as that which "is" when it is suspended and instituted in a signified, when it is placed into question in a category—for example, the category of "substance." Only when it is contained in a concept can the materiality of thinking be "weighed" and put into doubt. As a "representation," the materiality of thinking can be "counterbalanced," but not when it is a "thing" beyond objectivity, beyond and before the word, a "thing" that grazes [*rasante*] materiality.

From the first meditation up until the "I was" (I had a name) in the second mediation, we gradually enter this grazing [*rasante*] materiality. Throughout this passage, every "trace" is erased and "traditional knowledge" and the Latin school are "demolished." We enter little by little into the wasteland, not seeking the quagmire but rather as a kind of baptism that anticipates the bestowal of a new name, a new objectivity, a new tongue, a new regime of appropriation, a practice that harbors the new by conferring on all "mixing and confusion" the title of the "old" that is to be expunged.

In Descartes, the demolition of traditional "life" housed in the heteronomy of faith never risks complete renunciation of the concept, the empire of "the signified." In the end, "methodical doubt" does not lead beyond the concept. Certainly the Cartesian project silences the "old metaphysics" by withdrawing the words from that which "is," which metaphysics once used to make habitable that which "is" in morality, urbanism, medicine, or law. Its operation is to conquer for that which "is" the silence needed for the modern word to emerge and grow, which will make that which "is" habitable in modernity.

Only in this silence can "methodical doubt" undertake the weeding out of all old utterances that "entrusted" morality and industry to the "supernatural light" of "faith," that is, to purely "probable" [*verosímiles*] principles. It is a weeding necessarily prior to the pure position of a "clear and distinct" knowledge, the French "order and measure" that would "conduct life" from then on.

Descartes never renounces order. Even the dust cloud that rises from the fall of the old order contributes to the new one. It contributes to the disdain for the irrational as the possibility of that which "is," a possibility impotent before the courts and moorings of finite, Cartesian rationality.

For Descartes, the project is about acting out that which "is" and never becoming that which is acted upon, "for we do not praise automata, although they respond exactly to the movements they were designed to produce, since their actions are performed necessarily. We praise the workman who has made them because he has formed them with accuracy."[57] The project is about escaping every automatism, stitching that which "is" and its possibility into the machine, theater, politics mounted by the subject.

We are subtracted from that grazing [*rasante*] materiality by the Cartesian table of categories, the "simple and universal" elements that enclose the silence of that which "is," a silence once monitored by methodical doubt. This silence, we now see, was sometimes sought instrumentally at the behest of Descartes's project for the complete "conduct" of "life" and "nature" on the basis of the table of categories, a project now regulated not by the hyperbole of an absolute knowledge but by a will that limits itself to the categories of understanding and similarly limits the world piece by piece (*"peu a peu"*). It is a project now rendered accountable by "affirmation" and "negation," by judgment and the will restricted to the "light" of "simple ideas," the discourse on method, the firmest means to consolidate the hoped-for domination of all that which "is" through "pure understanding" subjected to the constant surveillance and autonomy of doubt.

We find traces of this change in will in the disregard for the possibility that the irrational might constitute the proper rhythm of that which "is," the disregard of the longing for an absolute truth—desire's beautiful soul— one made explicit in the *Objections and Replies*. Such a will abandons the dream of "infinite knowledge" as the means of total mastery over that which "is," and instead subordinates itself to whichever artifice, in its finitude, most effectively satisfies its bottomless hunger, if only gradually.

Thus the first properly Cartesian words—"I am, I exist"—are spoken in the conditional mood: "This proposition 'I am, I exist' is necessarily true every time I utter it"[58]—or write it, since that is, in fact, what Descartes is doing—"every time" I produce it, "every time" it is an expression of the Cartesian "pure understanding" that first appeared in the "Second Meditation"; unquestionable words "provided that" they are well protected against the irrational; "certain" words "provided that" "God or nature" or that which "is" is no match for the enclosures of finite reason, "provided that" that which "is" "no more [than it] belongs . . . to the nature of a mountain . . . to have a valley, or to the nature of a triangle to have angles whose sum is greater than two right angles,"[59] which would imply the impossibility of my concept, the technical factic impossibility of that which is omitted; "provided that" that which "is" is not free to claim "it is not true all the lines drawn from the center to the circumference are equal";[60] "provided that" the "clear and distinct" "subject" in its technical application to daily life is not occluded by the possibility of that which "is" and in fact automates and administers those possibilities, triumphantly performing that which "is"; "every time" that which "is" is mortgaged to the museum of Cartesian reason, the simulacrum of immortality he inaugurates; "provided that" "clear and distinct" knowledge is not simply an allegory referring to that which "is" but an effective apparatus to which that which "is" succumbs, digested.

When the "performance" of doubt reaches its zenith, it inventories all of its possibilities, and the universe of "conceptions" takes flight like a shadow unmoored. When the materiality of doubt is most reduced by its estrangement in signification, that materiality becomes certainty, that which cannot be contradicted. This is not the certainty of the word but the certainty of that to which words try to refer, the certainty before and beyond every linguistic code, prior to "proposition," "utterance," "conception," and "praxis," prior to "letters," "morality," "religion," "science," and "philosophy," prior to all production from "finitude," which remains nonetheless the only way to refer to materiality.

The investigation of truth in the "First Meditation" eagerly sought an unconditional discourse of that which "is" as the groundwork for its true appropriation. In the "Second Meditation" this investigation takes a turn. The very possibility of an objective discourse unconditionally replicating that which "is" proves to be impossible so long as objectivity and unconditionality cancel each other out, since objectivity is always a conditional framing from some point of view. That investigation, which began as a hunt for the unconditional replica, for the neutral repetition of some official procedure for completely possessing that which "is," soon recognizes that no word is capable of rendering the unconditionality and totality demanded of it. This turn takes place right at the start of the "Second Meditation." The first certainty is not "proposition," "utterance," "conception," or "praxis." The first certainty is before and beyond the concept and thus before and beyond *The Meditations*, although it can only be seen from them, from the hunting blind of the text that it elaborates.

We call "true" that presupposition before and beyond the word, the silent *cogito* before the word that is later reduced to the word. But this "truth" is not the same as when we speak of the "truth of a proposition." We call a presupposition "true" as we would something that is not a concept but that presumes the concept's referent. It does so to ameliorate the oppressive silence and convince us that we are not speaking into the void, or else it does so simply to omit or reduce that which "is" to a sphere of familiarity and control, since what falls outside the objective reality of thought cannot be logically defined so as better to understand its nature.[61] For the same reason, that which "is," the silent *cogito*, even if it is "clear," as "when, for instance, a severe pain is felt, the perception of this pain may be very clear,"[62] lacks all definition for finite objectivity even though it is "distinctly" reduced to the "objective reality" of thinking. Thought suffers its self-difference as "objective reality" and "material reality."

In the "Second Meditation," we call the written *cogito*—"I think, I exist"—"true." But the "true" here is something else. "True" is a proposition: "The proposition 'I am, I exist' is necessarily true." "True" are the words, the voices that appropriate that which "is" (the cogito before the word); "true" is the eruption of the table of the categories; "true" the writing "*ego cogito ego sum.*" "True" is the proposition "The proposition 'I am, I exist' is necessarily true." And it is true "every time I utter it,"[63] that is, provided [*siempre que*] it is controlled by the "utterance," which is itself controlled by "conception," the table of categories, and the phonetic alphabetic writing that Descartes thought he could escape through the *mathesis universalis* of analytic geometry.

In the *cogito* written as "true" is the economy of the table of categories. Moreover, it is the successful praxis of that economy, the Cartesian capitalization of the wasteland through the ex-position of the category of tables.

The written cogito is "true" provided that [*siempre que*] the application of the table of categories to that which "is" cancels whatever resistance arises; it is "true" provided that that which "is" surrenders to the Cartesian Daedalus; provided that the Cartesian possibility excludes or capitalizes on every other possibility; provided that the Cartesian writing of the silent *cogito* makes every other writing impossible. We call "true" the proposition that can be voiced in whatever words are available, words that are not necessarily adequate to that which "is" but are the necessary adequation of that which "is" to the "clear and distinct" "artifice," to the materialism of Cartesian reason, to the shift in truth as "comparison"[64] to that which "is," to the technology for capitalizing piece by piece that which "is."

The wasteland that precedes the modern true (word), the old true (word), every true (word), and domination-denomination does not rely on or adhere to the principle of noncontradiction. That which "is"—now, finally—is that which is yet to be named, the residual supplement of the technology, that which remains to be digested, unending difference. The written *cogito*, now inside Cartesian capital, is the violent omission of that which "is" assuming the risk involved in defining and molding the possible into a mathematical procedure; it is the disposition of that which "is" by the procedures of the finite understanding of the mechanical arts; it is the growth of the category of tables over the wasteland; it is the establishment of the here-and-now order of the "objective artifice of the idea," now cast into the wasteland.

Applied Research, Basic Research

As metaphysical meditation or questioning of the ground, the modern Cartesian university became primarily an epistemological university that interrogated the methodological principles of the condition of the subject of knowledge and of power. These two tracks of knowledge, which, on the one hand, apply methodologically to positive field knowledges and, on the other hand, act as reflective distance from the method's principles (methodical doubt), constitute the two tracks of modern university research: "'end-oriented' or applied research" and "basic research."[65]

Reflection on the grounds of the scientific method, the hopeless search for the ground and the ground of the ground, becomes apparent in the modern university's constant state of crisis, the institution's provisional, progressive, revolutionary charter. This French aspect of the modern university will be highlighted "spiritually and speculatively," in contrast to "Napoleonic" Cartesianism, by the German "idea" of the university in the context of the creation of the University of Berlin in 1810.

In Descartes, the debating and putting in doubt of the principles of method ("First Meditation"), which prevents acritical reliance on them and their automatic application, seeks to avoid the professional closure of knowledge to the mere operativity and technical performance of those axioms. Methodical doubt, the "evil genius," metaphorizes modern discomfort with subordination to any principle, even one's own. This discomfort concerns those axioms that restrain freedom, for freedom does not tolerate obstacles presented by either heteronomy or autonomy, even when those obstacles derive from that freedom. The subject can only be considered modern if it applies the axioms without axioms also applying to it. Already in Descartes, the modern university is philosophically laid out as a critical university that must give an account of its knowledge, a "knowledge of knowledge." In this sense, it is laid out as a "zealous and totalitarian" university (Nietzsche), eager to control its ground too.

As a critical university, the modern university will be enlisted to the "rallying cry" of modern wisdom: "Everything has a reason."[66] This rallying cry or "principle"[67] orients the modern university, which responds structurally to the call "to give reasons." "To give reasons" represents the universality of the secularizing university.

So little by little, the medieval university, which had once persecuted Descartes and his hyperbolic knowledge, embraces him as a brother. Little by little, the university becomes Cartesian, replacing the *transcendentia* with transcendental progress.

State Apparatus

Under the universality of progress and the universal progress directed by science, the university is yoked to the practical teleology of achievements useful for modern political power. As Althusser will emphasize, it is deployed as a state apparatus. Now universality leads, not as dehistoricization of an originary truth but as suprahistorical progress toward some goal yet to be achieved. Applied research and teaching will slowly become the primordial alveoli of the progressive *universitas*.

Slowly the university will become the state technical university, defining itself in terms of the progressive metanarrative that gives it direction. It is under the direction of this metanarrative that one must understand the nineteenth-century explosion of the four classical faculties (theology, law, medicine, and philosophy or arts) into more than fifteen faculties, each sub-divided into departments and programs.

The university's metaphysical movement from an earlier universal sub-stantiated as origin to a promised utopian universal presupposes another movement on another plane: the autonomization of certain regional languages as national languages and the formation of national states, languages, and histories. Under the universality of progress and universal political-economic progress of the nation-state and its language, the university serves as the modern state's techno-professional civil servant and critical spiritual guide.

Civil service and leadership appear, however, to be contradictory opera-tions. As civil servant, the university is professionally articulated by the heteronomy of needs for the enlightened state's economic progress. As reflex-ive guide, as autonomous university, it is articulated as critic of the needs of the state understood as an economic apparatus of knowledge and power. Together these universities form the antagonism of the capitalist university.

The Cartesian university ultimately will become Napoleonic and then Comtean. The Cartesian idea of the university, its French Enlightenment idea, will be historically carried out by the state pedagogical university ruled by the interests of the state, a center for the formation of secular bureaucrats, adepts of administration. The decapitation of the king will be followed by the emer-gence of disciplinary society, the society of disciplines that will micro- and macrophysically govern the prophylactic surveillance of the social contract.[68]

6

✦

The University of Berlin:
The Modern, Philosophical, German University

> With respect to the modern German university . . . we should
> point out the following crucial moments: The structural trans-
> formation of Germany's political economy in response to the
> French invasion; Prussia's political will to resist that invasion;
> and the rebirth of German national consciousness through the
> decision to oppose Napoleon's politics of truth with *Bildung*
> and the truth that Germans believe is native to them.
>
> —Patricio Marchant, "Sobre la necesidad de fundar un
> departamento de filosofía en (la Universidad de) Chile"

Napoleon defeated the Prussian army outside Jena on October 14, 1806. The
Universities of Jena and Halle closed. "Napoleon wrote to the sultan: 'Prussia
has disappeared.'"[1] In 1806, the empire vanished, even in name. "That year,
sixteen German princes [united in the Confederation of the Rhine] under
Napoleon's protection. On the first of August, they announced their separation from . . . the [Imperial Diet] of Regensburg. On August sixth Franz II
answered by laying down the German [Imperial] crown."[2] In 1807, the Peace
of Tilsit restricted Prussia to the eastern shores of the Elbe. "'French was the
official language up to the Elbe.'"[3] In 1808, Napoleon spoke to Goethe at
a meeting of princes in Erfurt and invited him to Paris: "'Come to Paris, I
demand it of you. There is a larger view of the world there.'"[4] In 1809, Napoleon suffered his first major defeat at the Battle of Aspern. Fichte delivered his
Addresses to the German Nation. Friedrich Schleiermacher's sermons made
him the preceptor to Berlin society. A delegation sent by Schmalz from the
University of Halle had an audience with Friedrich Wilhelm III of Prussia
requesting that the university be refounded in Berlin. Friedrich Wilhelm III is
said to have assented with the apparently apocryphal statement, "The state
must replace what it has lost in terms of material resources with intellectual
power." K. F. Beyme, one-time minister, briefly chief minister, and confidant

of Friedrich Wilhelm III, solicited essays about a new teaching institution from eminent professors, some of whom he had met through private lessons, among them Fichte and Schleiermacher.[5]

The modern German university has its political and historical origin in the Prussian will to "spiritually" resist the philosophical truth guiding Napoleon's educational policy. For the Germans this meant politically and philosophically situating the university on the margins of French universality and the French university, subtracting themselves from the growing impact of French metaphysics, resisting the Napoleonic translation of the Cartesian desire to "build the city," "the state," the "university," the "new house," and "the most perfect moral science"[6] in the form of the professional university.

German philosophical thinking on the university surrounding the creation of the University of Berlin opposes the Cartesian tendency of knowledge toward its instrumental application; it confronts the operation of truth that functions practically and technically as the fruit of the "highest level of knowledge;" it distances itself from the will to subordinate the speculative moment to practical and technical interests; it rejects subordinating the speculative principle to the knowledge and interests of the state. For the Germans conceive the speculative principle of philosophy and the sciences as the principle of the state and the university, and not the reverse, as in Descartes's crystallization in Napoleon. They conceived of the state as an effect of philosophy instead of philosophy as "state religion."[7] If they fear narrowly defined nationalism and the utilitarianism and positivism that guides public authorities in matters of science, it is because, according to them, the subject of knowledge is not the sovereign people incarnate in the state, as in postrevolutionary France, but the speculative spirit incarnate in a *system* (Schelling, Fichte) or *encyclopedia* (Hegel).

For these thinkers, especially Fichte and Humboldt, the peak of the university and truth is "spiritual."[8] Internal truth begins, develops, and culminates in the spirit.[9] Science is interested only in science. The interests of truth do not transcend truth itself. Lacking this essential interest and concentration in itself, knowledge and the university run the risk of dispersing across the diversity of empirical interests and activities without principle, unity, or gathering.

The philosophical university of "German idealism" emphasizes what the Germans believe is the only safeguard of the unity of knowledge and the systematicity of the field. The philosophical discourse of the German university adopts, explicitly in Humboldt and Fichte, Aristotle's rhetoric of knowledge from and for itself, which was so controversial in Descartes's *Discourse on Method* and in the later "Letter to Picot." In this discourse, the university will be, above all else, the university of the sciences, not the professions.

Even so, the German philosophical university knows itself to be the incomplete historical totality of knowledge. It knows its ideal is not yet fulfilled. This is a dual knowledge: the knowledge of what it knows and of what it does not.[10] Thus, any empirical university is an "image" of its unfulfilled totality, a synthesis in process (Kant) in the progress of absolute knowing (Hegel).

In both Fichte and Humboldt, the knowledge "won" by university research, before it tends toward instrumentalization as in Descartes, must stand on its own and so exceed itself while still maintaining its goals as the foothold for new research. In this sense, they define the "idea" of the university by strictly separating science from profession, reflection from determination. The orientation of the philosophical university is typically motivated by the search for truth while resisting the interests of the state, which constrain research to its practical necessities.

The state's interest in truth must become an object of university analysis and not its commanding subject. The speculative essence of the German philosophical university is revealed in the strict obligation to reflect on instituted truth as the executive power of the state. This point is clearly made by Fichte and Humboldt, as opposed to the apparent reconciliation of science and profession in Schleiermacher. If they cannot achieve full autonomy from the interests of the state, "universities . . . should be abolished immediately."[11] In fact, they would be abolished the moment they professionalized, since the idea of "science" is contrary to that of the profession. The professional university must remain excluded from the scientific university. "Solitude and freedom" will be the university's guiding principles.[12] Isolation so that the spirit will continually refer back to itself in the arduous search for truth, and freedom as a guarantee that research will not be constrained to external ends.[13]

Rather than subordinating the university to its interests, the state should subordinate itself to the interests of the university. For that reason, the university should not be thought of as "simply higher grades of school," the peak of professional interest. On the contrary, the modern state is obliged to subordinate professional interests to critical-reflective interests.[14] This does not necessarily mean, however, that knowledge's disinterested search—a question as foreign to the state as to everyday people—is not in some way linked to moral and political life. The fact that scientific activity aspires to "derive everything from first principles" finds its practical corollary: "Everything must be developed toward an ideal."[15] According to Humboldt, the legitimate subject of the German university can only be formed on the basis of the synthesis— "The principle and the ideal should always be connected in a single idea"—a synthesis ensuring that the scientific search for true causes continues to coincide with the search for just ends in moral and political life.[16]

Schleiermacher's Position

Schleiermacher appears to distance himself from the tenet that excludes the professional from the university. But this is ultimately a strategic move to defend the university as a totality of the sciences and not of the professions in a political economic context that gradually makes any nonprofessional state university project unworkable. Schleiermacher privileges the teleology of autonomous spiritual research over a heteronomous state teleology, and just like Humboldt and Fichte, he rejects out of hand the progressive instrumental direction heralded at every turn as the modernizing state's standard policy requiring the university to act as a "factory" for professionals, that is, as public mediator of labor power for the development and progress of the economy and the nation's history. This instrumental tendency, the preeminent object of Nietzsche's critique in *Anti-Education: On the Future of Our Educational Institutions* (1872), is not only the inheritance of "Napoleonic" Cartesianism but also of the technical medieval university, which, through the "higher" faculties of theology, law, and medicine, granted primacy to the university's professional officialdom, the "executive power" (Kant) represented by those faculties, and demoted to the status of the "lower" faculty the dialectical principle of the faculty of philosophy or arts.

According to Schleiermacher, the state fears the sterility and linguistic monstrosity of research when left to chart its own path. The state fears "that if it leaves them to themselves everything will soon wheel around in a circle of fruitless learning and teaching, far distant from life and practice, the desire for practical affairs will be replaced by the pure, disinterested thirst for knowledge, and no one will want to be involved in civil affairs."[17]

It also turns out to be politically "dreadful, a terrible thought" to organize an educational system that "supposes that already at school, or as they leave it, a split is to be made between those who are capable of the highest scientific culture and those who are allotted to a subordinate echelon, and that for the second group special institutions are to be established where they would be further cultivated for their particular area of knowledge in a more mechanical, traditional manner and without the philosophical guidance of the university."[18]

It is therefore not advisable to strictly impose hierarchies by decree, "especially if the goal is to preserve them."[19] An invisible apparatus would be preferable, one that ensures the hierarchy is naturally fixed and regulated. The university would educate everyone equally, without distinction, within the ascendent spiritual-teleological horizon of science and philosophy. Every university student, whatever path he may take, would be guided by the reflexive faculty's theology. And the distinction between scientists and bureaucrats would be marked by "knowledge of knowledge" and "knowledge of nonknowledge." In this way, once the professional has been completely incorporated into the theological horizon of pure science, he may then decide how to realize his own potential within that horizon. At the same time, this would spontaneously generate in him an interest in the totality of knowledge that circumscribes his and all other professions. This also interests the state to the same extent that it entrusts experts and technocrats with the business of leadership wherein the vision of totality is whatever is adequate.[20] Besides, not instituting hierarchies is not the same as eliminating them. Those who are "superior" will necessarily rise to the top, and those who are inferior will willingly adopt a subordinate position in any institution that enables each person to achieve what his powers will allow.[21] In this way, natural difference is preserved alongside political equality.

For its part, the state must favor a university politics of this kind and must not "through false concerns and through structures based on them, nurture those misunderstandings of scholars occupied among themselves with expansion of the sciences, [for] the schools will lose their foundations."[22] If it does, "over the long run the state will rob itself of the most essential advantages that the sciences afford it. That is, the longer the situation persists the more the state will lack people who can conceive and carry out great enterprises, who can astutely uncover the roots and connection of all errors."[23]

In a university ever more inclined toward the professions by economic state interests, Schleiermacher wanted to ensure that the instrumental horizon would be institutionally circumscribed by the speculative one, and that this horizon would leave its mark on professionals. Rather than a concession to professionalism, what he sought was to subordinate professionalism to science and philosophy. Thus, the schools would become a propaedeutic for the university's deepening of science and broadening of critique and not a propaedeutic for greater specialization and professional enclosure.[24]

7

✦

Kant's Architectonics

Upon entering into *The Conflict of the Faculties* (1798), every category appears as a key. According to the key one turns, the text opens into a variety of arrangements and proportions. The first key we turn, which will spirit us away, is "conflict." Guided by this category and our interests, we will translate concepts that emerge from the text—for example, the "university." Here the university is articulated as conflict, a conflict among physically defined dispositions, between "Left" and "Right." Inside the university, the Right is organized around the "upper faculties" (theology, law, medicine), the "government," "officials" that administer the state, and the Left emerges as the faculty of philosophy, which questions the government (executive power) and constructive pedagogical knowledge.

The text in question begins with a long paragraph that narrates its origin story. The narrative implicates the text's author, Kant, in his role as university professor. Kant the philosopher tells how Kant the university professor became an object of disfavor and censorship by the government of Friedrich Wilhelm II of Prussia because of "how irresponsibly" Kant had acted "against your duty as a teacher of youth" and "against our paternal purpose,"[1] having "misus[ed] your philosophy to distort and disparage many of the cardinal and basic teachings of the Holy Scriptures and of Christianity" in a book titled *Religion within the Limits of Mere Reason* (1793).[2]

The anecdote referenced in the text sets in motion the "conscientious account"[3] that a philosopher, Kant, feels obliged to give due to an official "misuse" committed by a teacher, Kant, who as an "instrument" of a government institution owes allegiance to the law of the land, in this case, to the king. The misuse apparently consisted in having reflected—philosophized, invested with a public character—in a definitively nonreflexive space, thus sowing doubt in the "*civil* community," an act the law only permits in the "*learned* community."[4] This is not just any anecdote but a university anecdote, a specificity derived from its medium, the body that is the central concern of *The Conflict of the Faculties*'s reflection.

Nevertheless, this "conscientious account" exceeds the empirical university, returning us to themes that, although they may not be directly academic, nonetheless shape the architecture in which its Kantian possibility crystallizes. These themes—already stated several times—can be sampled from among the following: "state," "people," "publicness," "truth," "language," "power," "autonomy," "reflexivity," "technics," "history," "progress," and other derivations.

According to the essential secondary literature,[5] *The Conflict of the Faculties* inaugurates the German tradition of "great" philosophical writing on the modern university, a tradition that will conclude with Heidegger's *Rectoral Address*.

Despite the fact that the text's "account" emerges from a specific conjuncture, it is not preoccupied with the university's sociological and historiographical aspects: How was it that it was created? Where were its first scholars educated? How were they credentialed? etc. Summarizing a long and arduous history and clinging to the postulate that the university is not a product of chance but a technical artifact resulting from a determinate "principle contained in reason,"[6] Kant instead dwells on the transcendental conditions of the institution, its relation to the state, the people, history, language, and truth. Thus, his "account" responds transcendentally to an empirical event, sketching the "transcendental architectonics" of that event and of all modern university *empirie*, which for the documentarian would be an endless task.

So the university is related to a conflict. That conflict leads us to the contingency that the state confronts with regard to its specific "end" of "influencing the people . . . [b]y public teachings,"[7] and relying on "the people's confidence in their teachers,"[8] since through teaching the state "can exercise a very great influence to uncover the inmost thoughts and guide the most secret intentions of its subjects."[9] What's more, "through the academic instruction of those who were to become the people's public teachers," the state can quietly advance or delay reforms as needed.[10]

Of course, "the government . . . does not itself teach."[11] It merely reserves the right to "sanction teachings"—those doctrines expounded in public. It indicates what is teachable to those who teach without worrying about the truth of what is taught. And upon occupying a public position, professors are required, "contracted," to perform according to government directives.[12]

Doctrine—that knowledge designated as teachable by the government—and the functionaries of that knowledge constitute a mediation between state and "people," an instrument deployed in the narrow field of the state's interests. As a teaching institution that makes all established science public "by *mass production*,"[13] the university is complicit with the state, representing its extension into civil society. It follows that some scholars or university professors are construed "as tools of the government . . . who are not free to make public use of their learning as they see fit, but are subject to the censorship of the faculties."[14] Not having the "right" to "reflect" or critique doctrine in public—thus availing themselves of their investiture by the state—they restrict themselves to simply repeating it. Relative to knowledge, professors are mere "technicians" of the doctrines the state capriciously authorizes for dissemination: "in accepting its offices, [they] have contracted to teach what it wants (whether this be true or not)" playing the role of "businessmen" more than men of science.[15] In this way the influence that professors exert on the public is "legal," bound to law and king.[16] The professors are the university's executive power and, therefore, strictly monitored.

The government gives the most attention, support, and import to this moment of heteronomy, which "secure[s] the strongest and most lasting influence on the people."[17] These are the higher faculties.

In order to carry out and control the uniform extension of the teaching "executed" by the upper or official faculties, the state provides a "text" and a "canon" for standardizing teaching.[18] "Such a text (or book) must comprise *statutes*, that is, teachings that proceed from an act of choice on the part of an authority," granting it authority and engendering respect.[19] The function of the upper faculties is unreflexively limited to the reproduction of that text, remaining subject to an external principle. As a medium of doctrinal expansion, the teaching faculty exists not to reflect on what it teaches but to convince and placate any doubt about it. It lacks autonomy. Thus the faculty of law does not question the justice of the law, nor does the faculty of theology question the truth of God. It seems "nonsense" to the practicing lawyer to prove whether the regulations are just or to search for the law in reason's reflexivity.[20] The lawyer looks for law in the code. According to his contract, the technician of the upper faculty—lawyer, physician, clergyman—cannot "philosophize" while he performs his public duty. And although it is not the upper faculties' specific role to raise doubts about the code, they can do so if and only if those doubts are not made public. The upper faculties can adopt a reflexive function, proper to the faculty of philosophy, but they cannot communicate it to the public without prior authorization from the government. The government's authority does not leave open the possibility of institutionally judging what is just or not. If these instruments of state (the professors) get carried away beyond their legally defined role, "the seeds of insurrection and factions are sown."[21]

The responsibility of the upper faculties means there is a direct relation between their "incursion" into "the civil community," which is nothing but the incursion of the state through them into civil society, and the socialization of the state's particular point of view universalized.[22]

By law, state professors are subject to the government. And the power of the state? Is state power subject to that law, through which it publicly acts as government? Is power perhaps irrational (not free) when it comes to its own dominion? Or does it possess critical distance, the activity of reflection that, putting off the public performance through which it is instituted, interrogates the law, agitating for its reform?

Without that freedom, power comes to a standstill in the technical automatism of its established capacity. It "could rest undisturbed." It is not an unsubjected subject or critic of the law who acts but a dogmatic machine.[23]

In this reflexive activity, power becomes autonomous from the government and its established order. It enters an "open field" of possibilities beyond the public establishment. Such a reflexive activity, proper to modern power, would be esoteric to the *conatus* [*conato*] of government. Power does not expose itself when it is reflexive. It lacks (executive) power. It does not determine but only listens to the "internal principle" of reflection. As the modern subject of power, the state is itself a conflict between the public possibility of serving as the law and its reflexive possibility or critical distance: a conflict between "reflection" and "determination."

From the perspective of power, one's "autonomy" consists in imposing the law without it being imposed, subjecting without being subjected, permitting so that what is permitted is not the same as what one permits oneself. The "autonomy" of power may be located primarily in the (esoteric) reflexive activity beyond positive law, writing, doctrine. This is a different or deferred instance of positive law, where the condition of the law may be considered.

But the autonomy of power not only presupposes the ability to reflect on its public position. It also supposes the ability to determine social establishment according to a proposition it decides, its interest. Thus, what power esoterically reserves as infinite reflexive judgment it discloses in small doses as order and doctrine.

The government or determination of the public is then a particular game of power, a game defined, on the one hand, by the technical requirements of contingency and, on the other, by the "open field" of reflection. This particular game through which power establishes its government by excluding other games and orders is not for that reason "dogmatic" or "arbitrary" because it is grounded not in the government itself but in open reflection, which, by illuminating the limits of action, recognizes and inscribes itself as a necessary particularity in an inconclusive totality.

The act of reflection is indispensable for an "enlightened" but not "despotic" government, that is, an enlightened absolutist one. But it cannot be properly practiced by the government alone since it is a critical and not an executive act. The act of reflection must be carried out by an official agent, although not governmental or invested with executive power, an agent that, although inscribed in and recognized by public institutions, critically solicits them, exceeding the performative system wherein power is governmentally established and exposed. Critique of the university institution, critique of executive power and of the law have an institutionally recognized place in the university. As we will see, for Kant that place, the faculty of philosophy, must constitute the university's highest institute and gathering principle. Publicly established, the faculty of philosophy solicits the government's particular game from without, from beyond its technical circuit, beginning from its language, which "is bound to be dangerous both to the government and to the public itself."[24]

We already know the government is that partial order through which power becomes public in the form of regency or "reality." The faculty of philosophy, as reflexive judgment, questioningly withdraws from any particular game of power. In withdrawing from the government's particular disciplining—and in fact, from all disciplining, as we will see farther on—the faculty of philosophy represents the possibility of publicness, reflexively open to every unsociable unnamed in every sociability. It is raw publicness before it is pacified into a defined legal or contractual artifact, publicness in that temporality that is open to reflection. In the temporality of reflection, the possibility of publicness and philosophy become one.

The faculty of philosophy is reflection on and "deferral" of government and any particular object. What is "written" holds no sway there, and the imperative and external speech are unwelcome, except for the constitutive command that its institutional dignity not be put to public use. The faculty of philosophy can "speak out publicly"[25] only on the fringes of the publicness it ultimately grounds. It is defined by the fact that "we can never accept [a practical teaching] as true simply because we are ordered to (*de par le Roi*)."[26] It only responds "to the principles of thought in general,"[27] never to a dictated statute. It rests on no doctrine or definitive concept, and it is in this sense autonomous.

Taken to its logical extreme, the reflexive faculty formulates no technical code on which it can rely. Given its interest in truth and the truth of truth, it resists translating its inquiry into determining language. The truth is technically undetermined in reflection, that is, in the faculty of philosophy. (The question as to what kind of language would be appropriate to such a faculty and the relationship of that language with the aesthetic faculties remains unanswered.)

The faculty of philosophy's role is to reflect on the technical domestication of the truth by disciplinary specializations. In doing so, it questioningly gathers them all and sets itself up as knowledge of the discipline's knowledge and nonknowledge. For the same reason, it lacks a specialization and is untranslatable into curricula. This faculty is therefore the center of knowledge's autonomy, the vortex from which the historico-technical actuality of truth, the "right-wing" of science, the established present are all questioned. "What is Enlightenment?" is therefore a question about the present [*actualidad*][28] that is out of date [*desactual*].

Useless (not executive) and deferring, the faculty of philosophy is not, however, sterile. It is the source of the unregulated questioning of the conditions of possibility of rules and principles. Thus, everything depends on the faculty of philosophy, which presides over the upper faculties.

Power cannot reflect in public, so it cloisters its reflexivity in the faculty of philosophy, making room for the critique of power within the technical workings of power. With Kant, reflection, the critique of power and knowledge conquer the institution's center without a center. The "anarchy" of reflection enters the institution without being subjected to it; it exceeds it and slowly expands it without provoking panics or revolts against the order in which power is experienced. Thus, in addition to serving the expansion (extension), reproduction, and strengthening of the law (upper faculties), the university is the critical condition of their autonomy.

It is said that the upper faculties serve as the people's unmediated guide. But their doctrines do not coincide with reason's reflexive difference. This gives rise to the structural conflict between the upper and lower faculties. The upper faculties publicly promote doctrine, defending against dissent. The lower faculty critiques the conditions of "the truth" on which the upper faculties' public promotion relies.

This structural conflict of the faculties, maintained inside the scientific community, hidden from civil discourse, cannot be resolved by a friendly accommodation. It needs a court case, a judge, and a lasting verdict. That judge, we now know, is pure reason, which regulates the conflict between Left and Right, nature and doctrine, truth and technics, nation and state.

Unfolding through reflexive judgment, determining reason does not become automatic but remains dynamically autonomous yet unmoved.

The constant progress that issues from the conflict between the spatial executive and the temporal reflexive, between "Right" and "Left," will lead civil society to a state of perfection that will do away once and for all with the restrictions and mediations between reflection (faculty of philosophy) and the people, nature, and society. Society itself will become the ecstatic space of infinitely determined reflection (temporality), in other words, "the kingdom of God on earth."[29]

8

✦

Nietzsche: From the Faculty of Philosophy to the Faculty of Genealogy

But how could we reproach or praise the universe! . . . In no way do our aesthetic and moral judgements apply to it! It also has no drive to self-preservation or any other drives; nor does it observe any laws. Let us beware of saying that there are laws in nature. There are only necessities: there is no one who commands, no one who obeys, no one who transgresses. Once you know that there are no purposes, you also know that there is no accident; for only against a world of purposes does the word "accident" have a meaning. Let us beware of saying that death is opposed to life. The living is only a form of what is dead, and a very rare form.

—Nietzsche, *Gay Science*

Genius [is] the final result of the accumulated labor of generations.

—Nietzsche, *Twilight of the Idols*

In many passages,[1] Nietzsche refers to the painstaking manufacture of universality, mobile multitude of anthropomorphisms, effect of "a sum of human relations which have been poetically and rhetorically intensified, transferred, decorated and which, after lengthy use, seem firm, canonical and binding to a people."[2] The universal has neither origin nor objective. It has only a genealogy. In Nietzsche, "origin" and "objective" are illusions sustained by an alchemy of little mechanisms,[3] the frugality of a genealogy of sources when compared to the solemnity of metaphysical origin and universality. Those empirical beginnings must be investigated to see how the "great" universals and the institutions in which they are embodied came about piece by piece, by which means they were expanded and stabilized, according to which local hybridizations and purifications.

The universal is dissolved as a substantive anteriority or promised posteriority. A version of the universal as an effect of forces—"states of force" that first conquer themselves, sanctioning their identity—has expanded to capitalize on territories and languages, small universalities that from their local emergence have gone on to build empires (the state, the self, the truth) upon the condition of forgetting their genealogy.

Within the framework of "invention" as the uneven and unstable ground of the general, the history of universals since Nietzsche has become the history of an empirical struggle, dominance, and mixing of localities, a history of trivialities in which, through jeering, pettifoggery, and incantations, a few gurgling, shrill noises have stabilized into emblems, idioms, and styles, becoming planetary, even interstellar.[4] Organized under the concept of "invention" is the "ideology" that the universal has no more universality than what it can conquer and no more identity or substance than what can be derived from the force and territory gathered under those terms. The universal is circumscribed to its own genealogy, its historical outline and factic transformation. Without a basis in community, its origin is grounded in the avatars and positionings of ephemeral imperatives and activities.

Along this path, nothing ensures a priori a universal community or history, for it is by forgetting their origins in unstable and fickle forces that tradition, sedentariness, and customariness arise. On the basis of the concept of "invention," to converse, translate, share, and agree are above all else to battle, dominate, digest, and regurgitate. "The rulers . . . say 'this is so and so,' they set their seal on everything and every occurrence with a sound and thereby take possession of it."[5] Every generality is the result of "a particular struggle."[6]

In this context, the university—its ethics and truths—is a thin veneer over customariness [*verosimilitud*], maintained and fostered by the forgetting of the extrauniversity motives and forces that sustain it. It is a veneer of verisimilitude that, on condition of this forgetting, serves as the true nature of all things, as an "assumption" or *universitas*. The university becomes a mode of encryption, the rigidity and sedentariness of life forces, which could bristle at any moment like "the back of a tiger."[7]

The text by Nietzsche to which we now turn, *Anti-Education: On the Future of Our Educational Institutions* (1872), oscillates between a Romantic and a genealogical critique of the modern university and state. (A Nietzsche scholar would likely categorize the text as the former.) The commentary that follows maintains this ambiguity, for it is indebted to a broader analysis of the relations between genealogy and Romanticism in Nietzsche's critique of the Enlightenment. This analysis, we feel, breaks from genealogy and adopts a Romantic tone in those readings that materialize the "actual history" in which genealogy dissolves universals; it adopts a Romantic tone toward those readings that fail to consider, for example, that the dissemination effected by genealogy is also in every instance [*en cada caso*] an "insemination" or construct that in turn requires another genealogy. The "step back," genealogy's memorious and dissolving return in each case [*en cada caso*] to the forgotten sites of the "emergence" and "origin" of institutions, is also a "step forward," inventive and constructive of those emergences and origins, a step forward that in turn demands its own genealogical dissolution and so on indefinitely. The Romantic temperament, on the other hand, in its search for a new historical epoch, enacts a critique of classicist ideals, a critique that, even knowing that it will never return, comes to rest on the longed-for homeland, an idealized Middle Ages.

Questions of Style

In a series of lectures delivered in Basel between January and March 1872 and later collected into the book, Nietzsche foretells the destruction or at least the radical mutation of the university.[8] The lectures do not offer an empirical examination of these establishments, in which the author declares himself "inexperienced."[9] They do not offer a diagnostic based on a systematic "measure" or "classification" upon which concepts guaranteed and backed by this accounting of the field will be later erected, concepts from which "guiding" questions, "timetables," and organizational "charts " are then deduced.[10]

From the very start, Nietzsche distances his style of evaluation and reading from the professional university's current style, which is primarily argumentative, expository, and verifying. He indicates this Enlightenment university style as the symptom he plans to analyze. He will read the secret, "the entrails"[11] of this style that is widely and centrally promoted by the modern, professionalizing state. He will also read this style—how else—in another style (genealogical? Romantic?) that is neither professional nor of the university.

From the start, Nietzsche's factic evaluation positions itself as a reading and knowledge practice different from the one gradually spreading in up-to-date teaching institutions and gradually, pedagogically penetrating provincial populations and mother tongues.

A first sign of this enlightened university style of assessment and interpretation is the brutal greediness to understand, a greediness that latches onto anything in its "blind desire" to measure, possess, and calculate everything "at any cost," a totalitarian logic lacking in "taste" (*sapore*) and wisdom [*sapiencia*—Trans.], incapable of distinguishing "those things which are . . . worth knowing" from those that can be simply ignored.[12] This style is driven by a demonstrative religiosity, cautious not to make missteps or leave loose ends; a foundational reason that is greedy, zealous for certainty, full of the tyranny it establishes over all *empirie*, dull and out of breath from such an overwhelming task,[13] a reason driven by utilitarian moralizing, by the total encompassing of things and temporalities as "things for" and "times for." Against such an all-encompassing horizon, anything that lacks a readily distinguished "for-that" is considered disposable, worthy only of being processed "for the benefit of."

To this instrumental style that gradually becomes dominant, Nietzsche opposes a style whose reading and speaking do not proceed with the rigor of measurement and precision. It is a style whose a priori holds that "life," that which "occurs," is in excess and inexact. It is a style unworried by "verification," the "*adequatio*," "argumentation," and gathering. It is a style capable of discerning "from afar" that between one phenomenon and another there are analogical and symptomatological certainties, a style whose discursive intention is disagreement and the reorientation of objects toward their points of "origin."

This style may be considered "pre-" or "post-" modern, but in any case, it is always untimely vis-à-vis any present dominated by the instrumentalist "tendency" of the primordially Socratic state Enlightenment in which it appears.

Rejection of the Enlightenment

Nietzsche's text critiques the Enlightenment, the way it cloaks the present in a peculiar logic that is universalized through higher education institutions. His rejection is not general or vague but attends to the way the Enlightenment sets up a progressive universal truth (Hegel), subsuming provisional and irreducible experiences and perspectives to a common logic. Another mode of enlightenment, of interaction between different homelands of experience and linguistic niches could just as well apply, a way of making connections that is neither "true" nor statist but erratic and anarchic, connections, for example, between the music of the Greek dialect and that of German Romanticism, a different way of linking modern universality to local heritage.

The Addressees

If not the lectures themselves, then the book that contains them specifically addresses the "wasteful"[14] ones who are prepared to read it, forestalling Enlightenment "haste,"[15] endlessly deferring the time of the ruling facticity. These readers are capable of ruminating leisurely on a book. They are aloof from an instrumental interpretation of reading, immune to the logic of efficiency that conceives of "time as money," at odds with the teleology of profit's ability to encompass all actions and things. They are readers who are not formed by the statist interpretation of thinking, who can meditate on thinking beyond the ken of dominant professional motives and the modes of reading that the modern university offers up as the only "serious" ones.

The explicit mention of these addressees gives the lectures an epic, confrontational arrogance to the extent that these readers, who in "isolation" and "mistrust" "suffer inwardly" the present,[16] might be incited by the book to radicalize their difference from the present.

Reading the Present

The lectures do not offer a historiographical or sociological examination of present institutions. Instead they treat the dominant tendencies of the German educational *factum*, tendencies that construct that *factum* by distracting it from the "lofty impulse"[17] that presided over its foundation, an impulse disfigured by the innovations imposed on it at the hands of the modernizing state.

That erstwhile lofty impulse was connected, not without coercion, to a regime that sought to exalt and free the possibilities of the "mother tongue,"[18] "fertile soil,"[19] irreplaceable "homeland"[20] of "genius,"[21] creativity, and history. A homeland and a genius threatened with being "emptied" and "cloaked"[22] by the colossal, universalizing, pedagogical apparatus for mass enlightenment promoted and managed by the state and dedicated to replacing maternal memories and experiences, in excess and inexact, with efficient university experience and professional specialist languages.

More than an examination of institutions, the text offers a reading of actuality, of the "entrails of the present."[23] In those entrails, which always refer back to other entrails and so on endlessly, one can read the "sense" promoted by the enlightened state, the future of the Enlightenment. What Nietzsche "predicts"[24]—that which is to come [lo por-venir] from current tendencies—is the destruction or at least the mutation of the modern, enlightened, statist university into a form that, today, can barely survive without dominating, lacking any notoriety, and which, strictly speaking, one could say is not alive.[25] If it lives, it does so only on tomorrow's credit.

With the gesture of foretelling, of launching into another present, Nietzsche's prediction activates the ears of the listening public, opening up a distance from the present that is indispensable for speaking about it, that makes it audible and visible as an object. Prophecy is, then, a rhetoric of distance that readies the sclerotic eardrums in the auditorium to listen to the present. Nietzsche exiles the listening public with untimely anecdotes—something that happened, something that will happen—habituating them to strangeness, building a bridge of empathy between his "natural" condition as a stranger and the public (including Burckhardt) that he addresses.

Temporality and Affect

Up to this point, the text has opened three axes of temporal and affective relations: (1) a "purer age"[26] in which the university and the mother tongue

established relations of mutual reciprocity, a past whose remembrance produces "nostalgia" for the mother tongue, dead mother supplanted by the
language of the wet nurse, the university-state stepmother; (2) a present
dominated by academic language that activates the pathos of "horror" and
"amazement" in folkloric modes of speech and behavior; (3) a future, proph-
esied from "hope"[27] or "despair,"[28] in which language will be unhinged from
its university frame.

Up to this point, the text treats a struggle in and for the present. At this
moment, two antagonistic tendencies sustain this struggle: (1) that of the process of professional universalism, incapable of solidarizing the heterogeneity
of linguistic provincialisms, which colonizes and educates that heterogeneity
by establishing the center—state enlightenment—everywhere; (2) the affirmation of the fertility of the mother tongue as the ground of particularisms,
solecisms, and alterities threatened with oblivion.

The exiled condition of Nietzsche's lectures becomes explicit when he con-
fesses his feelings about the present: "horror,"[29] "amazement,"[30] and "fear."[31]
Horror and amazement that none of his listeners shares, since they dwell in
the present as on an "estate."[32] Fear that would be the pathos that accompanies modernization not through the experience of its internal logic but rather
through the experience of that which this logic performs, that is, tongues and
maternal memories. Horror would be that feeling that attends "difference"
when faced with imminent elimination by its context. It is the feeling of the
stranger in a xenophobic climate, the feeling of the foreigner on the eve of
his reeducation.

As we have pointed out, "reading" demands as a condition of its possibility
a distance that makes it autonomous from that which is read. This distance,
if it is to constitute a principle of reading, cannot be consumed by the feeling
of fear. Even though it denotes impertinence and marks distance, fear falters,
blinds, absolutizes that distance, and impedes reading. In order to read the
"entrails of the present" and deploy that reading as "resistance" and "confrontation," one must make faltering into an epic. At the same time, reading
the "entrails" of a phenomenon evidences a certain weakness that can be
read in its secret. And if, as Nietzsche intends, the enlightened present can be
revealed so that its strategy does not go unseen, it is because the present has
been weakened. Essence is weakness, and the Enlightenment's weakness lies
in its drive to reduce everything—including its origin or "foundation"—to
the laws of its knowledges, its desire to display itself entirely in an illuminated vitrine,[33] in the transparency of understanding, to fully reveal itself,
unsheathing its epistemic mastery. To fully ex-pose its mastery is also to place
itself outside, without reserve.

Enlightenment modernity overlooks rural languages and maternal memories, imposing on them grammatical customs, stylistic codes, information
architectures that will bear fruit with their professionalization through a process of emptying and "rattling" preuniversity and illiterate experiences.

The merciless application of professional customs to the provincial is the Enlightenment's French legacy (Cartesian-Napoleonic), the theoretical primacy of analytic geometry, which must forget whatever it subordinates by plugging it straightaway into calculation (*ratio*).[34]

The *curriculum* is the university ethic in which disparate languages are disposed. To enlighten is to enter into specialization. And whoever wants to act upon the enlightened terrain of a profession—everyone does, thanks to a state strategy, as we will see—must circumscribe himself to a specific discipline.[35]

Crying Out from What Is Assumed

The Enlightenment dominates the present rather effectively by making itself invisible as that which is assumed, an assumption that only the isolated and the exiled are able to counter, as they are not absorbed by the instrumentalist medium but rather frightened of it.[36] Nietzsche takes for granted that the public listening to his lectures has been formed by this instrumental present. He understands that his words will sound unfamiliar and strange, as if they issued from a different "estate." He warns that he has little chance of being heard. He senses the risks entailed by any unfamiliar sound. From Socrates's well-known "case," he knows that, having concentrated the power of interpellation, speaking strangely carries the risk of death, for even that context is surprised and rattled by the strangeness of critical discourse. The familiar defends itself from the unfamiliar as soon as it surfaces. Family problems.

Strategically, Nietzsche pours honey into the ears of the auditorium. He must prevent the listeners from "turn[ing] their back"[37] after the first sentence. So he rhetorically disguises his discourse in anecdote, while also noting that what he will say is not entirely related to the immediate context but rather to the untimely [*lo extemporáneo*], whether "purer age"[38] or "eventual victory."[39] Only by means of the fiction of untimeliness [*lo extemporáneo*] can the present catch sight of its own fictitiousness, contingency, and accidental eventuality.

Part of the foreigner's power is making clear from the start that he speaks another language, that his organs are unfamiliar or made up of a different integument. Unfamiliarity must make itself known on the "threshold" of a different "estate," like presenting a "coat of arms" as well as the "arms" one carries.[40] Presenting arms [*la ilustración de las armas*] is the first courtesy, the immediate protocol among estates.

Nietzsche opens by stating his impertinence to a present that rules as that which is assumed. It does so in the most violent manner that can still be heard by a host comfortably ensconced in the invisible habits of his home, that is, revealing that edifice as a hostile illusion, revealing the history of its origins and construction, recalling the motives on which it is based and which it promotes, and foretelling its death and the aesthetic of its demise.

Structure of the Assumed

Two drives issue from assumed Enlightenment: the "drive" toward maximum expansion, according to which Enlightenment "extends . . . to an ever-wider circle," and the drive to "weaken it" or toward specialization, by which the Enlightenment monopolizes the entirety of the individual in a codified field of action.[41]

Both drives—expansion and specialization—are subordinated to the interests and directives of the state, which seeks the Enlightenment's renunciation of its supreme claims to "autonomy" and "anarchy," thus preventing any person from enlightening himself as he sees fit and Napoleonically requiring him instead to subordinate himself to state interests.

In addition to decrying our dwelling in assumption and highlighting the drives on which that assumption rests, Nietzsche proposes perverting assumed Enlightenment and its drives with counterdrives, a task these lectures outline:

(1) The "constriction" or restraint of Enlightenment, a constriction that does not suggest rendering its expansion elitist—as Habermas would have it[42]—but instead resists the performative will to professionalize everything, leaving nothing untouched, unenlightened. This constriction resists the Enlightenment's determined penetration into every experiential layer of maternal rootedness and affect and, as we will see, the consequent annihilation of the in-excess and inexact principle (genius) of poetry and arts. Nietzsche affirms the watchword "Enlightenment for all!" so long as nonprofessional spaces free from Enlightenment—maternal, genial, genealogical spaces—are safeguarded. It is in this second sense, leaving some spaces untouched, that Nietzsche speaks of a "higher education" opposed to "higher education" in any official state sense. Nietzschean "higher education" opposes education as a means for the state to produce a professional people with the aim of improving the national economy and shoring up the national happiness. This university procedure for state improvement impoverishes the individual. And in this sense, the "true" higher education opposes the "great mass of people"[43] or the massification of professionalism so that the state comes to mediate the individual, transforming every life into a statist life.

(2) Enlightened "autarchy," that is, leaving each locality to its own Enlightenment, promiscuity, and influences. Each locality may in-corporate whatever Enlightenment it chooses. These acts of in-corporating "other" knowledge are not overseen or organized by the state or any other centralizing power.

One might say that Nietzsche is still concerned with Prussian state-led Enlightenment, now no longer conceived as the pedagogical colonization of "false" givens (*empiries*) from a position of transcendental "truth," but rather as an Enlightenment that remembers its truths are effects of the unstable ground it seeks to discipline, an Enlightenment that attends to the contingency and arbitrariness of its emblems, a scenario in which "there were eternities during which [such a value] did not exist," in which its disappearance will go unnoticed, in which the destiny of all things in general is oblivion.[44] It is about assuming from the outset that all truth and every general principle is "nothing other than an aid supplied to the most unfortunate, most delicate and most transient of beings";[45] that the truth of truth, or any truth at all, is "vague and capricious," "a mobile army of metaphors, metonymies and anthropomorphisms, in short, a sum of human relations which have been poetically and rhetorically intensified, transferred, decorated and which, after lengthy use, seem firm, canonical and binding to a people";[46] that the university's wisdom "has no further mission that might extend beyond the bounds of human life"; and that only its "progenitor regards . . . with such pathos, as if it housed the axis around which the entire world revolved."[47] These are necessary effects, however, given the spectacle one flees through them, like some refuge of pitilessness, greed, insatiability, murder amid indifference "clinging in dreams . . . to the back of a tiger."[48]

State as Enlightenment Subject

At first, it is the state that appears as chief instigator of transcendental ideals. Factically what follows from this, however, is the professionalization of the majority of individuals such that the university expert becomes an "up-to-date person" [*individuo corriente*] in the same way one speaks of "valid currency" [*moneda corriente*]: modern teaching institutions must make sure that each person becomes as "up-to-date" or professional as possible.[49] "German 'higher schooling' is in fact a brutal form of training that tries to process a horde of young men as quickly as possible for use—and abuse—in the civil service,"[50] who are constantly exhorted, "'Wake up! Become conscious! Be smart!'"[51] and be "up-to-date," and that presents the plan of the state, in different guises, as an unavoidable necessity and "natural"[52] to the point that, rather than opposing Enlightenment, they clamor to receive it: We all want to be enlightened!

The dominance of the state speaks to this willingness to be enlightened as a matter of course. It is the state that engages in the "saber rattling . . . [that] naturally makes as strong an impression on most people as the voice of eternal truth written in stone, the primal law of things."[53] It thus disguises its ambitions as universal and eternal tasks. It is the state that takes "measures to send as many students as possible to gymnasiums" to the point of "overcrowding."[54] The generalization of Enlightenment figures among the "dogmas" that the modern state forcefully repeats. These focuses are rooted in the national economy according to the following formula: the greatest possible enlightenment, leading to the highest production, the most wealth, and the greatest happiness.[55] Utility is defined as "the highest possible income,"[56] as means and end of national Enlightenment.

The most effective strategy for achieving this expansion is the state's linking of public and military posts, high and low, to the school system, a mechanism that defines education in instrumental and utilitarian terms as a means of survival and educational institutions as "institutions for overcoming the struggles of life," institutions that "claim to create civil servants or shopkeepers or soldiers or businessmen or farmers or doctors or engineers."[57] By playing the part of "mystagogue of culture"[58] the state guarantees the public's unconditional "submissive obedience,"[59] predisposing its servants to take up the torch of official Enlightenment as universal Enlightenment.

The enlightened university interpretation of the meaning, language, and history that spreads throughout the modern educational system centrally articulates every "native language,"[60] depopulating their nomadic senses, exiling them from their contingency into academic necessity, where, cut off from their "native" alterity and banished to the university wasteland, day after day the untiring maw of a press they will one day join repeats: "'We are culture! We are education [*ilustración*]! We are the pinnacle! We are the tip of the pyramid! We are the apex of world history [*historia universal*]!'"[61]

By means of the two structural drives of Enlightenment (expansion and specialization)—drives that embrace one another in journalism and the university curriculum—the modern state, creator and promoter of culture and identity in general, wants the provinces to abandon their "mythical images,"[62] "religious instincts,"[63] their vernacular at once inexact and in excess and abruptly adopt instead the national and supranational state's "cultured," true, professional form of life; to entrust errant words to the performative regulation of state interests; and to forget their particular ground of shifting interests and the possibility of a discontinuous, unsettled enlightenment.

The state is interested in dissolving local interests in the general interest. For this to happen, it is indispensable for the "effective history" of general interest to go unnoticed. The state must hide the genealogy of the university's universality, naturalize the bloated wineskin of truth, obviate the accident of its origin in life's unpredictability, an accident nonetheless indispensable for the fantastic animal that, unlike others, needs a reason, a poem that protects and gives meaning to the pain of its existence. The poem of universality is a means of preserving the species.

The totalitarian desire to gather everything to its style and according to its teleology "whatever the cost," sets the enlightened university against the nonuniversity. The university rises up against its genealogy, its genial progenitor, the inexact genius in excess of nomadic pursuits on which is erected the university's machine of moral taxonomies for measurement, methodologies for discernment and application.

Nietzsche does not blame the university's system of passions (desire, avarice, pride, forgetfulness) nor the actions that proceed from them. The notions of good and evil, justice and injustice have no place in the close listening of genealogy.

One could read the *Genealogy of Morals* as the genealogy of university good and evil, a genealogy that dissolves the ethics and universality of the university into the matrix of forces and passions that precede it. Nietzsche dissolves the imperial university apparatus by "reading the entrails," revealing what that apparatus represses and forgets. This is a reading that makes intelligible the simulacrum of university "truth," as well as the necessity of that simulacrum.

Thus university teleology and theology are returned to the prospective perspective of the life forces that dominantly deployed them. The state history that enacts the metanarration and sedimentation of an empirically shifting body into disciplinary and hierarchical taxonomies is genealogically exposed in the act of its disguise. Through its "truth and lying in a non-moral sense," university universality is genealogically shown to be a life strategy. When this becomes apparent, the university's transcendental performance becomes an immanent constellation of shifting rhetoric and representations that arise from these forces as from flowering trees and songbirds.

The university, in its all-consuming greed to gather all points of view into one, will not tolerate genealogy. Genealogy weakens the statist university's theological strategy, dissolving it into the shifting sands of interest. It reveals that the universal deployed by the university is an immanent medium of facticity, that if nothing matters transcendentally (nihilism in action), factically nothing is indifferent, and it is in this factic discrimination that we should situate the "true" (erratic) university.

The state, as a principle that articulates the ephemeral in the "eternal," opposes the (dissolving) geniality of genealogy as well as the genealogy of geniality. The geniality of genealogy is its memorious return, which defers every arrival and subjection. In this sense, genealogy constitutes an epic and a "methodology" with neither beginning nor end, a deconstructive epic that returns from professionalizing state subjection to the nomadic fluidity and atheism that the university represses.

Recall that the enlightened state requires internal cohesion for its maintenance and consolidation. On this basis, it joins the provinces to one identity and national language. But Nietzsche makes special mention of a state objective that goes beyond the requirement of internal cohesion and the irreversible conversion of provincial into national forces. That objective is interstate competition.[64] To survive the desire of states to dominate one another leads them to cast enlightened uniformation[65] and national identity as professional identity. Toward that end, a state must attenuate as much as possible its internal disagreements.[66] Thus the principle of interstate and imperialist competition induces the state to eliminate endogenous difference.

But if the state's objective is to triumphantly hoist its distinction above the fray of interstate competition, this presupposes a difference or identity as yet undefined relative to "other" national identities. It appears incoherent, then, that the state would promote internally an Enlightenment that settles (*uniforma*) its internal disagreements. It appears incoherent that the state university would bury national diversity, the only principle that distinguishes it in the generalized conflict among nationalities.

Perhaps the state is not the subject of Enlightenment, a subject that in teaching the general metanarrative of professionalism and progress cloaks native characteristics in disciplinary ones. Perhaps the inverse is true: the principle that disguises fluid language and provincial homelands as the enlightened, professional, national state is Enlightenment itself and its productivist economy. Thus, when nations refracted through their enlightened university interpretation face one another in interstate struggle, they are already emptied of any difference, rendered the same by a planetary Enlightenment. In this way, the result of this movement is that national cultures increasingly appear the same.

One must take care not to confuse the vernacularizing inclination of Nietzsche's critique of the Enlightenment with the propensity toward a linguistic casteism, a racial or spiritual purity.

> [One speaks of] "purity" only in connection with a people's highly developed sense of language, which, in a large society, establishes itself, above all, among the aristocracy and educated. Here it is decided what is to be considered as provincial, as dialect, and as normal; viz., "purity," then is positively the customary usage of the educated in society, which received its sanction through the *usus*, and the "impure" is everything else which attracts attention in it. Thus, the "not-striking" is that which is pure. . . . A very important question arises of how the feeling for purity gradually is formed, and of how an educated society makes choices, to the point at which the whole range has been defined. It evidently acts according to unconscious laws and analogies here: a unity, a uniform expression is achieved. . . . In periods of language growth, one cannot speak of "purity" of speech. . . . Barbarisms, repeated frequently, finally transform the language; thus, the *koinē glōssa* . . . arose, later the Byzantine *rōmaikē glōssa* . . . and finally the completely barbarized new Greek. Who knows how many barbarisms have worked in this way to develop the Roman language out of Latin? And, it was through these barbarisms and solecisms, that good rule-bound French came about![67]

Identity is not language's point of departure but rather a retroactive sanctioning of language that issues from it. The origin of language is also an expression of force: "The rulers . . . say 'this is so and so,' they set their seal on everything and every occurrence with a sound and thereby take possession of it."[68]

Otherwise, it would be impossible to become enlightened, to travel from one place to another without incorporating alterity. Enlightenment, like travel, presupposes the promiscuity of self and other. One cannot travel without carrying one's self and without changing along the way, without overcoming the dialect from which one departs and without modifying it by taking leave of it. It is futile to try to pinpoint where Enlightenment begins and ends, where identity begins and alterity ends. Along the journey, any place may be the beginning, middle or end, identity or alterity, unstable and in movement. One travels, one is enlightened through, with, in, and against dialect. One cannot change places without taking oneself along while also losing or diluting oneself, unless—and this is what a purifying university Enlightenment hopes to achieve—the journey is the slow dispossession and elimination of difference [*lo desigual*]. The enlightened state achieves the equivalence of difference [*la igualación de lo desigual*] along the educative-curricular journey understood as "rattling" of alterity, the statist journey that pulls the differential ground out from under one's feet, filling the void with professional habits.[69]

Classical philology, the academic anchor of statist Enlightenment, sought to leap backward to ancient Greek language and culture by methodically and persistently seeking the "true" Homer and the "true" Sophocles. In its desire to establish a "pure" supralinguistic relationship with the "truth" of that culture, it purified every "interpretive" bias and silenced the "sound" of any dialect. Upon the reader's supposed virginity and purity, university philology enacts the ideology that it is possible to read the truth of any text or any dialect at any time. Philology believes—and it is founded on this belief—that thanks to method, its study is free from the subject of enunciation, the sound of dialect, whether the philologist's or the author's. Philosophy harbors the dual idea that the truth of a culture or a text is prelinguistic, an idea that will also dominate philologizing university philosophy.

"True enlightenment" demands "strict linguistic discipline" of the sound, rhythm, melody of its dialect.[70] "Take your language seriously! If you cannot feel a sacred duty here, then you have not even the seed of higher culture within you."[71] Taking one's language seriously does not mean "anatomical dissection";[72] erudite, historicist treatments; or grammatical, philological exercises. Taking seriously is the opposite of "taking universitarily."[73] To take seriously one's language means to feel revulsion at "the 'refined diction' of our literati and the 'elegance' of style so beloved and praised in our novelists and mass-producers of journalism," revulsion at certain words and turns of phrase in art criticism and academic parlance.[74] Only this feeling can show us how to "stride" genealogically through language and history.[75]

Genealogy versus Reflection

Learning to see and to think is one of the tasks for which we need educators: "People must learn to see, they must learn to think . . . getting your eyes used to calm, to patience, to letting things come to you; postponing judgment, learning to encompass and take stock of an individual case from all sides . . . not to react immediately to a stimulus. . . . [T]he essential thing here is precisely not 'to will,' to be able to suspend the decision."[76] Every nonspirituality "is due to an inability to resist a stimulus—you have to react, you follow every impulse."[77] The ability to postpone judgment, decision, stimulus is at once aristocratic and noninstrumental, "reason's rest." On the other hand, the vulgar is recognized because of its steadfast maintenance of its advantage and because this inclination is stronger than the drive to act without a specific goal.

An education in postponement instead of efficiency would be the first line of a Nietzschean opposition to the modern statist university. The genealogical Nietzschean university and the critical reflexive Kantian university would stand together against the Napoleonic Cartesian university. They part ways, however, due to the theological and teleological method of the latter vis-à-vis the atheistic genealogy without gathering and without end (a-telos) of the former.

Kant's reflexive faculty of philosophy teleologically deferred judgment, law, concept in its search for the end without end, a search for the final judgment, reason's architectonic system. The teleology of reflection leading to the final judgment, to a final "gathering" of judgment, enthusiastically regulates the modern university. Genealogical critique defers without origin or objective. It dissolves memoriously, knowing full well that memory is active and inventive and that what it designates as a phenomenon's point of origin and emergence will in turn require its own genealogy if it is not to be substantialized. These "points of origin and emergence" to which genealogy leads are not a fixed origin scene but the effects of a "false" memory for which "points of origin and emergence" must be continually reinvented . . . and so on endlessly with neither objective nor origin. The genealogical procedure does not administer any sense of university stability or gathering, whether statist or historical. Uni-version, uni-versity, and uni-versality all disappear in the di-version and per-version of shifting factic forces that echo meaning effects like possible life strategies.

In short, genealogical di-version versus reflexive theological uni-version. The "eternal return," eternal memorious deferral in the university's discontinuous facticity, such as di-versity, ad-versity, per-versity. We might think genealogy's eternal return as the faculty of philosophy, henceforward the faculty of genealogy. Finally, regarding di-version:

> Learning to think: our schools do not have any idea what this means. Even in the universities, even among genuine philosophy scholars. . . . Just look at German books: there is not even a dim recollection of the fact that thought requires a technique, a plan of study, a will to mastery—that thinking wants to be learned like dancing . . . dancing in every form, being able to dance with your feet, with concepts, with words; do I still have to say that you need to be able to [dance] with a pen that you need to learn to write?[78]

III

*The Non-Modern Transition
of the Modern University*

9

✦

Transition from State to Market

> We do not conserve, return, or progress; we hear the song of
> the sirens in the marketplace.
>
> —Nietzsche

The Latin word *transitio* (change of place) is declined in various ways: "This kingdom *will fall* into their hands" (Tacitus); "The smell of leaves *impregnated* the clothes" (Catulus); "Insatiable are the animals in whom food *passes directly* from the stomach into the straight intestine" (Pliny); "It *changes* into earth, stone, water, tree" (Ovid); "Water mixed with honey *transforms* into wine" (Propertius); "He was pretending to *cast off* our opinion" (Livy); "Thin wine is *expelled* more quickly as urine" (Horace); "He *ennobled himself* with patrician gestures" (Cicero); "The weasels do not *cross* the path" (Plautus); "He has *passed the limits* of shame" (Cicero); "The years quickly *elapse*" (Tiberius); "These images do nothing more than *pass by*" (Boethius); "Nothing *changes* lovers unnoticed" (Statius).

We searched in Latin dictionaries for a declension of *transitio* in which alteration was not a part of movement, a transition that would escape the polarity of self/other and would be bound up instead with the idea of "secretion" without the action implying a mutation, whether of that which is secreted or of that which is secreting, where the point of emptiness is also the starting point. We could not find one, and it is unlikely that such an absurdity exists in Latin since its metaphysics is typically formulated in statements of identity, in which the subject moves [*transita*] toward the predicate without revolution, without anything new emerging in the predicate that would modify the subject, only to exhaust itself by specifying itself in the same terms.

In modernity the "transition," understood as the passage from one place to another, alludes to the experience of revolution and change. It references modern experience as such, the experience of experience that Kant called "synthetic judgements," where predicate B is alien to subject A and "this connection is thought without identity," although it is not for that reason arbitrary.[1]

In modernity, we give the name "experience" to an event that moves us from the everyday to the unprecedented, throwing "habit" (Hume) or "verisimilitude" (Todorov) into crisis. We call "experience" not only the event of the new and unprecedented but also the event of the new and archaic—for example, when we notice something that happened to us unawares, the unseen clue that we suddenly see belatedly resignify past events and possibilities that were, not by omission, unheard thoughts (Benjamin), now activated in the memory of signs.

"Experience," accordingly, is not just that which occurs daily amid the familiar but rather that which occurs in an untimely manner and changes course. It changes the course not of this or that routine but of the limits and conditions of routine. Experience is an occurrence that introduces an impossible time into the present, the *conatus* of another series into the series in *conatus* [*en conato*].

"Transition," like "experience," can be assimilated to "modernity." Transition is experience and modernity that departs from the "self" and progresses toward the "other," establishing along the way a translational tradition, never full or finished, that links its points of departure and arrival.

For us—and it is impossible to determine where "us" begins and ends—the word "Transition"[2] fits neither the medieval nor the modern meanings we have referenced. It does not evoke bucolic sensibilities (*aesthesias*)or epic quests and feats. It suggests, on the contrary, the weariness caused by asymptomatic illnesses that worsen over time, and that by the time we notice them have weakened us such that we lack sufficient morale to treat them.

It is likely that our apprehension of the term "Transition" comes from the fact that we use it, not innocently, to refer to a state of affairs that neither changes [*transita*] nor plans to; a state of affairs we sense will not suffer any displacement [*traslación*] or that has already definitively passed [*transito*] and, having done so, will never pass [*transitará*] again, threatening us with its unyielding stasis. The current use of the term "Transition" attributes movement and transformation to a stationary and intransitive reality, a misattribution we are all guilty of.

We are then living with the effects of an improper name for the present. We should add that in certain domains of language the word retains a modern and experiential charge and a memory linked to change, revolution, and progress, which, as we pointed out, no longer exist. We linguistically constitute our present on the basis of an accessory homonym. And I believe that this contradiction is the thread we must tug on when it comes to our trepidation in the Transition.

Today's Transition does not move; it is a state of conservation that persists, not to be followed by another. The experience of the new is a memory we retain only as information. The Transition hosts all guests, however foreign they may be. In this way, the variations the Transition harbors, innumerable and diverse as they are, evince a circular reiteration of the familiar that bars experience of the new.

In the Transition, nothing new happens in any modern, transformative sense. Nothing happens that changes and would thereby expose us to the unexpected, the surprising, the unforeseeable. The multiform spectacle of its multiplying variations produces, as in a kaleidoscope, the weariness of a fixed rotation that incorporates and subordinates every event. As diverse as they may be, events become indistinguishable from the Transition, which remains identical in its multiplicity. Modernity was history's entertainment, the expectation of and enthusiasm for the inassimilable revolution. The Transition is the absolute boredom of an endless common sense [*verosimilitud*].

The Transition is not only a local phenomenon. At different times it has affected (or will have affected) different places across the planet, if not the planet itself. For example, we need only look to the report authored by Simon Nora and Alain Minc (1976) about "how to lead the computerization of society. . . . how to promote it and put it at the service of democracy and human development," a report commissioned by French president Valéry Giscard D'Estaing in 1975 to ensure the preeminence of the French state in a telematic world;[3] or Lyotard's *The Postmodern Condition* (1979), written in response to a similar request by the Conseil des Universités to the Government of Quebec;[4] or like the documents and publications by José Joaquín Brunner, who headed the scientific advisory council on the modernization of Chilean education; or, at a different level, what Foucault and Deleuze formulated as the crisis of modern categories for the analysis of power and knowledge: a crisis of the location of power-knowledge (the state), its proprietorship (the dominant class), its expression (the law), its modes of action (ideology and repression), its structure (determination in the last instance by "superstructure" or by "base"), a crisis of modern categories and, ultimately, a crisis of the category of crisis.[5]

The world already is, and within it the possible, the compossible, and the "incompossible" (Leibniz).[6] No qualitative value transcends the economic game. Its entire substance would be but special effects of the market economy. There is nothing "beyond" capitalism. Late capitalism has no outside. "The previous model of antagonistic blocs has met its end."[7]

If the world already is, and any exchange of objects and subjectivities—a conversation, this very text—is immersed in commercial activity and serves some form of capitalization or valorization, then everything that can be debated or discussed exists only in the market's immanence. That means the demand for political justice, economic justice, social restitution are not demands from or for something "beyond" but demands immanent to the heteronomy into which the market recedes, consolidating itself. In this regard, we should highlight the contemporary irrelevance of "ideologies"[8] and value systems when compared to the modern context in which the "use value" of an ideology opposed its "exchange value."

Since the Transition, the world is one amid the many forces that configure it. Nothing occurs outside the global economy and the transcultural order that accompanies it. Focusing on its constitutive cultural and symbolic framework, the world is one, diverse and dispersed, irregular and unstable. Its unity is complex, and its conflicts are complicated to the point of undecid-ability. It is in this context of all-worlds-in-one that locality is forged,[9] that the not-so-simple relationship between the local and the global comes into play. The sovereignty of nations and subjects is circumscribed by the new cosmopolitanism of the global economy. The point of departure of every dif-ference is heteroclite identity, articulated pluralism that disguises the general equivalent of postnational capitalism.

Late capitalism demonstrates that it will work with many political regimes and not only democratic ones, that in the unstable process of its ebb and flow it embraces, uses, and produces in every instance [*en cada caso*] any kind of governance over bodies and populations that serves abstract financial profit. Neoliberal capitalism would be, then, facticity without essence, which some-times produces, sometimes questions the very conditions of the essence that it produces and questions. Facticity without essence reflects ethics, aesthetics, sexualities, epistemes, producing and arranging them this way or that way, in every instance [*en cada caso*], according to the requirements of financial profit.

In this context, democratic rule often stands out as an encouraging indica-tor: "The new world order not only proclaims but demands democracy and the opening of local economies to the free market; by means of its transitions, the new world order spells the end of tyranny and anarchy: neither dictator-ship nor social collapse; neither terrorism nor the military boot; instead the political self-organization of society through its justly elected and legitimate representatives."[10] Advanced capitalism politically clings to its democratic frame [*verosimilitud*] (Fukuyama).

Nothing is essential to contemporary capitalism. Capitalism has no canon, it lacks a "frame" [*verosimilitud*], its boundaries do not give form. If a world always constitutes a diversity of "compossible" qualities (Leibniz) that dis-tinguishes the *conatus* of another world or series already in *conatus* and that threatens to unworld it, then planetary capitalism today, seen from the moon, does not constitute a world at all. Unworlding is immanent to its inclusive logic, in other words, its financial profitability.

"The best of all possible worlds" was not the "best" for its moral qualities and even less so for its hospitality. It was the best because it was "the most varied,"[11] for having united in its "series" the greatest possible heterogeneity. And if in its *conatus* this world were to triumph over every other world that also clamored for existence, by virtue of its qualitative "weight," contempo-rary planetary capitalism would be the nonworld in which "possible worlds" and "series" coexisted insofar as they are useful for financial profit. This is the way we should think about democratic pluralism and neoliberalism's effective [*fáctica*] deregulation, which does not exclude arbitrary, circum-stantial laws. Neither has anything to do with modern democracy or modern liberalism, which directed funds (public or private) toward increasing access to things like education, health, social security, etc. The social contract, class struggle, politics, the state, the division of knowledge, the division of labor, the distribution of the sensible are not the "subject" of capitalism, as was believed in modernity. Today they are revealed to be its objects, its financial fuel.

We assign the name "liberal democratic" to neoliberal capitalism's financial facticity lacking world and aura, to its plasticity and ability to adopt any ideological posture. And we confuse this democracy, this liberality or plasticity of limitless financial subsumption, with modern democracy and modern liberalism, whose function was rather to underwrite all kinds of consumption, subsuming the unspecified financial to a single use.

Our local sociology assigned the name Transition to the process of redemocratizing Chilean society after the military dictatorship, a process that supposedly started with the end of the dictatorship and culminated with the recuperation of full democracy. Sociologically speaking, the start of this Transition "coincides with the last phase of the military regime . . . beginning with the authoritarian plebiscite of 1988 . . . and ending with the inauguration of the democratically elected government in December 1989."[12] The same can be said of the university's "transition": it begins with the end of military intervention and lasts until the full, or at least fuller, recuperation of its autonomy, now understood as the Chilean university's new heteronomy within finance capital. The idea that the political and university transitions started with the end of the military regime and its puppet university rectors and that it would end with a fuller democracy shows just how trivial our sociological definition of the word is.

This understanding of the term "transition" coincides with the approach taken by twentieth-century "transitology" to transitions to democracy. Transitology mapped an empirical field of study and posited transnational typologies that cover everything from war theaters (the European transitions to democracy after the First World War; the postfascist transitions to democracy in Germany, Italy, and Japan); transitions to democracy after military dictatorships, with or without sporadic warfare (Greece, Spain, Chile, Argentina, Brazil, Paraguay); the transitions of Eastern Bloc countries, beginning with the USSR, which transitology specifies as a transition to democracy in the absence of its historical memory; etc. Transitology maintains that the origin of the transition to democracy is not democratic, that its roots lie in wars, defeats, military coups, economic disasters, and a host of other calamities.

What sociology calls transition does not correspond to the period of the *translatio* from the modern state to the poststate financialized market (something that happens through wars and dictatorships and a host of calamities). Rather it corresponds to the postdictatorship period—in other words, a time when there is no *translatio* at all. Properly speaking, Transition for "us" does not name the transfer of governance from dictatorship to democracy, but the transformation of economics and politics effected by the dictatorship: the displacement of the state as the center and subject of national history and its replacement by the ex-centric, poststate, postnational market. This displacement presupposed, more generally, the loss of modern history's articulating categories: the state, the people, revolution, progress, democracy, interest, history, ideology, hegemony, dissent, autonomy, locality, politics, pedagogy, nationality, etc. In this sense, the Transition undermines the modern categorial institution, exhausting its referential ordering.

In this way we want to indicate that the transition from the modern state to the poststate market coincides with the transition and definitive collapse of the modern university built on the Kantian division of labor between the "higher faculties" ("applied research") and the "lower faculty" ("basic research"). In modernity their conflict and its network of meanings were represented by the university wall that demarcated the institution's temporal separation from the present. The financial university annuls the temporal difference at its core. The financial university overhauls the modern university's every quality—its aura, its difference—in service of financial profit.

If the "conflict" or "class struggle" between "physical-technical labor" (*physis*) and "intellectual-critical labor" (*meta-physis*) constituted the antagonistic axis of modern history, modern politics, and the modern university, then the end of that history-politics-university will come when that conflict is extinguished. In the Transition—the one effected by the dictatorship—this difference will be exhausted in the real subsumption of every conflict to finance capital. In the transition understood as the end of history, as the end of the social division of labor, capitalism will remain and difference, the unequal, will vanish.

End of the Action/Meaning Difference

Once the conflict of the faculties is contained by the "process of capital valorization" and the folds of critique fail to unmask "capital in process," intellectual work, the "lower faculty," will have disappeared into the automaton of the technical "upper faculty," which now carries out real subsumption in the division of labor. "The real agent of the labor process taken together" becomes undifferentiated "labor-power" organized into a planetary "cooperation" or "collective laborer" that "increase[s] the functions of productive labor-power directly subsumed to Capital" such that "it is quite immaterial whether the job of a particular worker . . . is at a greater or a lesser distance from the actual manual labor."[13] The division of labor, the conflict of the faculties now constitute "limbs of this 'aggregate worker'" in its *immediate productive consumption by capital*."[14] Marx continues, "Some work better with their hands, others with their heads, one as a manager, engineer, technologist, etc., the other as overseer, the third as manual laborer or even drudge.

An ever-increasing number of types of labor are included in the immediate concept of productive labor, and those who perform it are classed as productive workers, workers directly exploited by capital and subordinated to its process of production and expansion."[15]

Derrida writes, "It was once possible to believe that pure mathematics, theoretical physics, philosophy" and also "poetry," "literature," and others constituted writing events "inaccessible to programming by the agencies or instances of the State . . . or capital interests" and counterpoised to the end-oriented technical writing subsumed by them.[16] This "opposition" or division of labor, this class struggle between "the technological" and "the theoretical," the lower and the upper faculties, "is difficult to maintain . . . with thorough-going conceptual as well as practical rigor."[17] (A stark example is the fact that intellectual property law prevents us from citing at length, as we would have liked, the Derridean text that we are now commenting on, paraphrasing, quoting piecemeal.) Everything seems to transpire as if it were impossible to "maintain the boundary that Kant, for example, sought to establish between the schema that he called 'technical' and the one he called 'architectonic' in the systematic organization of knowledge," a boundary that maintained the structural possibility of the university as a conflict between the theoretical ends of the "lower" faculty and the technical ends of the "upper" faculty.[18] Basic research (theoretical physics, astrophysics, chemistry, molecular biology) has "never before . . . been so deeply committed to ends that are at the same time military," "national and international security," and "telecommunications" ends.[19] But also "literature, poetry and fiction in general" can be made useful in "ideological warfare," "the theory of commands," "military pragmatics" and thereby made to bear witness to the "original intermingling of metaphysics and technics."[20]

A bit later in the same text, Derrida proposes undoing [*desistir*] the subsumption to technical equivalence, the antagonism, conflict, polarity of the theoretical and the end-oriented, the lower and the upper. At the same time, he proposes desisting from [*desistir*] the simple maintenance of such an antagonism. Through this double renunciation [*desistencia*], Derrida proposes a "community of thinking" in which the dividing line between lower and upper, theoretical and technical would not be clearly established, such that "the border between basic and end-oriented research would no longer be secured."[21] Such a "community of thinking" would not be a faculty of the sciences or philosophy. Rather than a "community of," this would be a community "in the broad sense—'at large'—" since the values of science as much as philosophy are so often "subjected to the unquestioned authority of the principle of reason."[22] It is unclear if such a community—which would question "the essence of reason and of the principle of reason," which "would attempt to draw out all the possible consequences of this questioning"—would "bring together a community or found an institution in the traditional sense of these words."[23] Rather it "must rethink what is meant by community and institution" as well as the plasticity and "ruses" of technical reason, "the paths by which apparently disinterested research can find itself indirectly . . . reinvested by programs of all sorts."[24]

Corollary to the Transition

For "us Chileans," the dictatorship—understood as the Transition's stage upon which the modern state subjects itself through dictatorship to abstract financial markets—has a corollary that points in the following general directions:

(a) The transition of public or private funding for primary, secondary, and tertiary education from its subordination to the nation-state's economic and ideological ends to the subordination of primary, secondary, and tertiary education to abstract financial profitability. As with health, pensions, water, electricity, and every other sector, the goal of education will transform into its use value for abstract financial profit. This change to the category of education from preschool to university (and of categories in general) was directed "by General Pinochet himself" and had been in preparation since September 11, 1973, in the form of the "instruments and prior bases" for the *Presidential Directives on Education* (1979);[25] in the political constitution approved without electoral record keeping in 1980; in the dictatorship's Basic Law on Universities; in the constitutional amendment of 1989; in the Brunner-Frei reforms;[26] in the Guaranteed Student Loan (Crédito con Aval de Estado) promulgated in 2006 by the government of Ricardo Lagos; in the latest education reforms enacted by Michele Bachelet and Sebastián Piñera (2011–18). All this slowly produced—in the sense of advanced and naturalized—the transition from the right to education and the pedagogical state to the principle of freedom of teaching[27] and the pedagogical society. In other words, financial profit comes to subordinate every category.[28]

The modern state university's standardization of worker subjectivity is thrown into crisis when confronted with a form for standardizing subjectivity no longer articulated by state hegemony and the chain of institutions that embodied it in modernity. Today the demand for financial profit would be the mode of articulation, a demand that liberalizes national and state definitions and canons of consumer behavior, a demand for the rescaling of standards of behavior, another plane of possibility for worker behavior and subjectivity in general subordinated to the profitability of finance capital.

It is this new commercial apparatus that deregulates the activity of political economy and the "standing"[29] of the modern state, making room for activity that has been liberalized to become functional for abstract finance capital. The gradual (dis)articulation of the behavior of the modern populace, the functionalizing of bodies as vehicles for abstract financial profit unfolds assemblages that far outstrip the working style associated with the wage.

How much remains today of the modern wage and modern work, of formal and real subsumption to capital compared with the corporeal assemblages of unwaged, abstract financial profit? What remains of the modern wage's movement understood as the capitalization of state hegemony, when the categories of public and private, the use value of a body, have been converted, whether directly or indirectly, into the milkmaids of abstract finance capital?

In this sense, the financial enterprise becomes microphysically panoptic in relation to the bodies that valorize it (Foucault); it winds around, rattles, and drops them; it opens up and seizes every esoteric fold.

(b) As something that has already occurred, transition implies a mutation in the mode of meaning making. This displacement would affect not only the comprehension of some concepts by which modern power-knowledge-work traditionally has been articulated but also the use of our entire lexicon. In the transition, concepts would suffer a change in the stabilizing axis of meaning, with all the irregularity and aimlessness one could imagine. We would now be patients, and the language that always possesses us would be in each instance [*en cada caso*] the performative agent of a homonymic unfolding of names. The referential principle of our names and terms—notably their modern categorial use and those categories such as sovereignty, state, people, truth, history, technics, experience, representation, etc.—detaches from its modern meaning. This is significant particularly for those critical pragmatics that hold onto the living memory of those categories' modern referentiality. Chile's predictatorship democracy was organized around the axis of the state as the discursive subject that sought to regulate the economy and national history in the ever-changing theater of the international conflict for planetary hegemony. Predictatorship democracy was essentially—or rather eventally—discursive, still inscribed in the central ideological battle over the regulation of abstract capital's rate of profit. Predictatorship democracy played out as the discursive confrontation of historical life projects that represented particular and conflicting social interests. Before the dictatorship, ideologies, sensibilities, metanarratives, the core conflict between the philosophies of history of modern capital still dominated abstract finance capital. In that context, real conflict—hegemony, the formulation of arguments, modern philosophies of history that shape, discipline, and implement forces—regulated and articulated capital's rate of profit. Or at least it tried. Only from a perspective that pays attention to the meaning and discursive subordination of capital's profitability can we say that planetary capitalism is still a world: a capitalist world in two hot wars and one cold one, a capitalist world turned imperiously planetary by a process of unworlding worlds that is at once extensive (formal subsumption) and intensive (real subsumption).

The Transition or dictatorial modernization of the Chilean state consisted in extending its role in subordinating and regulating financial profit and, at the same time, subordinating modern state capital to the profit motive of abstract finance capital.

The transversal *medium* in which this Transition takes place—even if its empirical catalyst was murder, torture, the disappearance and violation of bodies disciplined in accord with the modern paradigms of capitalization and state wealth distribution—institutes itself and regularly functions, ever more imperceptibly and familiarly, through the temporal apparatuses of abstract finance that render bodies profitable. Whether by the coup or the modern subordination of the social body to the wage, these insubordinate, modernized, temporal apparatuses refunctionalize state capital and the modern disciplining of bodies for a functional organization of the state and of modern populations for abstract financial profit.

A powerful exposition of this completed transition in our university environment can be found in raúl rodríguez freire's *La condición intelectual*.[30]

10

✦

The Categorial Crisis of the University

In December 1994, the Office of the Academic Vice Rector of the University of Chile convened a seminar on the university for a dossier in the first issue of the sixth volume of the *Anales de la Universidad de Chile*, the university's journal founded in 1843. The call for papers invited written contributions and conversation in response to the following questions: "What is the National University today? By what right can the University of Chile continue to call itself the National University? What is and what should be the relationship between the University and the State? What should we understand by the term productivity when this concept is applied to university work? How can said productivity be evaluated?" Although this event underscored the exceptional crisis in which the university was mired—a crisis that would affect the overall design of the university as a modern state university, a crisis that would force it to ask this series of questions about its meaning, its historical necessity, and its relevance, about the pertinence of its style, its disciplinary and generic structure, its constitution, and the contemporary prerogatives of its tradition—it seemed at the same time to want to neutralize said exceptionality and rally us to its norms, its normality, by including with the call for papers a "style sheet" to which solicited texts needed to adhere. With this regulation, the university seemed to be taking precautions against "outside" speech unrecognizable to it, still unpresentable in its cloister so long as the modern, disciplinary, linguistic constitution of knowledge could be preserved amid that vertiginous facticity which has no appreciation for memories, styles, plans, and traditions. At the moment that it is subjected to the extramural, poststate market, the university defends its tradition and defends itself with that tradition.

Nonetheless, the tone, topics, and questions of the call for papers incited us to transgress academic boundaries, putting on the table questions that are normally kept under the table, except in times of crisis so as not to impact the university's daily workings—for example, the significance of the university outside the university, its foundation, the extradisciplinary forces that make the university necessary beyond its walls.

At the same time, it raised for us the lexical question about how, in what language to write about the university, since to write about the university as it would write about itself would be to betray from the start the intent to refer to it.

To speak in nonuniversity terms about the university was, I believe, the real challenge of the call for papers, and the most attractive insofar as it was also the most daunting. We did not have any meaningful language other than university speech. To repeat the formula from the beginning of this book: How to speak nonuniversitarily of the university? In what language should we read university language? How should we avoid adopting its style so that for once we might slip through its fingers and gain discursive autonomy from it? And were we to do so, how would we make the university hear us? How to be heard without allowing oneself to be assimilated? And how to avoid assimilation yet still be taken into account?

The call for papers was an incitement to speak and think the university with inscriptions and ideas that in principle would overflow the academic. Glimpses that would allow us to perceive the limits, the law, the language and sense, the necessity and exclusivity of the university in this context, to give an account of its signifier. The call invited us to think the university event from a position subtracted from within it, such that this thought that had never before been thought could orient the university in the events in which it was mired, perhaps forever, ignorant about the essentials that one must know in modernity: about what is happening, and what is happening to the university amid what is occurring; about how history, its history, moves; about the present or its impossibility. One would have to know what permitted the university its freedom of movement in the midst of contingency.

Finally, I believe that the call for papers urged us to resist modernization by invoking modern questions. In other words, it urged us to resist conservatively, as if we had reached an era in which all resistance must adopt the form of conservation, return, memory.

By means of the call for papers, the University of Chile snubbed the Transition's habitual performance,[1] whereby modernity decides to abdicate—this being its final decision—all responsibility and self-determination, giving itself over to the heteronomy of facts, that is, to modernization. The University of Chile resisted transferring its meaning to mere action and reaction, to market stimulation or lack thereof, demanding instead a metathinking of the university event. In the Transition—that definitive step away from modernity, as we shall see—the call for papers demanded that we think in modern terms, perhaps to succumb by thinking modernly the death of the modern university.

Of course, the event to which we were so enthusiastically and cordially invited never took place. And although it could have taken place—a small consolation—it would not have been realized. The event would have exceeded the call for papers, falling outside modernity into full modernization. Even the call for papers had fallen into modernization when it demanded we think modernly and with "urgency": "In recent years we have noted the urgent need to build a body of thought that reformulates the mission and raison d'être of the University of Chile. . . . We continue to see how our historical position is being eroded, and we seem incapable of constructing another. It is therefore urgent to debate the necessity of our place, the very possibility of this space."

The call demanded thinking that would allow us to grasp the urgency into which the University of Chile had prolapsed. Such urgency relates to the impossibility of the university to think itself and its context, perhaps because there is no longer any context. An impossibility that leaves the university adrift among transitional events that had steered it and the educational system in general away from nation-state regulation and toward transnational market irregularity. Immersed in those transitional events, expelled from the state's refuge to the market's streets, dislocated from its habits, its paradigm, its tradition, the university urgently demands a thinking that would orient it in the midst of this forest of a market.

From the start, the urgent character of the call discomfited thinking immersed in its own analytic rhythms behind university walls, the modern critical distance presupposed by the modern university. The urgent tone suggested that it was not the university itself doing the convening from within its self-possessed interiority but rather the heteronomy of the university disseminating itself into the market.

The absence of foundational thinking about the university is not just a problem of the current conjuncture, in which the university transits from state to market while the state transfers to the market its responsibility to educate—what is officially called "educational modernization."[2] Even when the University of Chile was a pedagogical apparatus of the state, it raised no such fundamental questions. Not only was Chile's national university not reflexively autonomous relative to the interests of the modern state; it was, by and large, the state's accomplice.[3] It was necessarily an accomplice when the university collaborated in founding the modern state. It has been an accomplice during periods of democracy, during dictatorship, and it is now at the moment of the "state's extinction." It is imperative to analyze the reason why the modern university in Chile lacked this foundational thinking, the thinking of the faculty of philosophy in the Kantian sense, and why only in the moment of the state university's extinction—an extinction at the hands of the modern state that chooses "self-extinction," that is, the poststate transition to the market by means of military regimes—why in this moment questions arise that had not and could not have arisen before, not even at the founding of the modern university in the nineteenth century. The University of Chile has never thought its foundation, not even in its "foundational" moment in Andrés Bello. It was unnecessary, even impossible insofar as the university in Chile never needed a philosophical foundation, since here what had been established by European modernity[4] was merely repeated, more or less parodically.[5] If the university was established here, it was not due to some modern reflexive decision but rather to an inertial and instrumental interest, the urgency of orienting the Chilean nation-state in modernity, in its "creole" reiteration of European philosophy, liberty, and progress.[6]

The most important thing about this call for papers when compared to others—an importance that could also be a market illusion—was its repetition of the original questions that founded the modern European university. Only now it repeats them mechanically and in Spanish according to that need which draws every event near to death.

Modernity/Modernization

Throughout the modern tradition, autonomous reflection has demanded that thought staunchly commit to and strictly obey its *internal forum*. For modernity this *forum* was never something guaranteed in advance. On the contrary, modern thought had to constantly fight for its autonomy, producing the conditions of its internal freedom in the external *forum* of the prejudices and pressures to which it has been historically subjected. This relates to the idea that the rational is less the power to submit events to calculation and measure and more the principle that permanently protects our freedom. Hence, modern thought affirmed itself as critical theory, as a thought not exhausted and consumed by the event but rather capable of thinking the event by tracing back beyond its conditions and from there orient itself. Therefore, the preeminence of modern critical theory has never meant imperviousness to its context, as if it were the soul's soliloquy. Modern reflection, the thinking of critique consisted in seeing the arbitrariness and contingency of everything that appeared necessary and eternal, seeing the constraint and necessity of everything that claimed for itself autonomy and free will.[7]

I want to treat expressly this aspect of modern thought, the emptiness of this thought, in our current modernizing moment by sketching the concepts of "modernity" and "modernization."

If in modernity, scientific, political, artistic, educative practices, everyday tasks, and life itself were accompanied and directed by transcendental, meaningful narratives, by philosophies of the subject's emancipation through the production and invention of its own life (Lyotard); if these were also critically accompanied by hyperbolic doubt about the conditions and limits of every methodological or ideological orientation; then in our current moment of modernization, we would be experiencing the waning of said narratives and philosophies of history accompanied by unease about the critical possibility of the thought that ensured our distance and autonomy from them. At the same time, "the decline of narrative can be seen as the blossoming of techniques and technologies."[8] A rough translation of the term "modernization" could be the increasing effectiveness and efficiency of practices lacking a meaningful metanarrative or theory of the ground (or abyss) that underpins (or does not) their guiding method. In contrast to "modernization," we could call "modern" any practice (political, academic, domestic, etc.) that not only is guided by the practical immediacy of its method but also is oriented, in the last instance, by a philosophy of history or an ideology permanently determined by "hyperbolic doubt"[9] about its conditions. Modern are the science, politics, and education that are thought in terms of progressive emancipation and that simultaneously think the conditions of emancipation and progress (Kant). Modernization, then, would name the transition of a reflexive, ideological modernity to a modernity without ideologies or critical hyperbole. In this sense, modernization would be the act of taking distance from the modern, not approximating it.

Nonetheless, anyone can see that ideologies have proliferated in the context of modernization. Modernization must become gradually more pluralist, tolerant, democratic when it comes to the ideological and the critical. The idea that any ideology must be admitted to the democratic slate so long as it behaves is one of the clearest symptoms of the decline and death of modern ideology. The ideological is diluted as it diffuses. How does this happen?

The ruin of the ideological as the guiding principle of practice makes possible the proliferation of ideologies. Insofar as no one ideology presumes to direct life, it would be easy for them to array themselves in a row as if the rarity of their heraldry enlivened some costume party without participating in it. Ideological tension, conflict, confrontation, and censorship derive from a context in which ideological reflection is believed to direct the state, history, education. In modern terms, ideological debate and dispute regulate events. Modernization, however, perceives any ideological influence in politics, education, etc., as the tyranny of ideology over facts (the market), as an obstacle that must be liberalized at the risk of losing dynamism. Modernization would be the context in which the ideological proliferates, no longer in its commanding role but now as mere variation, a menu of consumer choices, symbolic ornament, marketing tactic, or background triviality. It is a question of the proper attire for *discourse*. The ideological, with its semantic density, is vanquished, but in the same instant it is redeemed by its syntactical weightlessness.

Facts rule. "The crisis of modernity refers to the defeat of ideologies by facts. But in modernity, too, facts had triumphed over ideologies. One could even claim that facts have always outstripped meaning. In modernity, however, it was possible to recover from the intrusion of facts and the domination of their logic. Modernity was characterized and therefore could be defined by this ideological and discursive overlaying of events."[10]

The specificity of modernization consists in the impossibility and undesirability of discursively and critically capturing events. It is neither possible nor desirable to recover discursively from what happens. It is impossible to constitute oneself as a subject on the basis of discursive subjectivation or some point of view autonomous from whatever is happening. The tripartite division of the fields of reality, representation, and subjectivity no longer holds.

The interaction of semiotic, material, and social flows takes place beyond any possible recuperation by a linguistic corpus or theoretical metalanguage.[11] Modernization annuls every modern illusion, installing us in the blinding clarity of facticity. Modernization leads us from the modern enthusiasm that deals with programs for steering events to the disillusioned cynicism that inhabits the event with the clarity and "humor" of indifference.

And whether or not what is happening globally today is called "advanced capitalism," "postindustrial society," or "integrated world capitalism," capitalism would not count as an ideology. In contemporary society, capitalism is characterized by its intranscendence, its prediscursive facticity, its ability to work technically without reflexivity, that is, technologically. Contemporary capitalism shows that every ideology, including socialism, served as the factual medium for its postideological reinforcement. Democracy need not be essential to capitalism, *pace* Fukuyama. It has been deployed by all kinds of dictatorships (Guattari).

Modernization not only points to the crisis of ideologies. It also points to a categorial crisis. Modern categories for representing and reflecting on what happens in university terms have been on the decline. When we speak of the crisis of modern education, we are really talking about the total or partial inapplicability of these categories for the analysis and understanding of contingency. We are talking about the passage of knowledge, power, education, and practice beyond the modern categorial scope of the university and politics. The collapse of the modern university and modern politics are inseparable so long as the modern architectonics of the university coincides with the modern architectonics of politics. This is a (nonprogressive) crisis of modern categories for the analysis of knowledge that is also a (nonprogressive) crisis of the analysis of power.[12]

The non-modern crisis—that is, the crisis of modern crisis—also refers to the breakdown of representation, a topic to which we have alluded. The crisis of the university would coincide with the impossibility of its relation, of any totalizing narrative that would systematize its positions and authorize its hierarchies. Every attempt today to represent or give a discursive account of the state of knowledge (and of power) is exceeded by a facticity that cannot be translated to a general cartography. Not only does the modern code not pertain, no code does.[13] The non-modern crisis refers to the impossibility of a general mapping of the current state of affairs. It is not about some conceptual crisis upon the emergence of a new, substitute categorization, or the emergence of a new map with the obsolescence of another.[14] The non-modern crisis is the crisis of the categorial full stop, a crisis that for the same reason cannot be represented. We lack the categories for analyzing the event of the crisis of categories. In this sense, we must recognize that we do not know what is happening to the university or to politics. We lack a knowledge that would orient us in the facts; "we are lost in them like journalists in the news."[15]

Thinking in Facticity

It is impossible to think the university's present or the present in general. Today, the Kantian gesture in the questions "What is the Enlightenment? What is the present?" is impossible.[16]

The formula "urgent thought" prompted a foundational or metanarrative thinking in order to retreat and reorient toward commercial events without the redundancies that lead to friction and delays. What kind of thinking would this be—if it existed—that would allow us to "think" from events themselves the irretrievable fall of modern thinking into contingency?

To conclude, we will organize a few traits prefigured in what has been said already. This would be a thinking neither categorial nor synthetic; genealogical more than teleological; not narrative, argumentative, reflexive, or critical; neither generic nor disciplinary; neither representational nor transcendental; but a contingent thinking that defers the apparatus, a commercial disposition in which it is mired, undifferentiated from facticity.

If, when it comes to the university and politics, everything already "makes no difference" transcendentally, categorially speaking—"God is dead"[17]— then, factically speaking, nothing is indifferent. Redundancy or resistance in the apparatus is at stake in each gesture. The ruin of transcendental duplication places us in the factic empire of stimulation. The goal would be to not "let go," to defer the stimulus. When we look at the current "emergencies" of the University of Chile, the stimuli to which the university has succumbed strike us as immediately apparent. These stimuli must be deferred if the goal for the university is its non-modern autonomy in facticity.

IV

Pinochet's Signature

1. In 2005, journalist María Olivia Mönckeberg published an investigation titled *La privatización de las universidades* (The privatization of the universities). In many regards, the book bears witness to more than what its informative narrative conveys.[1] It bears witness to the coup d'état's sovereign, dictatorial refounding of Chilean education through a double movement that, first, derogated the law and opened the exception between 1973 and 1979 and, then, naturalized the exception as law, a movement first evidenced by the 1979 publication of the Presidential Directive on Education (Directiva Presidencial sobre Educación; DPSE) in the daily newspaper *El Mercurio*.[2]

Until 1979, the neoliberal juridical refounding of education lacked three elements: (1) the constitution, which was put to a vote in 1980 in a plebiscite that lacked voting records; (2) the dictatorship's General Law of Universities, enacted on January 3, 1981; (3) the 1989 amendment of the constitution. These laws and directives subordinated the *right to education* and the pedagogical state to the principle of *freedom of teaching* and the pedagogical society. This became clear in the 2006 high school and university student uprisings that rallied around the slogans "Down with profit!"[3] and "Universal free tuition!" the same movement that reached a turning point in 2011,[4] when it questioned but did not exceed the neoliberal education framework established in 1979, a framework developed and naturalized over more than thirty years that continues into the present as a kind of interface looking to fuse with each body.[5]

2. In the opening talk delivered at "The (Im)Possible University," a conference that took place in 2016 at the Universidad Metropolitana de Ciencias de la Educación (Metropolitan University for Educational Sciences; UMCE) in Santiago, Peggy Kamuf invoked her experience of "the apocalypse of the university" in the United States, which may preview the American university's total capture, without resistance or reserve, by corporate finance capital's logic of equivalence. In a passage that merits extended citation, she also refers to the neoliberal transition of the Chilean university brought on by the 1973 coup, the dictatorship, and the Chicago Boys:

Ten years ago, in an essay titled "Accounterability," I reflected on
this question of the familiar analogy between the university and the
market. My question was simply: is there indeed an analogy here?
An analogy, of course, presumes some difference between the terms
or entities being compared, an interval that holds them apart and
thus allows the comparison. In 2006, I was concerned to analyze
the forces that were, and had been for some time already, seeking
to close . . . "the gap kept open . . . dispensing with it altogether so
as to close down a residual space of difference. The university . . .
must be found . . . must be *made* to occupy a space not just *like* that
of a market, but one which . . . saturate[s] every domain of possible
experience without remainder . . . as the universal value equivalent.
In the United States this translation is largely complete. Only pockets
of resistance remain, here and there, notably in 'the' university. Now
it is time to close these down.[6]

Not long after I conjured up this apocalypse of the university, sometime the following year, I read Naomi Klein's *The Shock
Doctrine: The Rise of Disaster Capitalism*. I recall that it provided
something like the worldwide master narrative within which to place
the disappearing gap between the university and the market. Klein is
not concerned directly with the university's corporatization, although
others, of course, have been writing about that for far longer than ten
years. But I was reminded when I leafed through Klein's book again
recently that the university nevertheless played a key role in what her
narrative positions as the opening salvo in corporate capital's war on
the public interest and the public sphere. For, as I no doubt do not
need to remind many of you here, in Santiago, that opening salvo
targeted Chile and its weapons were students and professors. . . .

[T]he story begins at the University of Chicago's department of
economics where Milton Friedman and a hard-core circle of anti-
Keynesians were eager to prove their theories on the ground. But
in the mid-1950s the U.S. economy was booming under essentially
Keynesian principles that kept corporatism in check. So Friedman
and his gang were left out in the cold, no one listening to them at least
in Washington. But then came an opportunity to experiment with the
economic fortunes of another society. It followed upon a trip to Santiago by the then chair of Chicago's economics department, Theodore
Schultz, who was a true believer in the Friedman doctrine. Colluding
with an official of the U.S. International Cooperation Administration,
Schultz brought back to Chicago, as Klein describes it: "a plan that
would eventually turn Santiago, a hotbed of state-centered economics,
into its opposite—a laboratory for cutting-edge free-market experiments, giving Milton Friedman what he had longed for: a country
in which to test his cherished theories. The original plan was simple:

the U.S. government would pay to send Chilean students to study economics at what pretty much everyone recognized was the most rabidly anti-"pink" school in the world—the University of Chicago. Schultz and his colleagues would also be paid to travel to Santiago to conduct research into the Chilean economy and to train students and professors in Chicago School fundamentals."[7]

The "Chile Project" as it was called was officially launched in 1956 and over the next fourteen years 100 Chilean students went to Chicago and returned to Chile with their advanced economics degrees. By 1963, Klein notes, the Pontifical Catholic University (PUC) sported a new economics department in which twelve of the thirteen faculty members had degrees from the University of Chicago. "Now," Klein writes, "Chilean students didn't need to travel all the way to the U.S.—hundreds could get a Chicago School education without leaving home."[8]

As doubtless you know, this story of ideology transfer via the university had an important sequel. During the first year of Salvador Allende's doomed presidency, a group of the "Chicago boys"—a number of whom were current faculty at the PUC—got to work, with CIA sponsorship, preparing a manual for revamping Chile's national economy once the coup had wiped the slate clean, applying one of those shock treatments that Friedman had routinely advocated. These academics were ready, as soon as the blow had been struck, to, in the words of Orlando Letelier quoted by Klein, "supplement the brutality, which the military possessed, with the intellectual assets it lacked."[9] Or as Eduardo Galeano has written: "The theories of Milton Friedman gave him the Nobel prize; they gave Chile General Pinochet."[10]

3. Mönckeberg's book also bears witness to the effective deployment of the neoliberal juridical order during the Concertación governments that accommodated to democracy the dictatorship's university design, further consolidating a higher education system subordinated to abstract, profit-seeking finance capital and the transfer of public goods and institutions into private hands.

4. Mönckeberg also bears witness to the transition from the dictatorship to the Concertación, that is, the democratic consolidation of a parliamentary, juridical, and corporate apparatus designed by the dictatorship, an apparatus that under the military regime had been blocked from participating in globalization, even though neoliberalization can occur in any form of government. This passage from dictatorship to Concertación, from sovereignty to financialized accumulation, does not represent a crisis so much as a consolidation, development, and readying of the framework installed by the dictatorship and translated into the education sector, for example, in the report *Los*

desafíos de la educación Chilena frente al siglo XXI (Challenges for Chilean education heading into the twenty-first century), released in 1994 by the Committee of Expert Consultants to President Eduardo Frei Ruiz-Tagle and chaired by José Joaquín Brunner, who also chaired the Commission for the Study of Higher Education.

Mönckeberg's book is linked to a previous investigation she published in 2001, titled *El saqueo de los grupos económicos al estado chileno* (The sacking of the Chilean state by the private sector). This book also reveals that the passage from dictatorship to Concertación is not a crisis, rupture, refounding, or transition of the framework. Instead, we find a bureaucratic realignment, curation, cleaning, and primping, the maintenance and development of everything the dictatorship expropriated, distributed, and founded, of everything Pinochet signed with sovereignty with that signature that keeps signing. But what does it sign? It signs the assemblage of the sovereign nation-state and transnational corporate management, the terrain of the Concertación's and now the Alianza por Chile's sovereign-managerial government, which inherited everything Pinochet had signed.[11] The doctrinaire social sciences camouflaged this Pinochetista transition and endorsed the transition to the Concertación, obscuring Pinochet's signature on the constitutional framework of postdictatorship governments. Pinochetistas think and say as much when they demand recognition for Pinochet's transformation of the country. In this they are not wrong, except that they focus on the person more than the signature, that dead name that keeps signing long after the death of the one who bore it.

It was not hard for the Concertación to adapt to the social scientific doxa that supplied much of the discourse that made it appear as an agent of democratic restoration. But what kind of democracy did the Concertación help restore? None. Instead it epitomized the transnational, corporate, managerial machine for governing populations endorsed by Pinochet, setting up a parliament of limited-liability corporations that ruled not sovereignly but by commercial risk-assessment indicators and the opportunistic performance of republican rituals for the news media's glorification, aestheticization, and fetishization of the *new* mode of production, that mode of production without a mode that represents the managerial paradigm that has subordinated the sovereign paradigm to its bureaucracy.

In any case, the "trans-" prefix commonly employed in syntagmata such as transnational, transcultural, transdisciplinary, transversal, and transformer does not indicate a deconstruction of identity, that is, a movement that neither issues from nor returns to identity and that only occurs wherever identity, topologies erode without establishing *new* identities or destroying *old* ones. When we speak of the transnational, corporate, managerial paradigm, the "trans-" prefix is an identitarian event that is homogenizing, taxonomic, and regulating in its pluralism. In this it resembles exchange value, which—despite its infinite metaphorization being itself infinite metaphoricity but at different speeds and rhythms—is also an identitarian event in the dialectical terms of capitalization and government, the *katekhon* or containment of the universal satellite that, like the old artisanal sun, is always the same, never goes astray, never loses sight of capital amid the diversity it illuminates.

5. The coup happened not in Chilean history but to Chilean history, retroactively transforming its past and future anterior. If the social sciences generally see the coup as a parenthesis in the country's democratic history, that parenthesis would need to be inverted from the conventional "(. . .)" to ") . . . (". This inversion does not aim to demonize the coup d'état as something that erupts outside of history. It instead invalidates any attempt to explain the event of the coup as interrupting the country's democratic history. The inverted parenthesis establishes the dictatorship as the lens through which to understand two centuries of Chilean democracy as an oppressive and violent regime. It is violent not just because it makes use of arms, the force of arms, and the armed forces but rather because its monopoly on arms, the monopoly on violence—class, gender, racial, and species violence—is structural to sovereign democracy. It is defined not by a few gunshots but by the monopoly of arms.

6. There is a paradox at work in what the social sciences call the "Transition." I refer to the fact that the corporate, managerial paradigm for the governance of populations according to the financial calculus established by the dictatorship constitutes the limit of the government's sovereign, industrial, nation-state paradigm. But that same sovereign paradigm—the sovereign dictatorship in one of its characteristic expressions—takes sovereignty to the limit. It is as if the sovereignty that died with corporate management and calculus sought to exhaust itself in dictatorial hyperbole. By subordinating itself to the calculus of financial profit, sovereignty itself is allowed to die within sovereign dictatorship. Sovereignty is allowed to die by allowing it to live subordinated to the calculus of financial profit. The sovereign dictatorship establishes a constitution that redistributes sovereign containment amid the incontinence of corporate calculation and its postsovereign mode of accumulation.

7. What changes [*transita*] with the dictatorship is sovereignty itself. Not without resistance, this transition or mutation asphyxiates the modern university's regulatory schema—according to the speculative critique of the lower faculty of philosophy, which today goes by the names humanities, criticism, feminism—as the financial profitability of atopical capitals take hold.

8. Moving from the state as center and subject of national history to the ex-centric, transnational, corporate market presupposes the displacement of the modern university's articulating gestures and categories (as well as its governability): state, people, knowledge, technics, truth, responsibility, history, progress, language, and their derivatives, such as resistance or reflexivity. The dictatorship's transition disempowered the categorial institution of the modern university and its constitutive conflict between fundamental

and applied research, between critique and canonical knowledge, between modernism and modernization—in short, the conflict that governed the modern university's profession of modernist faith and that transformed both into reflexive relationships to power/knowledge.

9. Through the neoliberal interface, the Chilean university gradually ceases to represent a specific framework [rubro] for the production and reproduction of knowledge and is transformed instead into a vehicle of abstract finance capital. Finance capital lacks a determinate framework. It turns a profit in any sector [rubro] or in various sectors simultaneously according to its cycles of expansion. Thus, one financial holding can gather under a single profit motive a consortium of universities, a real estate company, a chain of pharmacies, schools, casinos, banks, an AFP,[12] a float of fishing trawlers, and many others too all at once.

10. In Chile's neoliberal university interface, it is not that the university is financed by capitals derived from different sectors [rubros] but that an indeterminate [sin rubro] finance capital subsumes to its profit motive whatever sector can be rendered profitable, among them the university, education, and health sectors [rubros]. In the neoliberal interface, the university's mission and standard of excellence becomes financial profit. Whatever yields the greatest profit at the least cost is deemed excellent. As a tenet of modernity, quality is impossible in the neoliberal university, or else it is only possible as resistance within impossibility. In the heteronomy of financial profit, every quality, every consumer good or university utility [usuariedad]—credentials, grades, research, teaching, extension—is treated as the academic value of the rate of profit or, more precisely, as the use value of an exchange value. If under liberalism a consumer good presupposed a quality, under neoliberalism the commodity—the educational, university commodity—represents consumption without a good or the consumption of a good that is mere financial profit.

11. The morality, function, and responsibility in and of the financial interface demands that profit should subordinate quality. It would be irresponsible to do otherwise. In this way, our neoliberal universities are excellent universities for the extraction of profit. Those institutions that either resist or fail to submit are seen as irresponsible. The only mode of resisting such a responsibility is by resisting it from within.

12. Like any extractive industry that projects endless profit, it must do so in every sector [rubro] or circuit according to the profit calculation for the average life in that sector or circuit. Calculation represents a relation to the living substrate that the interface necessarily touches, assembles, and consumes like a fuel measured in degrees insofar as that living layer is flammable material, combustible. If in the university framework, let's assume, that fuel releases heat, as in the 2011 student movement, finance capital will move out. Or rather it does not even move out since it is already in motion, for as we have suggested, it has no place, no aura.

13. Chile's neoliberal university interface could execute a cycle of extraction with the speed of a starving dog finally fed without ever distinguishing the stimulus. Even though in 2011 the temperature reached a breaking point and *the sky began to turn red*, this did not mean that neoliberal extraction suffered a structural reversal. It only retroactively indicated that another educational reform was needed,[13] that the rate of profit or the subjection by the state to private capital in the "education" sector needed to be intensified. It has brought about a slowing of the rate of profit and the destabilization of specific institutions but not of abstract finance capital.

14. The unconditional thinking of nineteenth-century Europe noted with typical pithiness that *essence is weakness* (Nietzsche). The neoliberal university interface revealed its essence, its event when the National Accreditation Commission (Comisión Nacional de Acreditación; CNA) was criminally indicted and its president, Luis Eugenio Díaz, was imprisoned on charges of "bribery, corruption, divulging secrets, and business dealings incompatible with the accreditation of higher educational institutions."[14] One might think that his sentencing would sound the death knell of the neoliberal university's common sense [*verosimilitud*], that the revelation of its fraud and uncontrollable drive to extract rent would lead to a devaluation of the exchange value of the goods in question: courses of study, diplomas, certificates, and university brands. It became clear to all that the university's mission, its framing [*verosímil*] was in no way academic or concerned with quality but only with financial profit in an inadequate but still serviceable modality, namely, fraud, crime, necrocapitalism as the condition without law, without the condition of the law and its condition.

15. The neoliberal interface became ominously apparent with the closure of Universidad del Mar sanctioned by the minister of education, Harald Beyer, in 2012. This demonstrated to vital populations that the quality of institutions, their users, and their products in no way resembled their publicity or stated juridical and social purposes. In the capitalist service sector, the customer is always right, and when he returns a product, his money must be returned too. In this case there was no product to return, and the contracts and their guarantees demanded continued payment even if your university or home had disappeared. And if you do not pay directly, you will pay indirectly, because the managerial state backs private companies with the tax money we pay when we drink a beer or buy a book.

16. The most ominous aspect of the neoliberal interface that appeared in those days was the popular recognition that almost half of Chilean university students—mostly those who ranked in the two bottom quintiles of the university entrance exam—attended nonuniversity universities or universities that could not be accredited even by the neoliberal accreditation system. They became students without university exchange value, slum dwellers swindled by the academic placebo they were sold through blanket advertising by Chile's neoliberal educational interface, by the National Congress that

legislated in favor of that interface, by the intellectuals who constructed and developed the model, by the governments that managed it, and lastly by the entrepreneurial state. The more these slum dwellers become aware of the fraud ensnaring them, the more they see how the academic quality they purchased through an engrossing, aestheticized ritual is sucked into the coffers of abstract capital. . . . But what can one do!

17. The university discrediting of neoliberal Chilean universities is not absolute. It is produced by the collision of this paradigm with the idea of the modern university, whose mission and excellence are not financial profit but a critical stance in relation to society, language, knowledge, technics, history, understanding, memory. In *Anti-Education: On the Future of Our Educational Institutions*, Nietzsche ironically describes the modernization of the German university and the loss of its critical, genealogical conflict: the more enlightenment, the higher the production; the more profits, the greater the happiness. The principle of the Chilean neoliberal interface is more convoluted: the lower the quality, the more publicity; the more publicity, exponentially more professional and university students; the more exponential the growth, the greater the profit. . . . And happiness? That can be translated as entertainment:[15] a university entertained with learning how to learn, the dematerialization of the book and reading, the translation of writing into ranking. Unhappiness too is like an underpainting incapable even of eliciting sadness.

18. The neoliberal interface not only transformed the modern university, state, government, and democracy. Even the mountains and the sky were transformed. Like virtual clouds of gold and silver spray, the air-conditioned greenhouse-skyscrapers of the new urban centers of accumulation are an open-air cinemascope reflecting the sunset, multiplying it in a kinetic collage of shades like the simultaneity of the geometric progression of mirrors turned toward one another, a cinemascope open to its infinite immanence with no outside. Meanwhile, twenty-four hours a day, seven days a week, the mantras of the news cycles and advertisements that organize the neoliberal urban landscape are projected over living slums. This is an endoscopic landscape for these new populations that hurry across zebra crossings, descend staircases into the subway, perform acrobatics at stoplights, watch out windows, switch on flat-screen TVs as they sink into armchairs, or fly by on high-speed highways casting sidelong glances at the trash-can fires down below as the moon rises to shine above the air pollution. On every street corner, one encounters the animated liquid-crystal murals that leave no trace, make no palimpsest—that is, the hatred for memory that is the lodestar of Southern Cone neoliberalism, which shines above the transgenic wasteland the region has become.

19. In the Transition, political, aesthetic, economic categories and the everyday activities of a world akimbo coexist alongside, intermingle with, or are transferred to the emerging world order. The same utility [*usuariedad*]

that inheres in the names of institutions utterly transformed often persists. When this happens on a large scale, we are confronted with aestheticiza-tion. Aestheticization means the wholesale transfer of the categories of one mode of production to another. The transition of paradigms effected by the dictatorship broadly applies the qualities of the modern university—and medieval-theological, even Greek qualities—to the neoliberal university interface. In the same way, the everyday occupations and preoccupations of the neoliberal worldview are aestheticized with auras and superstitions that hail from any period thanks to the growing cartoon network[16] of advertise-ments that wash over vital populations.

20. The year 2011 marks a moment of inflection when university and nonuniversity populations realized that the mission of Chile's neoliberal edu-cation was to obtain the greatest profit at the lowest cost, that financial profit constituted its quality assessment. In that same year, José Joaquin Brunner and Carlos Peña coedited an anthology titled *El conflicto de la universidades: Entre lo público y lo privado* (The conflict of the universities: Between pub-lic and private).[17] In their prologue, an essay that extends over fifty pages, the authors try to endow the underpainting of the financialized university interface with an aura by using the appearances, watchwords, values, and functions borrowed from the pre-state, medieval European university and what they call the postmodern university. In their text, the modern state uni-versity disappears, reduced to a totalitarian institution whose only remaining value for the authors is as a kind of secular guardian of anti-endogamic universalism.

21. The rhetoric of the essay is historicist. "Once upon a time," they tell us. Once upon a time "as historical research demonstrates"[18]—and I will paraphrase their text—European universities had an origin. . . . Once upon a time in the thirteenth century, the university was born in Europe, and it spon-taneously spread like a fungus across the body of an unnamed civil society. The universities possessed a marked communitarian sensibility, were oriented toward the public good and financed, of course, largely by their students. . . . Once upon a time these universities grew from preexisting schools that were clerical in nature . . . or else professors who hosted in their houses students who purchased instruction from them. . . . Once upon a time the students were responsible for the entirety of the cost. . . . Once upon a time we find the following predecessors . . . the universities of Salerno, Bologna, Paris, Oxford, Montpellier, Padua . . . the first imperial university in Naples, the first pon-tifical university in Tolosa . . . the *studia generalia*, the *ratione fundatorum*, *ratione privillegorium*, the *ius ubique docendi* . . . the *studium, sacerdotium*, and *regnum* . . . the *translatio imperii* and *translatio studii*, the *potestas sec-ular* and the *sapientia scholastica* . . . the *litterati* or "word vendors." . . . Once upon a time, students from the same geographic region formed nations to negotiate more favorable conditions from professors who taught for a fee. . . . Once upon a time, everything changed, and the *Kulturstaat* came into

being, that fusion of *studium* and *imperium*, the Prussian and Napoleonic universities[19] . . . the growing concentration of secular power in the hands of the modern state . . . the monopoly on physical violence, the capture and distribution of the gross domestic product, and the administration of the means for achieving national integration . . . the weakening of the cosmo-politan idea of the medieval university . . . state bureaucracy . . . ministries of education . . . a severe and oftentimes military discipline, strictly organized and controlled by an enlightened despotism that governed every detail of the curriculum, the granting of degrees, and conformity of academic imagina-tion to official doctrines, including personal habits such as the prohibition on beards among members of the university (just like during the years under Pinochet). . . . Once upon a time, the rhetoric and ideology of the Latin American pedagogical state borrowed from nineteenth-century France. . . . Once upon a time the entirety of the educational system answered the specific needs of the labor market. . . . Once upon a time the Humboldtian model, the most influential in Europe and the United States in the nineteenth century and in the rest of the world in the twentieth century. . . . Once upon a time the *Bildungsbürgertum* . . . the enlightened, paternalistic, pedagogical state (*Erziehungsstaat*) . . . the modern university seeking harmony with the form of the nation. . . . Once upon a time *Wissenschaft* and *Bildung* . . . Friedrich Wilhelm III . . . Napoleon in Jena. . . . Once upon a time only 4 percent of the income of the University of Berlin came from tuition . . . an 84 percent state subsidy for the same university . . . and 86 percent for the University of Heidelberg. . . . Once upon a time around 1850, very few universities pos-sessed an endowment sufficient to cover their operating costs . . . Oxford and Cambridge. . . . Once upon a time in the nineteenth century, the modern university transformed into the paradigmatic representation of the public . . . into a powerful tool of the welfare state. . . . Once upon a time postmodernity dawned . . . the restructuring of the state in the era of globalization . . . the ascendence of economics over national politics . . . changes to the infrastruc-ture of human communication . . . the rise of a globe-spanning society . . . the shrinking of the world. . . . Once upon a time, we finally come to universi-ties as we understand them today in all their diversity . . . products of state action or civil society initiatives . . . the appearance of many private institu-tions of higher education . . . the growing importance of private financing . . . higher education is incorporated into market dynamics . . . the yearning to express diverse forms of life. . . . Once upon a time there was no necessary relationship between the public and state universities. . . . no belief that all universities produce public goods or should seek state financing. . . . Once upon a time it was indispensable for the state to have a handful of institu-tions that represent the plurality of society. . . . Once upon a time Brunner and Peña in 2011. . . .

22. "It is not by chance that those who rule locate their future in the past and that this past should become the place where what they consume

is repeated in advance. To avoid the consequences for what they have per-
petrated, to clean the stains and cover the traces of the present by means
of a regress blurs the outlines of contemporary history, thereby undoing
the very concept of history. The victors, whose corporeality has been thus
eroded, return festively to embody the past by mirroring the triumphs of
their ancestors. Fashion plays the matchmaker to this revival. With its pomp
and its science it restores, reviews, and orthopedically replaces the dateless
immateriality of the newcomers with the easy, indolent reincarnations of
luxury. In the same manner as before, fashion makes them equivalent to the
same equivalents as always. In the likeness of illusion, they reproduce their
vacuousness."[20]

23. In this way, Brunner and Peña intervene into the lead-up to the 2011
student uprising's inflection point, advocating with their prologue the neoliberal interface that replaces quality with profitability and makes excellence
equivalent to income. They skirt the genealogy of the financial university,
which did not come into being in the commercial relationship between professors and students centuries ago, but rather with the sovereign coup d'état
that divvied up the state treasury among corporations, businessmen, and
their relatives.

24. Since 2011, the persistent uprisings of high school and university
students has transformed the discourse of the Ministry of Education. It has
modified the usual educational discourse that has imbued bodies over nearly
thirty years of usage and fine tuning, reproducing itself as it produces and
contains them. It modifies that language by revisiting what has fallen behind.
To the extent possible, there is no functionalism in this mutation, no dead
who bury the dead. Nor is there a predetermined end, a script that guides
this change. Power, enunciation, transformation are one and the same in this
minor [menor] uprising that exposes and denaturalizes the primary [mayor]
language through which it works. It charts its metamorphosis on a fabric
or rather a screen full of clichés like some invisible church, which, having
achieved its evangelizing mission, erases its genealogy and works on populations like nature itself. The clichés, slogans, decrees, contracts, and fine print
are everywhere. From within neoliberal semiotics and semantics, this change,
this uprising, the students' story, forges a path with and against the categories
and control of the neoliberal laboratory, its mass media, its pay scales, its
investment capacity, its police.

25. If the primary [mayor] language of the Ministry of Education moves
from content to expression—*what is well conceived is well spoken*—this
minor [menor] language by which the student movement charts its path as
first uttered, expressed, traced and only then conceived, in order to insist on
that which is beyond conception. There is no script for a sustained uprising. Nor can it be improvised. Neither scripted nor improvised, its *conatus*
[*conato*] has forged a path and transformed the quality of the interface that
once contained it, by surpassing it, making it visible, because it could. In

this sense, the students' power derives not from the voice or language of the oppressor now wielded against the oppressive paradigm, but rather from the affirmative uprising of multiplicities realized within the medium of the dominant language.

26. Little in the uprising happened according to script; the act of enunciation preceded the enunciation itself. Little in the uprising was improvised. Much of what happened followed an exacting performance that took up most if not all of the stage. At the same time, nothing was done without risk. The principle was gestural, going back to the underpainting. There can be no reform of nonreform without edge work, without getting to the underpainting and running the risk of getting stuck there. For that reason, the uprising's rigor, its performance, must get to the underpainting and, in that same medium, trace a figure.

27. The reflexive, modernist gesture of the modern university becomes impossible with the neoliberal subsumption of its forces to a modernizing, abstract profit motive along with the fetishization of its realm in the form of a canon of objects and practices turned profit-yielding merchandise.

Stated in metaphysical language: it encounters the limits of its aperture, its (im)possibility with the revelation that basic research, which the modern university had counterpoised to applied research, was in fact the wellspring of applied research, thus sharpening the modern university's conflict of the faculties between knowledge and truth, modernization and modernism.

28. Above all else, the modern university experiences its non-modern crisis—the crisis of the conflict between modernism and modernization—through the revelation that its purported openness is an androcentric closure, a revelation offered by the mass performance of feminism to this androcentric horizon. The modern university and the modernizing university experience this non-modern and non-modernizing crisis through the return of that which their androcentric horizon, with all the force of its categorial exceptionality, had excluded from inclusion or else included as exclusion. This is the imperial violence of a reflexive, modernizing, Western, androcentric horizon revealed by a feminist violence that cannot be pacified by that horizon, a feminist violence at least as intense as the horizon given by androcentric givenness.

In the wake of many posthumous predecessors, the event of the affirmative, feminist crisis of the modern university (modernist/modernizing)—a crisis that promises resistance that will destroy neoliberal capitalism's abstract profitability—took place in 2018 in what has become known as the *mayo feminista*, to which we now turn.

AFTERWORD TO THE SECOND EDITION

In 1996 a roundtable about the first edition of this book was organized by its publisher, Cuarto Propio. I participated alongside Federico Galende, Pablo Oyarzún, and Guadalupe Santa Cruz. The roundtable was printed in the book albeit outside the body of the text as an appendix. There Guadalupe Santa Cruz made the following point:

> I am somewhat uncomfortable with the silences in the text. In a short quotation at some point in the text, you refer to feminist thought.[1] . . . Precisely when it comes to nature and culture, the entire social contract leaves us women out. So the discourse is ungrounded: Who is speaking? Who is being spoken about? Celia Amorós, a Spanish philosopher, says that the social contract categorizes women as nature in an ambiguous manner that at once exalts and excludes. On the one hand, we are legitimating nature . . . inside the home, in private spaces . . . guardians of virtue at the center of the family. And on the other hand, we are that nature which must be dominated, controlled. . . . Not being part of the social contract is something that apparently has made us women into a problem. So when one speaks of the social contract of the "modern subject," who is being presupposed? For me, this "modern subject" needs to be conjugated, particularized, geographically and historically situated.[2]

> In the two moments you point out [Santa Cruz is referring to Federico Galende, who has suggested that philosophy and politics are born together]—the Greek polis and the French Revolution—we women are absent. We are out of sync with philosophy. Geneviève Fraisse offers an interesting reflection on precisely this absence of women from philosophy. She underlines the historical fact that philosophy is delayed, conferring on us certain attributes—for example, subjectivity—only when they have been "weakened" . . . when they have already lost some of their political power.[3]

"Women," "feminism," and "subaltern" are names Santa Cruz uses for those who remain outside the social-university contract and upon whose repression institutions and institutes are erected that determine which knowledges, practices, embodiments, sexualities will participate or not in university life, and according to which hierarchies they will do so. Reading the book against the grain, she highlights the closure on which its explanatory democracy depended.

Reading the roundtable again in the wake of the *mayo feminista* of 2018 and in tandem with a constellation of texts that have been debated over the last several decades, texts that in turn reread and translate other, older, seminal texts, Santa Cruz's intervention arrives in retrospect like the future anterior of a non-modern crisis of the modern university that remained beyond the thematic scope of *The Non-Modern Crisis of the Modern University* that was published in 1996. "The silences in the text" to which Santa Cruz alluded, that which remained in the shadows of what the text thematically illuminated, involved the modern university's anthropological, heterosexual, Western framing—its idea and imperiality in all the singularity of its concrete expressions. Her intervention touched on the question of the frame, the style of the canvas onto which the modern university had been painted—the shards, ruins, the broken vessel of its idea—a style that the book could not shake (off). If it had, I would have written about a different non-modern crisis, a different crisis, a different book, one that this epilogue to the reedition highlights as absent, in the way one notices what could have happened but did not. That book, the missing one, would have displaced into the descriptive field of its performance: the modern university's anthropological frame with its naturalized understanding of the binary gendered difference of man/woman, masculine/feminine; the social pact and university contract that "leave women out"; the gendered class struggle distributed and naturalized and furthered de facto through roles and hegemonic hierarchies—a class struggle that disappears as such in the mythical immediacy of a dynamic, androcentric present that everywhere is produced and reproduced, publicized and modernized, assigning functions, poses, movements, everything from the clearest and most obvious to the most minuscule and diffuse—that exiled women from the "public" to the "private spaces . . . of the family" in the form of the teleological, unwaged reproduction of the labor force, of knowledge power, political power, and cultural power. Such a book would have undone the fetishizing metonym "man" as the supposedly neutral and generic name for heterosexual humanity, man/woman.

The mere fact that this humanity cannot be called by the metonym "woman," that "woman" should seem an implausible metonym for "humanity," makes clear the nonneutrality of the metonym "man" and the masculinity that traverses the usership [*usuariedad*] of the word "humanity."

The insidiousness of the "man" metonym is overwhelmingly apparent in the inscription of the proper name for the "human" in the question about the "proper name of man"—What is man? What is humanity?—throughout the long series of writings on that question—itself anthropological—that consigns it to memorable formulations like "the rational animal," "the political animal," "the mimetic animal," "privileged creation," "the thinking thing," "individual," "subject," "production and mode of production," "Dasein," up to and including its treatment as "thing," as "X" that, subtracting itself from every determination, in each instance [*en cada caso*] enables those same determinations according to its unique reception and elaboration. But then, and this is its insidiousness, this "X" or anasemic "thing" comes already anthropologically framed in the form of the question of man's name.

For their part, sexualities and genders—including lesbian, gay, bisexual, trangender, intersex, and queer—reveal the nonneutrality of the metonym "heterosexual humanity," that alliance within the dominant fiction that negates them as perversion. At the same time, sexuality, *minor* embodiments,[4] affirmative paraphilia that navigate, maraud, and contaminate identities without ever settling into one, disrupt with their tracing not only sexual boundaries but also the boundaries of nations, classes, races, and species— with this we are nearing Derrida's notion of *Geschlecht*. Sexualities and minor embodiments make visible and circumscribable the nonneutrality, the arbitrariness, the violence-become-the-rule of anthropological identity with its humanity, categorial distribution, and hierarchy of all existing things. This is a minor embodiment that allows itself to be affected and infected by a monstrosity that unworks the anthropological stabilization of the normal/ monstrous distinction among a columbarium of categories and taxono- mies;[5] a minor embodiment that makes an anomalous critique reverberate, a performance that, enunciating without enunciation, traces the enunciative performativity of the Western alphabet. That would have been a book in constellation with the indispensable writings that would have made it pos- sible, texts that had already deconstructed the anthropological stabilizers of sexuality and the modern university,[6] a book that would have answered in its own *manner* Guadalupe Santa Cruz's inquiry about the 1996 edition of *The Non-Modern Crisis*.

The subtitle to the 1996 edition of *The Non-Modern Crisis of the Modern University* reads *Epilogue to the Conflict of the Faculties*, an allusion to Kant's 1798 text. The book conceived of itself as an epilogue to the transcendental conflict between the higher, technical faculties and the speculative, lower fac- ulty; an epilogue to the event of the modern philosophical university, which, at least as an idea, spread from Kant to Althusser and beyond, marking with those written milestones the unfolding of its modern event.[7] The instability of this event grows in proportion to the emergence of another event that encom- passes it, an event no longer modern or at least not only modern and certainly incomprehensible to modernity. The prologue to the first edition also referred to Heidegger and Derrida as written milestones of nonmodernity that decon- structed the event of the modern, Kantian university; postfacing readings that rendered visible the fact that the conflict of the faculties, the modern dispute between the (critical) faculty of philosophy and the (executive) technical faculties, between basic research and applied research, between understanding and thinking had become indifferent to the operational equipping of the university in accord with the hegemony of the principle of sufficient reason; postfacing readings that, schematically put, stepped back from the technical, philosophical university and installed a difference between university and thinking (Heidegger), between university and unconditioned writing (Derrida).

Guadalupe Santa Cruz's observations highlighted the exclusion of women and subalterns from the university contract. But more than that, her observations identified a dispute between feminism and the university (its patriarchal event), between feminism and anthropology, feminism and humanities, feminism and Occidentalism, similar to the dispute between an unconditioned writing and the technical university. The event of feminism cannot be reduced to merely problematizing one sector of the phenomenal world. Stepping back, listening from a noumenal body, desisting feminism will not be simply distributed among the phenomena of that which is patriarchally arranged. It also seeks to retrace the interminable digest of that phenomenality, gesturality, handwork, regardless of the object under examination. Retracing the handwork, the arrangement [*disponibilidad*], the apparatus [*dispositivo*] of man and humanism constitutes the impulse that the unwritten book—the other non-modern crisis of the modern university understood as the non-patriarchal crisis of the patriarchal university—would have followed in the wake of Guadalupe Santa Cruz's comments.

NOTES

Translator's Introduction

1. Walter Benjamin, "Theses on the Philosophy of History," in *Illuminations: Essays and Reflections*, ed. Hannah Arendt, trans. Harry Zohn (New York: Schocken, 1968), 257.

2. Joseph Vogl, *On Tarrying*, trans. Helmut Müller-Sievers (London: Seagull Books, 2011), 48.

3. A particularly rich passage that plays on the polysemy of this term can be found in "Not Speaking Universitarily, the Faculty of Philosophy Gathers the University (Kant)."

4. Willy Thayer, *Technologies of Critique*, trans. John Kraniauskas (New York: Fordham University Press, 2019), 8–10.

5. See "The Modern Franco-Cartesian-Napoleanic-Comtean University" and "The University of Berlin: The Modern, Philosophical, German University."

6. See pages 66–68, 90.

7. See pages 115–120; see Gilles Deleuze and Félix Guattari, "What Is a Minor Literature?," in *Kafka: Toward a Minor Literature*, trans. Dana Polen (Minneapolis: University of Minnesota Press, 1986), 16–27.

8. "A critique is never a subject that transcends the field of immanence but a fold within it, 'immanence of immanence,' writes Deleuze, 'absolute immanence . . . whose very activity no longer refers to a being [that is, a substance or subject] but is ceaselessly posed in a life': an impersonal critique without subject, although singular, that erodes the plane opening up virtualities within the closely woven density of blockages and contracts." Thayer, *Technologies of Critique*, 113–14.

9. One of its more important arguments takes aim at such periodizing notions as "post-dictatorship" and "transition to democracy," claiming that 1973 represents a coup against historicity itself by installing an intransigent transition, that is, the perpetual present of an always mutating capitalist order. See "Transition from State to Market."

10. See page 8.

11. For an assessment of the movement in relation to its most radical sectors, see Bret Leraul, "Surplus Rebellion, Human Capital, and the Ends of Study in Chile, 2011," *A Contracorriente* 14, no. 2 (2017): 283–307.

12. This narrative has not been uncontested both before and after the September 2022 plebiscite that roundly rejected the first draft of the new constitution. See Alejandra Castillo and Sergio Villalobos-Ruminott, "Una constitución menor: Conversación con Willy Thayer," in "Dedicado a Willy Thayer," ed. Sergio Villalobos-Ruminott, *Papel Máquina* 13, no. 16 (October 2021): 3–34; Willy Thayer, "Revolt/Performance: The Performative Pause," *South Atlantic Quarterly* 122, no. 4 (2023): 849–54.

13. On facticity, see below, xiv.

14. See "Pinochet's Signature" and Afterword.

15. See page 108.

16. "If the world already is, and any exchange of objects and subjectivities—a conversation, this very text—is immersed in commercial activity and serves some form of capitalization or valorization, then everything that can be debated or discussed exists only in the market's immanence. That means the demand for political justice, economic justice, social restitution are not demands from or for something "beyond" but demands immanent to the heteronomy into which the market recedes, consolidating itself" (page 107).

17. For Thayer's take on citational practices and the archive, see *Technologies of Critique*, 117n1.

18. Page 110. Also: "In the Transition, nothing new happens in any modern, transformative sense. . . . The multiform spectacle of its multiplying variations produces, as in a kaleidoscope, the weariness of a fixed rotation that incorporates and subordinates every event. As diverse as they may be, events become indistinguishable from the Transition, which remains identical in its multiplicity. Modernity was history's entertainment, the expectation of and enthusiasm for the inassimilable revolution. The Transition is the absolute boredom of an endless common sense [*verosimilitud*]" (page 107).

19. See page 121.

20. A rich and exhaustive account of this scene, or more precisely scenes, can be found in the interviews and conversations gathered in Federico Galende, *Filtraciones: Conversaciones sobre el arte en Chile, 1960–2000* (Santiago: Ediciones Alquimia, 2019).

21. See Neil Smith, *Uneven Development: Nature, Capital, and the Production of Space*, 3rd ed. (Athens: University of Georgia Press, 2008).

22. "The historical curricular inscription of the faculty of philosophy into the university-technical division of knowledge carries philosophical language from the critical zone into one of the flawlessly equipped, instituted, communicative districts of sovereignty and actual university governmentality. The disciplinary constitution of philosophy forecloses the faculty of philosophy's critical possibility in the act of canon formation" (page 43).

23. "Deconstruction of identity . . . [is] a movement that neither issues from nor returns to identity and that only occurs wherever identity, topologies erode without establishing *new* identities or destroying *old* ones." (page 127).

24. See, for example, Gayatri Chakravorty Spivak's series Elsewhere Texts (Routledge / Seagull Press) and the Critical South series at Polity, which champion the translation of theory from the Global South. Long-standing interest in bringing Thayer's work to an anglophone readership culminated in 2020 with the release of his first book-length work in English. *Technologies of Critique* (Fordham, 2020) was the subject of his participation in the Critical Theory in the Global South initiative of the Mellon-funded International Consortium of Critical Theory Programs, a force for provincializing North Atlantic theory. For other English-language translations of the author's work, see Willy Thayer, *Technologies of Critique*, trans. John Kraniauskas (New York: Fordham University Press, 2020); Guadalupe Santa Cruz, Federico Galende, Pablo Oyarzún, Willy Thayer, and Elizabeth Collingwood-Selby, "Conversation on Willy Thayer's *The*

Unmodern Crisis of the University," trans. Alessandro Fornazzari, *Nepantla: Views from the South* 1, no. 1 (2000): 229–25; Willy Thayer, "The Possibility of Criticism: A Response to Nelly Richard's 'The Language of Criticism: How to Speak Difference?,' " trans. Alessandro Fornazzari, *Nepantla: Views from South* 1, no. 1 (2000): 263–67; Willy Thayer, "*The Non-modern Crisis of the Modern University,*" trans. Elizabeth Collingwood-Selby and Ramsey McGlazer, *Critical Times* 2, no. 1 (April 2019): 59–84.

25. See Marc Bousquet, *How the University Works: Higher Education and the Low-Wage Nation* (New York: New York University Press, 2008); Abbie Boggs, *Non-Citizen Futures and the U.S. University: A Genealogy* (New York: Fordham University Press, 2023); Roderick Ferguson, *The Reorder of Things: The University and Its Pedagogies of Minority Difference* (Minneapolis: University of Minnesota Press, 2012); Sandy Grande, *Red Pedagogy: Native American Social and Political Thought* (New York: Rowman and Littlefield, 2004); Jodi Melamed, *Represent and Destroy: Rationalizing Violence in the New Racial Capitalism* (Minneapolis: University of Minnesota Press, 2011); Fred Moten and Stefano Harney, *The Undercommons: Fugitive Planning and Black Study* (New York: Minor Compositions, 2013); Eli Meyerhoff, *Beyond Education: Radical Study for Another World* (Minneapolis: University of Minnesota Press, 2019); Chris Newfield, *Ivy and Industry: Business and the Making of the American University, 1880–1980* (Durham, NC: Duke University Press, 2003); Chris Newfield, *Unmaking the Public University: The Forty-Year Assault on the Middle Class* (Cambridge, MA: Harvard University Press, 2008); Chris Newfield, *The Great Mistake: How We Wrecked Public Universities and How to Fix Them* (Baltimore: Johns Hopkins University Press, 2016); David F. Noble, *Digital Diploma Mills: The Automation of Higher Education* (New York: Monthly Review Press, 2001); Conor Tomás Reed, *New York Liberation School: Study and Movement for the People's University* (New York: Common Notions, 2023); Jeffrey Williams, "The Need for Critical University Studies," in *A New Deal for the Humanities,* ed. Gordon Hutner and Feisal Mohammed (New Brunswick, NJ: Rutgers University Press, 2015), 145–59; la paperson, *A Third University Is Possible* (Minneapolis: University of Minnesota Press, 2017).

26. See "The Modern Franco-Cartesian-Napoleonic-Comtean University" and " 'Our' Actual Faculties of Philosophy."

27. Roland Barthes, "Lecture in Inauguration of the Chair of Literary Semiology, Collège de France, January 7, 1977," trans. Richard Howard, *October* 8 (Spring 1979): 7.

28. See page 36.

29. See page 116.

30. See page 9.

31. Pablo Oyarzún, "Review of the Unmodern Crisis of the Modern University," trans. Alessandro Fronazzari, *Nepantla: Views from South* 1, no. 1 (2000): 267. Compare Oyarzún's reading of the use of the conditional in Thayer's discourse to Thayer's reading of the conditional in Descartes in "Excursus on the "First Meditation," The 'Zero Degree' of Meaning," page 68.

32. Not only is Thayer's usage of the conditional idiosyncratic in Spanish, but its usage in Spanish and other Romance languages differs from English, which

recurs to unwieldy periphrastic formulations since it lacks specific inflections for mood.

33. Jesús Adrián Escudero, "Facticity (Faktizität)," in *The Cambridge Heidegger Lexicon*, ed. Mark A. Wrathall (New York: Cambridge University Press, 2021), 311–12.

34. See John Beverley, Michael Aronna, and José Oviedo, eds., *The Postmodernism Debate in Latin America* (Durham, NC: Duke University Press, 1995).

35. John Kraniauskas, "Translation Has Always Already Begun: Translator's Introduction," in Willy Thayer, *Technologies of Critique*, trans. John Kraniauskas (New York: Fordham University Press, 2020), vii.

36. See page 18.

I. The Non-Modern Crisis of the Modern University

1. A Few Things That Must Be Stated

1. These surroundings mark the point of departure not only today. The debates about the creation of the University of Berlin (1810), Kant's *The Conflict of the Faculties* (1798), Andrés Bello's *Inaugural Speech of the University of Chile* (1843), all are framed by the question concerning the relationship between the university and the state, progress, history, language, truth, etc.

2. Thayer's use of *verosimilitud* and *verosímil* harkens back to Tzvetan Todorov's analysis of *vraisemblance*, translated by Richard Howard as "verisimilitude." Tvetzan Todorov, "Introduction to Verisimilitude," in *The Poetics of Prose*, trans. Richard Howard (Ithaca, NY: Cornell University Press, 1971), 80–88. In Thayer's idiosyncratic usage, *verosimilitud* and *verosímil* connote the frame, horizon, scene, or the compossible (as in Leibniz) that go unnoticed, constituting a kind of habit, common sense, or customariness. The terms do not necessarily connote a relationship to truth or reality, as the English term "verisimilitude" suggests. I have therefore translated *verosimilitud* and *verosímil* according to context. When Thayer quotes the term, I have followed the English-language translation of the cited text. In all cases, I have provided the Spanish original.—Trans.

3. Which was walled off from which first? The university from society and politics or vice versa? Or did they both build the wall, giving rise to "critical distance" at the same time?

4. According to Thayer, the phrase *en cada caso* derives from Heidegger's *Being and Time*, where it is associated with the concept of *Jemeinigkeit*, a term translated into English either as "in each case" or "in each instance." For Thayer the term expresses the aporia of a "factic transcendental," the irreducible difference of each case of being thrown into the world each and every time. Although the English-language reader may hear a generalizing, even universalizing gesture, Thayer's usage decomposes this set phrase into aporetic literalness. It is marked throughout the text.—Trans.

5. See Friedrich Nietzsche, *Unpublished Fragments from the Period of Thus Spoke Zarathustra (Summer 1882–Winter 1883/84)*, trans. Paul S. Loeb and David F. Tinsley, in *The Complete Works of Friedrich Nietzsche*, vol. 14, ed. Alan D. Schrift and Duncan Large (Stanford, CA: Stanford University Press, 2019), 141; Friedrich Nietzsche, *Unpublished Fragments (Spring 1885–Spring 1886)*, trans. Adrian del Caro, in *The Complete Works of Friedrich Nietzsche*, vol. 16,

ed. Alan D. Schrift and Duncan Large (Stanford, CA: Stanford University Press, 2020), 147.

6. See Jacques Derrida, *Eyes of the University: Right to Philosophy 2*, trans. Jan Plug et al. (Stanford, CA: Stanford University Press, 2004).

7. Friedrich Nietzsche, *The Birth of Tragedy*, in *The Birth of Tragedy and Other Writings*, ed. Ronald Speirs and Raymond Geuss, trans. Ronald Speirs (Cambridge: Cambridge University Press, 1999), 75.

8. In this regard, Mayz Vallenilla's claim is suggestive: "To see institutions of higher education—and especially the university—erected on the foundation of a substantialist spatial morphology, the transformation implied by such a foundation, at a minimum, raises the following conclusion: 1.) the crisis of the representation of the university as an enclave or closed space (cloister, compound, *campus*). . . . As is well known, in opposition to the monadic spatial morphology, we find the proposed substitution of such a model by a higher education without institutions, or whose one institution would be the system." Ernesto Mayz Vallenilla, *El ocaso de las universidades* (Caracas: Imprenta de la Cultura, 2022), 188–89.

9. Marshall McLuhan and Quintin Fiore, *The Medium Is the Massage*, ed. Jerome Agel (New York: Penguin, 1967).

10. Jacques Derrida, "The Principle of Reason: The University in the Eyes of Its Pupils," trans. Catherine M. Porter and Edward P. Morris, in *Eyes of the University: Right to Philosophy 2* (Stanford, CA: Stanford University Press: 2004).

11. Like most Western European languages, Spanish distinguishes between the knowledge of facts and things (*saber*) and the knowledge of people and practices (*conocimiento*). Following Kant's division between the higher and lower faculties, Thayer uses *conocer* and its derivatives to refer to the ends-oriented knowledge of understanding and *saber* and its derivatives to refer to speculative knowledge. In those instances where Thayer's argument hangs on this lexical distinction, it has been marked in translation either as the difference between "knowledge" (*saber*) and "understanding" (*conocimiento*), as the difference between "knowledge" (*saber*) and "knowledges" (*conocimiento*) or through the inclusion of the original terms in brackets.—Trans.

12. To understand the connotations and importance of the term *tránsito*, see Thayer's argument in Part III. Although I have translated this term and its derivatives according to context, due to its importance, I have noted the Spanish throughout.—Trans.

13. In English in the original.—Trans.

14. See Derrida, *Eyes of the University*.

15. "Suppose, for example, that a firm such as IBM is authorized to occupy a belt in the earth's orbital field and launch communications satellites or satellites housing data banks. Who will have access to them? Who will determine which channels or data are forbidden? The State? Or will the State simply be one user among others? New legal issues will be raised, and with them the question: 'who will know?'" Jean-François Lyotard, *The Postmodern Condition: A Report on Knowledge* (Minneapolis: University of Minnesota Press, 1984), 6.

16. See Jürgen Habermas, *Knowledge and Human Interests*, trans. Jeremy J. Shapiro (Boston: Beacon Press, 1971).

17. Wilhem von Humboldt, "On the Internal Structure of the University in Berlin and Its Relationships to Other Organizations," trans. Chad Wellmon and Paul

Reitter, in *The Rise of the Research University: A Sourcebook*, ed. Louis Menand, Paul Reitter, and Chad Wellmon (Chicago: University of Chicago Press, 2018), 117 (translation emended).

18. See Derrida, *Eyes of the University*.

19. This "lateness" of the university could make it a center of resistance to the market. A slow university, technologically out of date, commercially deferred might be activated as a body that delays the productivist stimulus.

20. "To know all at any cost." Friedrich Nietzsche, *Philosophy in the Tragic Age of the Greeks*, trans. Marianne Cowan (Washington, DC: Regnery, 1962), 43.

21. Plato, *Republic*, trans. G. M. A. Grube and C. D. C. Reeve, in *Plato: Complete Works*, ed. John M. Cooper and D. S. Hutchinson (Indianapolis: Hackett, 1997), 1089.

22. Seneca, *Selected Philosophical Letters*, ed. and trans. Brad Inwood (New York: Oxford University Press, 2007), 4.

23. Gilles Deleuze and Félix Guattari, *A Thousand Plateaus: Capitalism and Schizophrenia*, trans. Brian Massumi (Minneapolis, University of Minnesota Press, 1987), 98.

24. Gilles Deleuze, *Negotiations 1972–1990*, trans. Martin Joughin (New York: Columbia University Press, 1995), 44–45.

25. Friedrich Nietzsche and Carole Blair, "Nietzsche's 'Lecture Notes on Rhetoric': A Translation," *Philosophy and Rhetoric* 16, no. 2 (1983): 109–10.

26. Émile Durkheim, *Sociology and Education*, trans. Sherwood Fox (Glencoe, IL: Free Press, 1956).

27. In English in the original.—Trans.

28. From Thomas Kuhn, *The Structure of Scientific Revolutions*, 3rd ed. (Chicago: University of Chicago Press, 1996): "No part of the aim of normal science is to call forth new sorts of phenomena. . . . Nor do scientists normally aim to invent new theories, and they are often intolerant of those invented by others. . . . [D]uring the period when the paradigm is successful, the profession will have solved problems that its members could scarcely have imagined and would never have undertaken without commitment to the paradigm" (24–25). "Normal scientific research is directed to the articulation of those phenomena and theories that the paradigm already supplies" (24). "A paradigm assures them [scientists] that the facts they seek are important. From Tycho Brahe to E. O. Lawrence, some scientists have acquired great reputations, not from any novelty of their discoveries, but from the precision, reliability, and scope of the methods they developed from the redeterminations of a previously known sort of fact" (26).

29. Mary Shelley, *Frankenstein* (New York: Open Road Integrated Media, 2006), 37, ProQuest.

30. *Conatus* is a term used by Benedictus de Spinoza to designate the will to self-preservation or power to act, which is also the ground of all affect. See Benedictus de Spinoza, *Ethics*, trans. George Eliot, ed. Clare Carlisle (Princeton, NJ: Princeton University Press, 2019). The equivalent term in Spanish is *conato*, which has been marked throughout the text.—Trans.

31. Friedrich Nietzsche, *Anti-Education: On the Future of Our Educational Institutions*, trans. Damion Searles, ed. Paul Reitter and Chad Wellmon (New York: New York Review Books, 2016), 35.

32. Gottfried Wilhelm Leibniz, *Monadology: A New Translation and Guide*, ed. and trans. Lloyd Strickland (Edinburgh: Edinburgh University Press, 2015), 26.

33. See Fritz K. Ringer, *The Decline of the German Mandarins: The German Academic Community, 1890–1933* (Cambridge, MA: Harvard University Press, 1969.)

34. See Serge Gruzinsky, *La guerra de las imágenes: De Colón a Blade Runner* (Mexico City: Fondo de Cultura Económica, 1994); Magdalena Chocano Mena, *La fortaleza docta* (Barcelona: Bellaterra, 2000); José Luis Becerra López, *La organización de los estudios en la Nueva España* (Mexico City: Universidad Nacional Autónoma de México, 1963); Mariano Peset, *Obra dispersa: La universidad de México* (Mexico City: Universidad Autónoma Metropolitana, 2001); Silvio Arturo Zavala, *Las instituciones jurídicas en la conquista de América* (Mexico City: Editorial Porrúa, 1988).

35. André Menard, "Universidad y brujería (entre las salamancas y la crisis (no) moderna . . .)," in *La universidad (im)posible*, ed. Willy Thayer, Elizabeth Collingwood-Selby, Mary Luz Estupiñán Serrano, and raúl rodríguez freire (Santiago: Ediciones Macul, 2018): "Current intercultural or decolonial projects that advocate the incorporation of Indigenous or subaltern cultural content into the university or directly through the creation of Indigenous universities (I am thinking of the Amawtay Wasi Indigenous University in Ecuador, for example) . . . have often been characterized by the aestheticization of the political and historical conflict between the university and Indigenous difference, transforming a horizontal symmetry of forces among enemies bound together by wars and alliances into a commensurability in terms of a common medium. The problem is that the medium by which Indigenous content might achieve visibility and legitimacy on a par with university content is itself the university medium. This means that, on the one hand, Indigenous cultural content is framed in the apollonian formats of the cosmological schema created by missionaries and anthropologists and that, on the other hand, the claims of racialized Indigenous subjects for access to the university coalesce into one body, such that the Indigenous academic is pigeonholed into the anthropological role of the informant, that is, the ethnological token that embodies and transmits the content of her culture" (78–79). A bit later in the same essay, Menard shows how the decolonial university project, its critical deficit, subsumes the other to the logic and language of the neoliberal university. In these neo-mercantilist institutions, "the schematic, catechistic aesthetic rooted in ethnology is juxtaposed to the commercial project-logic aesthetic and is categories of mission and vision, its methodological precepts and pedagogical projects. . . . 'Faced with coloniality as the legacy of modernization imposed on the peripheries of the world system, The Intercultural University Amawtay Wasi (UIAW) in Ecuador offers an alternative higher education model philosophically and conceptually grounded in an 'Abya Yala rationality' articulates the organizational, the symbolic, the whole, the complex, and the ancient through four principles: relationality, complementary duality, the existential-symbolic and reciprocity. Its mission, goals, and methodological precepts are founded on these principles as its actions and reflections on space and time derive from chronologies and dispositions bound to the ahead cosmological relation

of eternal time that moves in spirals. Its pedagogical model and curriculum are organized in accord with the square cross or *chakana*. . . . The epistemological component of this structure manifest in five specific elements that reflect the structural outline of the model and make up five Centers of Knowledge across the curriculum, but also the project of higher education in general. The components are: *yachay* (knowledge) which issues from the north as air and expresses the reason of understanding, interpretation, the use of a particular epistemology; *munay* (love) situated on the left is represented as water and makes space for passion, institution, desire, and the ability to think with the heart; *ruray* (action) which emerges from the south in the form of earth and speaks to the capacity to experience, build, produce, fashion and fashion oneself, to realize and materialize, to develop and experiment; *ushuay* (power) which complements as fire, the energy and power that enlivens; and finally the central coordinating axis, *kawsay* (life-origin), the broad wisdom that alludes to life as a unconditional experience, a permanent tension between opposites in harmony, a real basis for interculturality.' Paola Vargas, "Educación superior intercultural en disputa," *Polis* 38 (2014): 6." (78–79, n.17).

36. Sigmund Freud, *Beyond the Pleasure Principle*, trans. C. J. M. Hubback (London: International Psycho-Analytical Press, 1922), 26.

37. Thayer is referencing the chiasma of knowledge and power in the architectonics of the Kantian university. The faculty of philosophy is designated as the lower faculty because it is the site of fundamental research on which the higher faculties—medicine, law, theology—depend. While the latter are closer to the power of the sovereign, their knowledges are also beholden to it.—Trans.

38. In English in the original.—Trans.

39. See Derrida, "The Principle of Reason"; Martin Heidegger, *What Is Called Thinking?*, trans. J. Glenn Gray (New York: Harper and Row, 1968).

40. See René Descartes, *Search after Truth*, trans. Elizabeth S. Haldane, G. R. T. Ross, Marjorie Grene, and Roger Ariew, in *Philosophical Essays and Correspondence*, ed. Roger Ariew (New York: Hackett, 2000).

41. See Immanuel Kant, *The Conflict of the Faculties*: *Der Streit der Fakultäten*, trans. Mary J. Gregor (New York: Abaris, 1979), 11.

42. See Lyotard, *The Postmodern Condition*.

43. While the term *facticidad* could be translated according to context as "mere existence," "contingency," or "effectiveness," Thayer's sustained engagement with the thinking of Heidegger and his successors has warranted use of the philosophical term "facticity" in most cases. While in existentialist philosophy, facticity signifies the world that can be objectified from a third-person perspective, which is necessarily bound up with the transcendence or self-reflection that allows one's existence in that factic world to be experienced, in Heidegger's thought, facticity is the stuff of life itself, the thrownness (*Geworfenheit*) of being-in-the-world which discloses our being there (*Dasein*) first through our forgetfulness of ourselves in our practical absorption in the world. While Thayer's usage is informed by these understandings of the term, it is broader and not limited to either tradition.—Trans.

44. Pablo Oyarzún and Adriana Valdés, "Fragmentos de una conversación acerca de la universidad," *Revista LO* 1 (November 1992).

45. Willy Thayer, Elizabeth Collingwood-Selby, Mary Luz Estupiñán Serrano, and raúl rodríguez freire, eds., *La universidad (im)posible* (Santiago: Ediciones Macul, 2018).

46. See Friedrich Nietzsche, *Human, All Too Human: A Book for Free Spirits*, ed. Richard Schacht, trans. R. J. Hollingdale (New York: Cambridge University Press, 1996), 16.

47. See Martin Heidegger, *Kant and the Problem of Metaphysics*, 5th ed., trans. Richard Taft (Indianapolis: Indiana University Press, 1997).

48. Descartes, *Search after Truth*, 317 (translation emended); see also Karl Marx, *A Contribution to a Critique of Political Economy*, trans. N. I. Stone (Chicago: Charles H. Kerr, 1904).

49. In English in the original.—Trans.

50. Descartes, *Search after Truth*, 322.

51. André Lalande quoted in Giorgio Agamben, *The Man Without Content*, trans. Georgia Albert (Stanford, CA: Stanford University Press, 1999), 95.

52. Agamben, *Man Without Content*, 95–96.

53. Agamben, *Man Without Content*, 96–97.

54. Jorge Luis Borges, "John Wilkins' Analytic Language," in *Selected Non-Fictions*, ed. Eliot Weinberger, trans. Esther Allen, Suzanne Jill Levine, and Eliot Weinberger (New York: Viking Penguin, 1999), 231.

55. See René Descartes, *Discourse on Method*, trans. Donald Cress, in *Philosophical Essays and Correspondence*, ed. Roger Ariew (New York: Hackett, 2000).

56. Kant, *Conflict*, 27.

57. Kant, *Conflict*, 9.

58. See Antonio Gramsci, *Selections from the Prison Notebooks*, ed. and trans. Quintin Hoare and Geoffrey Nowell Smith (New York: International Publishers, 1971); Louis Althusser, *On the Reproduction of Capitalism: Ideology and Ideological State Apparatuses*, trans. G. M. Goshgarian (New York: Verso, 2014).

59. "How are your students connected to the university? We answer: Through the ear—they take part in university life as listeners. . . . The student attends lectures. . . . He can choose what he wants to hear; he does not necessarily have to believe what he hears; he can shut his ears if he does not want to hear at all. . . . The teacher, then, speaks to these listening students. Anything else he may think or do remains inaccessible to them, cut off by a monstrous chasm. He often reads while he speaks. In general, he wants as many listeners in attendance as possible, but if need be, he makes do with a few, almost never with just one. One speaking mouth plus many ears and half as many writing hands: that is the academic system as seen from the outside—the educational machinery of the university in action." Nietzsche, *Anti-Education*, 75.

60. Faculty for advancing experience in the imagination. See Theodor Adorno and Max Horkheimer, *Dialectic of Enlightenment: Philosophical Fragments*, ed. Gunzelin Schmid Noerr, trans. Edmund Jephcott (Stanford, CA: Stanford University Press, 2002).

61. In *The Dialectic of Enlightenment*, Adorno and Horkheimer maintain that every "anticipation," "association," "classification," is determined in advanced by the schematism of the "culture industry" and advertising industry.

62. Jacques Derrida, "Onto-theology of National-Humanism (Prolegomena to a Hypothesis)," *Oxford Literary Review* 14, no. 1 (1992): 4.

63. See Karl Marx and Frederick Engels, *Manifesto of the Communist Party*, in *Marx and Engels Collected Works*, vol. 6 (London: Lawrence and Wishart, 2010), 477–518.

64. State and para-state apparatuses; urban, planetary, domestic, conjugal communications media; creative industries; circuits of circulation and consumption; associations, unions, finishing courses, etc.; linkages and machinic equipment that produce the totality of one's subjectivity and life span. See Félix Guattari, *Schizo-analytic Cartographies*, trans. Andrew Goffey (New York: Continuum, 2012).

65. See Althusser, *On the Reproduction of Capitalism*.

66. See Guattari, *Schizoanalytic Cartographies*.

67. Karl Marx, *Capital*, vol. 1, ed. Ernst Mandel, trans. Ben Fowkes (New York: Penguin, 1976), 949–1086.

68. Marshall McLuhan, *Understanding Media: The Extensions of Man* (Berkeley, CA: Gingko Press, 2013): "Now, however, it is called information-gathering and data-processing. But it is global, and it ignores and replaces the form of the city which has, therefore, tended to become obsolete. With instant electric technology, the globe itself can never again be more than a village, and the very nature of city as a form of major dimensions must inevitably dissolve" (237). "If the work of the city is the remaking or translating of man into a more suitable form than his nomadic ancestors achieved, then might not our current translation of our entire lives into the spiritual form of information seem to make of the entire globe, and of the human family, a single consciousness?" (50). "By putting our physical bodies inside our extended nervous systems, by means of electric media, we set up a dynamic by which all previous technologies that are mere extensions of hands and feet and teeth and bodily heat-controls—all such extensions of our bodies, including cities—will be translated into information systems. Electromagnetic technology requires utter human docility and quiescence of meditation such as befits an organism that now wears its brain outside its skull and its nerves outside its hide. Man must serve his electric technology with the same servo-mechanistic fidelity with which he served his coracle, his canoe, his typography, and all other extensions of his physical organs. But there is this difference, that previous technologies were partial and fragmentary, and the electric is total and inclusive. An external consensus or conscience is now as necessary as private consciousness. With the new media, however, it is also possible to store and to translate everything; and, as for speed, that is no problem" (48).

69. Radioscopy, telescopic astronomy, telecommunications travelers, etc.

70. "In some parts of the world, the past half-century has seen the speed of intercommunication increase the rate of interpersonal interaction to such an extent that small towns and villages, with their local languages and dialects, have been erased from the map. Airlines have ignored the small town, the train no longer stops there, trade decreases and with it employment, and young adult speakers of the local idiom drift to the city and are eventually assimilated by its culture and language but also, like anyone anywhere with access to a television receiver, they absorb the mass culture of mass media. Culture as information and entertainment has become a commodity that can be bought and sold. Its content

is dependent on cost-benefit economics of scale. Production is geared to large markets likely to attract the greatest number of people. This limits the number of source languages and operating languages, resulting in a worldwide direct and indirect diffusion of cultural concepts, world views, meanings, associations and other elements of the few languages of those who produce and package such commodities as films, audio cassettes, video cassettes, television series, satellite broadcasts and other mass circulation commodities. The incremental growth of these communication networks and mass media cultures is bringing fewer and fewer dominant cultures into contact with hundreds of others." William F. Mackey, "Mother Tongues, Other Tongues and Link Languages: What They Mean in a Changing World," *Prospects* 22, no. 1 (1992): 43.

71. Paul Feyerabend, *Against Method*, 4th ed. (New York: Verso, 2010).

72. Nelly Richard, "Saberes clasificados y desórdenes culturales," in *La invención y la herencia* (Santiago: LOM-ARCIS, 1995), 31.

73. Patricio Marchant, *Sobre árboles y madres* (Buenos Aires: La Cebra, 2009), 115.

74. Lyotard, *Postmodern Condition*, 4.

75. See Jacques Derrida, "Mochlos, or, The Conflict of the Faculties," trans. Richard Rand and Amy Wygant, in *Eyes of the University: Right to Philosophy 2* (Stanford, CA: Stanford University Press, 2004).

76. Derrida, "The Principle of Reason," 145–46.

77. See Martin Heidegger, "Overcoming Metaphysics," in *The End of Philosophy*, trans. Joan Stambaugh (New York: Harper and Row, 1973), 84–110.

78. Walter Benjamin, "The Work of Art in the Age of Its Technological Reproducibility (Second Version)," trans. Edmund Jephcott and Harry Zohn, *The Work of Art in the Age of Its Technological Reproducibility, and Other Writings on Media*, ed. Michael W. Jennings, Brigid Doherty, and Thomas Y. Levin (Cambridge, MA: Harvard University Press, 2008), 22.

79. "But that Art of total synthesis which is the cinema, that fabulous newborn progeny of the Machine and Feeling, begins to cease its wailings and enters into childhood. Its adolescence will soon come to seize its intelligence and multiply its dreams. We want to speed up its blossoming, to hasten the coming of its youth. *We need the Cinema to create the total art towards which the other arts have always tended.* . . . I call attention to the fact that if Architecture, born of the wholly material need for shelter, showed itself highly individualized in advance of its complements Sculpture and Painting, Music, on the other hand, in the course of centuries, followed an exactly inverse process. Born of a purely spiritual need of elevation, of higher oblivion, Music is really *the intuition and organization of rhythms which govern all nature.* But first it showed itself in its complements. Dance and Poetry, taking thousands of years to reach its individual liberation as *music independent of dance and song*, the Symphony. As *the determining entity of all the orchestic of lyricism*, it existed before what we call pure Music, preceding Dance and Poetry. As all forms in Space are above all Architecture, aren't all rhythms in Time above all Music? Today the 'circle in movement' of aesthetics finally closes triumphantly on that total fusion of art called Cinematography." Ricciotto Canudo, "Manifesto of the Seven Arts.' " trans. Steven Philip Kramer, *Literature/Film Quarterly* 3, no. 3 (1975): 253–54.

80. Benjamin, "Work of Art," 22.

81. Friedrich Nietzsche, *The Gay Science*, trans. Josefine Nauckhoff and Adrian del Caro, ed. Bernard Williams (Cambridge: Cambridge University Press, 2001), 150, quoted in Maurice Blanchot, *The Infinite Conversation*, trans. Susan Hanson (Minneapolis: University of Minnesota Press, 1993), 154.

82. See Claude Lévi-Strauss, *The Raw and the Cooked: Mythologiques, vol. 1*, trans. Doreen Weightman and John Weightman (Chicago: University of Chicago Press, 1983).

2. From the Epic to Kitsch, From Enthusiasm to Boredom

1. See Pablo Oyarzún, "Universidad y creatividad," *Anales de la Universidad de Chile*, series 6, no. 1 (1995).

2. "An intimation, a historical sign (*signum rememorativum, demonstrativum, prognostikon*) demonstrating the tendency of the human race viewed in its entirety" toward progress. Kant, *Conflict*, 151.

3. Barzún, Jacques, *The House of Intellect* (New York: Perennial Classics, 2002)

4. See Lyotard, *Postmodern Condition*.

5. With the onset of financialization in Chile in the 1990s, paying in installments (*por cuotas*) has become common practice for everything from consumer durables to groceries. Thus, financialization provides the grounds for comparison between the university and the supermarket.—Trans.

6. See Lyotard, *Postmodern Condition*.

7. Nietzsche, *Anti-Education*, 16.

8. See Lyotard, *Postmodern Condition*.

9. Talcott Parsons and Gerald M. Platt, "Considerations on the American Academic System," *Minerva* 6, no. 4 (Summer 1968), 505.

10. Derrida, "Mochlos": "The Western university is a recent *constructum* or artifact, and we already sense that it is *finished*: marked by finitude . . ." (90). "A debate on the topics of teaching, knowledge, and philosophy could at least be posed in terms of responsibility. The instances invoked—State, the sovereign, the people, knowledge, action, truth, the university—held a place in discourse that was guaranteed, decidable, and, in every sense of this word, 'representable'; and a common code could guarantee, at least on faith, a minimum of translatability for any possible discourse in such a context. Could we say as much today? Could we agree to debate together about the responsibility proper to the university? . . . For if a code guaranteed a problematic, whatever the discord of the positions taken or the contradictions of the forces present, then we would feel better in the university" (87).

11. Nietzsche, *Anti-Education*, 3.

12. In this passage, *actualidad* has been rendered literally as "actuality" to emphasize the ontological valence of the term—as opposed to the more epistemological term "reality" or the more historical term "present"—relative to the phenomenological term of art "facticity."—Trans.

13. For the significance of this term, see Jacques Derrida, "Tympan," in *Margins of Philosophy*, trans. and ed. Alan Bass (Chicago: University of Chicago Press, 1982), ix–xxix.—Trans.

14. While the term *peripecia* denotes an accident or turn of events in theater or in life, it connotes the nomadic, restless wandering of its Greek root περιπέτεια (*peripeteia*), a connotation developed in the subsequent passage.—Trans.

15. Referring to the censorship of *Religion within the Limits of Mere Reason* that he received on behalf of Friedrich Wilhelm II of Prussia, Kant says: "I have done no harm to the public religion of the land. This is already clear from the fact that the book in question is not at all suitable for the public: to them it is an unintelligible, closed book, only a debate among scholars of the faculty, of which the people take no notice." Kant, *Conflict*, 15.

3. "Our" Actual Faculties of Philosophy

1. Would it even be possible to teach the calling into question of the present, the writerly, untimely gesture? The idea of writing as the repetition of the past event of the writerly gesture would appear to be the only incubator of critical thought. Is this teaching compatible with the current organization of the curriculum of the faculty of philosophy and its finances?

2. Barthes, "Chair of Literary Semiology," 7ff.

3. Marchant, *Árboles y madres*, 103.

4. Arthur Schopenhauer, *On Philosophy at the Universities*, in *Parerga and Paralipomena: Short Philosophical Essays*, vol. 1, trans. E. F. J. Payne (Oxford: Clarendon Press, 1974), 139–40. Reprinted by permission.

II. University, Universality, and Languages

Epigraph: Franz Kafka, "An Old Manuscript," trans. Willa Muir and Edwin Muir, in *Complete Stories and Parables* (New York: Schocken, 1983), 416–17.

1. In the second chapter of the fourth part of *The History of Sexuality, Vol. 1*, Michel Foucault recuses modern categories—unity, property, locality, centrality, subordination, expression—from the analysis of knowledge/power. Michel Foucault, *The History of Sexuality: Volume 1, An Introduction*, trans. Robert Hurley (New York: Pantheon Books, 1978). For a succinct exposition, see Gilles Deleuze, "A New Cartographer (*Discipline and Punish*)," in *Foucault*, ed. and trans. Seán Hand (Minneapolis: University of Minnesota Press, 1986), 23–46.

2. Nietzsche, *The Birth of Tragedy*.

3. See Friedrich Daniel Ernst Schleiermacher, "Gelegentliche Gedanken über Universitäten im deutschem Sinn. Nebst einem Anhang über eine neu zu errichtende (1808)," in *Gründungstexte. Johann Gottlieb Fichte, Friedrich Daniel Ernst Schleiermacher, Wilhelm von Humboldt*, ed. Rüdiger von Bruch and Engelbert Habekost (Berlin: Humboldt-Universität zu Berlin, 2010); *Philosophies de l'Université: L'idéalisme allemand et la question de l'Université. Textes de Schelling, Fichte, Schleiermacher, Humboldt, Hegel*, ed. Luc Ferry, Jean-Paul Pesron, and Alain Renaut, trans. Gérard Coffin, Jean-François Courtine, and Luc Ferry (Paris: Payot, 1979).

4. Not "politics is destiny," as Napoleon was supposed to have said to Goethe, but "Spirit is fate and fate is Spirit." Martin Heidegger, *Schelling's Treatise on the Essence of Human Freedom*, trans. Joan Stambaugh (Athens: Ohio University Press, 1985), 2.

5. Bartolomé de las Casas, *History of the Indies*, trans. Andrée Collard (New York: Harper and Row, 1971).

6. Andrés Ajens, *Poetry after the Invention of América: Don't Light the Flower*, trans. Michelle Gil-Montero (New York: Palgrave Macmillan, 2011); Andrés Ajens, *Con dado in-escrito* (Córdoba: Verbena Ediciones, 2009); Andrés Ajens, *Más íntimas mistura* (Santiago: Intemperie Ediciones, 1998).

7. "For not to signify one thing is to signify nothing, and if names do not signify, discussion with others is done away with, as in truth it is even with ourselves. For it is not possible even to understand without understanding one thing." Aristotle, *Metaphysics*, trans. and ed. C. D. C. Reeve (Indianapolis: Hackett, 2016), 55.

8. Georg Wilhelm Friedrich Hegel, *The Difference between Fichte's and Schelling's System of Philosophy*, trans. H. S. Harris and Walter Cerf (Albany: State University of New York Press, 1977), 91, quoted in Jean-François Lyotard, *Why Philosophize?* (New York: Polity Press, 2013), 44.

9. Lyotard, *Why Philosophize?*, 46.

10. Aristotle, *Metaphysics* (Indianapolis: Hackett, 2016), 14.

11. "Just as all men have not the same writing, so all men have not the same speech sounds, but the mental experiences, which these directly symbolize, are the same for all, as also are those things of which our experiences are the images." Aristotle, *De Interpretatione (On Interpretation)*, trans. E. M. Edghill, in *The Basic Works of Aristotle*, ed. Richard McKeon (New York: Random House, 1941), 40.

12. In this and the following passage, Thayer plays on the three terms in Spanish that denote what is singularly conveyed in English as "language." While the terms *lenguaje* (language) and *lengua* (tongue) are readily captured by English equivalents of Latin and Germanic extraction, the Greek-derived term *idioma* is not captured by the English "idiom," which is narrower in scope. Nonetheless the etymology of both terms from the Greek ἴδιος (idios)—meaning "own," "private," or "characteristic"—is important for Thayer's word play.—Trans.

13. See Plato, *Republic*, 1075. [The transliterations of ancient Greek come directly from Thayer's original.—Trans.]

4. *Transcendentia*, the Medieval University, and the Missionary Structure of the University (A Sketch)

Epigraph: Thomas Hobbes, *Leviathan*, ed. J. C. A. Gaskin (New York: Oxford University Press, 1998), 228. Reprinted by permission.

1. Michel Foucault, "What Is Critique?," trans. Kevin Paul Geiman, in *What Is Enlightenment? Eighteenth-Century Answers and Twentieth-Century Questions*, ed. James Schmidt (Oakland: University of California Press, 1996), 383. The Christian pastoral also introduces innovations to and deviations from the Platonic *orthótes*. In contrast to Schmitt, Foucault elaborates a radical distinction between Platonic and Christian pastoral power. For Foucault, the pastor's power is not exercised in a polis, understood as a sovereign territory, but over a flock, a multitude, a movement. If the Greco-Roman sovereign personified territorial power over a polis, the Jewish god accompanies his flock as they pass through those territories. Its affairs concern not territorial sovereignty but the securing and rendering disposable of individual and collective life. The pastor "gathers, guides, and directs" his flock by paying attention both to the herd and to each of his sheep. Insofar as the pastor must ensure the salvation of each and every one, he appears as a "benevolent" power who furthers life and makes live. Precisely

due to this "benevolence," Foucault considers pastoral power as the predecessor of the modern physician, who manages the health of the individual and the population, of individual and social bodies. Far from the judge who makes die or lets live, the sovereign who decides about the antichrist, the pastor is a physician of the mind and a public health expert who makes live, constantly caring for all with the aim of "improving" their lives. Seeing in the pastorate a central concern for the affirmation of life, it is understandable why the pastoral power is for Foucault the predecessor of educational biopolitics that work on the basis of similar strategies to make live and let die, to manage and govern the life of populations. For Foucault, government and sovereignty are technical concepts that should not be confused with one another to the extent that they correspond to different technologies of power/knowledge. See Rodrigo Karmy, "*Políticas de la en(x) carnación: Elementos para una genealogía teológica de la biopolítica*" (PhD diss., Universidad de Chile, 2010).

2. For example, the Juli Mission at Lake Titicaca (1578) was founded as a center for learning Indigenous languages and customs, as a propaedeutic for the evangelizer. Before beginning their evangelizing mission, the priests at Juli were required to learn two of the widely spoken languages in Peru. Learning Indigenous languages was indispensable for evangelization, since, in the words of the Jesuit priest José de Acosta, "*logos* can only reach men through human speech. Thus, the preacher who uses the Aboriginal language to convey his message captures the Indigenous person's attention and pleases him with his eloquence." And since the prevailing doctrine held that not all languages or ethnicities possessed *logos*, it must be introduced wholesale. Acosta believed for the same reason that sermons must be tailored to Indigenous capacities, since the doctrine the Jesuits sought to universalize entailed a cosmovision incomprehensible to the Indigenous: the kingdom of God above on a higher plane, the church as custodian of God's truth, and an underworld ruled by a Fallen Angel who possessed all those lacking universal *logos*, that is, the Indigenous whose "own" spirituality was evidence of their possession by the Devil. See Horacio Zapater, *La búsqueda de la paz en la Guerra de Arauco: Padre Luis de Valdivia* (Santiago: Editorial Andrés Bello, 1992).

3. Étienne Gilson, *La philosophie au moyen age* (Paris: Payot, 1922), 1:132.

4. Gilson, *La philosophie au moyen age*, 1:132.

5. The governance of medieval universities was generally constituted by the heteronomy of the chancellor, a leadership role that originated in those universities founded by the popes. See Antonio Alvárez de Morales, *La ilustración y la reforma de la universidad en la España del siglo XVIII* (Madrid: Ediciones Pegaso, 1985).

6. Nietzsche and Blair, "'Lecture Notes on Rhetoric,'" 109.

7. See Antonio Gil de Zárate, *De la instrucción pública en España*, vol. 3 (Madrid: Colegio de Sordo-Mudos, 1855).

8. Mayz Vallenilla, *El ocaso de las universidades*, 31–33.

9. Leibniz's monad abides by the principle "all things conspire" (σύμπνοια πάντα) or the confluence of the totality in every part and vice versa. It also abides by the restriction of the possible to noncontradiction (metaphysical necessity) and of that which exists to sufficient reason (moral necessity) and, ultimately, the discretion of the meta-reader (God) who reads the infinity of monadic reflections, making their mutual influence understood as "pre-established harmony" into a

principle of reason. The same goes for Aristotle. Every autonomy answers to the regressive teleology of the unmoved mover.

10. Mayz Vallenilla, *El ocaso de las universidades*, 34.

11. Mayz Vallenilla, *El ocaso de las universidades*, 35.

12. In 1525, the Sorbonne unanimously declared that allowing the partial or total translation of the Bible into regional languages and dialects was neither pertinent nor useful for Christendom and might even be pernicious such that it might be expedient to suppress those that already existed. In 1546 the Council of Trent declared Saint Jerome's translation and revision of the Latin version of the Bible (*Vetus Latina*), the Vulgate, to be the only authentic version. Pope Paul III began revising this text in 1546. Later, Pope Sixtus V (1585) published the Sixtine Vulgate. Pope Clement VII took up the work of his predecessors and published the Clementine Vulgate, etc. See González Porto-Bompiani, *Diccionario literario de obras y personas de todos los tiempos y países* (Barcelona: Montaner y Simón, 1967).

5. The Modern Franco-Cartesian-Napoleonic-Comtean University

Epigraph: Nietzsche, *Gay Science*, 110.

1. Jürgen Habermas, "Modernity vs. Postmodernity," *New German Critique*, special issue on Modernism, ed. Seyla Ben-Habib (1981): 3.

2. See Ángel Rama, *The Lettered City*, trans. John Charles Chasteen (Durham, NC: Duke University Press, 1984).

3. See Gianni Vattimo, *The Transparent Society*, trans. David Webb (Baltimore: Johns Hopkins University Press, 1990).

4. Descartes could not imagine that analytic geometry could be inscribed in one moment of alphabetic-phonetic writing—as Derrida will later conceive French—and that, so inscribed, it would be a nonuniversal language suspended in one very specific moment in the history of writing. See Jacques Derrida, *Of Grammatology*, trans. Gayatri Chakravorty Spivak (Baltimore: Johns Hopkins University Press, 1997).

5. Jacques Derrida, "If There Is Cause to Translate I: Philosophy in Its National Language (Toward a "licterature en françois"), trans. Sylvia Söderlind, in *Eyes of the University: Right to Philosophy 2* (Stanford, CA: Stanford University Press, 2004), 4.

6. Derrida, "If There Is Cause to Translate I," 6.

7. René Descartes, *Meditations on First Philosophy*, trans. Donald Cress, in *Philosophical Essays and Correspondence*, ed. Roger Ariew (New York: Hackett, 2000), 99.

8. "I could not do better than to try to get rid of them once and for all, in order to replace them later on, either with other ones that are better, or even with the same ones once I had reconciled them to the level of reason." Descartes, *Discourse on Method*, 52.

9. Descartes, *Discourse on Method*, 56.

10. Descartes, *Principles of Philosophy*, 228. Since the destruction of the foundation will bring down the entire edifice along with it. Descartes, *Discourse on Method*, 52.

11. Descartes, *Discourse on Method*, 51.

12. Descartes, *Search after Truth*, 320.

13. See René Descartes, "To Mersenne, 15 April 1630," in *The Philosophical Writings of Descartes*, trans. John Cottingham, Robert Stoothoff, Dugald Murdoch, and Anthony Kenny (New York: Cambridge University Press, 1991), 3:23: "It will be said that if God had established these truths he could change them as a king changes his laws." See also René Descartes, "To Mersenne, 27 May 1630," in *The Philosophical Writings of Descartes*, 3:25; René Descartes, "For [Arnauld], 29 July 1648," in *The Philosophical Writings of Descartes*, 3:358.—Trans.

14. Descartes, *Meditations on First Philosophy*, 104.

15. Descartes, *Discourse on Method*, 56.

16. Descartes, *Discourse on Method*, 51.

17. Descartes, *Search after Truth*, 321.

18. Descartes, *Discourse on Method*, 51.

19. Descartes, *Discourse on Method*, 48.

20. Descartes, *Discourse on Method*, 49.

21. Descartes, *Search after Truth*, 321.

22. Descartes, *Search after Truth*, [508], 321.

23. Descartes, *Discourse on Method*, 65.

24. Descartes, *Meditations on First Philosophy*, 135.

25. Descartes, *Meditations on First Philosophy*, 107.

26. Descartes, *Search after Truth*, 321.

27. Descartes, *Meditations on First Philosophy*, 105.

28. The brief history of philosophy outlined in the "Letter to Picot" makes manifest the goal of flattening meaning, Greco-Latin opinion, from Thales to scholasticism, a history that he condemns as "likelihood" (*verosimilitud*), "probability," and "uncertainty." Descartes, *Principles of Philosophy*, 222–31.

29. Descartes, *Meditations on First Philosophy*, 105.

30. For Descartes, metaphysics as "methodical doubt" consists in the discussion, questioning, and removal of any axiom or principle. For that reason, it is not positioned but questioning of every position.

31. Descartes, *Principles of Philosophy*, 228.

32. Descartes, *Discourse on Method*, 52.

33. "It would not really be at all reasonable for a single individual to plan to reform a state by changing everything in it from the foundations up and by toppling it in order to set it up again; nor even also to reform the body of the sciences or the order established in the schools for teaching them." "It is true that we never see anyone pulling down all the houses in a city for the sole purpose of rebuilding them in a different style and of making the streets more attractive." Descartes, *Discourse on Method*, 52.

34. Descartes, *Discourse on Method*, 79.

35. The objectivity of objects resides in subjectivity.

36. Descartes, *Discourse on Method*, 54.

37. Descartes, *Discourse on Method*, 69.

38. Descartes, *Discourse on Method*, 49.

39. René Descartes, "To Mersenne, On the Eternal Truths (April 15, May 6, and May 27, 1630)," trans. Donald Cress, in *Philosophical Essays and Correspondence*, ed. Roger Ariew (New York: Hackett, 2000), 28.

40. This method is exemplified in the fifth and sixth parts of the *Discourse on Method*, in the *Optics*, the *Meteors*, the treatise *On the World*, the *Principles of Philosophy*, and *The Passions of the Soul*.

41. Descartes, *Discourse on Method*, 74.

42. Descartes, *Discourse on Method*, 74.

43. Descartes, *Discourse on Method*, 75.

44. "In order to have experience of this in the question at hand, we first divide everything that pertains to it into two parts; for it ought to be referred to either us, who are capable of knowledge, or to those things which can be known." René Descartes, *Rules for the Direction of the Mind*, trans. Marjorie Grene and Roger Ariew, in *Philosophical Essays and Correspondence*, ed. Roger Ariew (New York: Hackett, 2000), 19.

45. Descartes, *Meditations on First Philosophy*, 103.

46. Descartes, *Meditations on First Philosophy*, 107.

47. Descartes, *Meditations on First Philosophy*, 104.

48. Descartes, *Discourse on Method*, 52.

49. See Descartes, *Meditations on First Philosophy*, 99.

50. See Descartes, *Meditations on First Philosophy*, 115.

51. Descartes, *Discourse on Method*, 56.

52. Descartes, *Meditations on First Philosophy*, 104.

53. Descartes, *Discourse on Method*, 56.

54. Descartes, *Discourse on Method*, 56.

55. Descartes, *Discourse on Method*, 52.

56. See Descartes, *Meditations on First Philosophy*, 100.

57. Descartes, *Principles of Philosophy*, 240.

58. Descartes, *Meditations on First Philosophy*, 108 (translation emended). The marker of conditionality is the phrase "toutes les fois que," translated into Spanish as "siempre que" and rendered by Donald Cress into English as "every time." Both the French and Spanish phrases convey more conditionality than the English. In some instances, Thayer uses "siempre que" in a strong conditional sense, which I have rendered as "provided that," another acceptable translation although farther removed from the standard English translation of Descartes. For reference, the clause in French reads: "Et tenir pour constant que cette proposition: *Je suis, j'existe*, est nécessairement vraie, toutes les fois que je la prononce, ou que je la conçois en mon esprit."—Trans.

59. Descartes, "Objections and Replies," 157.

60. Descartes, "To Mersenne, On the Eternal Truths (April 15, May 6, and May 27, 1630)," 30.

61. See "Meditation Three" in Descartes, *Meditations on First Philosophy*.

62. Descartes, *Principles of Truth*, 242.

63. Descartes, *Principles of Philosophy*, 108.

64. Descartes, *Meditations on First Philosophy*, 103.

65. Derrida, "The Principle of Reason," 143.

66. Gilles Deleuze, *The Fold: Leibniz and the Baroque*, trans. Tom Conley (London: Athlone Press, 1993), 41.

67. "Yet, without this mighty principle there would be no modern science, and without such a science there would be no university as we have it today. The university is grounded on the principle of reason. How are we supposed to conceive

this: the university grounded on a principle? May we venture such an assertion?" Martin Heidegger, *The Principle of Reason*, trans. Reginald Lilly (Indianapolis: Indiana University Press, 1991), 24.

68. Michel Foucault, "Truth and Juridical Forms," trans. Lawrence Williams and Catherine Merlen, *Social Identities* 2, no. 3 (1996): 327–42.

6. The University of Berlin

Epigraph: Patricio Marchant, "Sobre la necesidad de fundar un departamento de filosofía en (la Universidad de) Chile," in *Escritura y temblor*, ed. Pablo Oyarzún and Willy Thayer (Santiago: Editorial Cuarto Propio, 2000), 272.

1. Heidegger, *Schelling's Treatise*, 2.

2. Heidegger, *Schelling's Treatise*, 2.

3. Heidegger, *Schelling's Treatise*, 2.

4. Heidegger, *Schelling's Treatise*, 2.

5. See Daniel Fallon, *The German University: A Heroic Ideal in Conflict with the Modern World* (Denver: Colorado Associated University Press, 1980).

6. Descartes, "Principles of Philosophy," 228.

7. Schopenhauer, *On Philosophy at the Universities*, 143 (translation emended).

8. "In any case, as a fully formed scholar applying his education in his future life, he will someday live a life rooted solely in the ideal; he will view, shape, and organize reality solely from that standpoint, in no way admitting that the ideal must defer to reality." Johann Gottlieb Fichte, "A Plan, Deduced from First Principles, for an Institution of Higher Learning to Be Established in Berlin, Connected to and Subordinate to an Academy of Sciences," trans. Chad Wellmon and Paul Reitter, in *The Rise of the Research University: A Sourcebook*, ed. Louis Menand, Paul Reitter, and Chad Wellmon (Chicago: University of Chicago Press, 2018), 79. This principle of a knowledge that only attends to itself and only deepens itself sustains the basic idea of the university as "*schools in the art of putting scholarly reason to use*" and "the free and easy play of concept formation," which will not tolerate being affected by the mechanization, habit, or repetition that are typical of learning and training in the professions. Fichte, "A Plan, Deduced," 73, 76.

9. Ruled by the active principles of a creative intelligence, Fichte's idea of the university expresses the will to radically separate from the university and its idea all that which is not an active principle of creation. In other words, the separation of the professions "benefits as much this practical art, which is best learned through serious practice under the watchful eye of an experienced Master, as it does scientific art itself, which is purified and concentrated to the highest degree so that part of our school of art must be separated out and other independent institutions made for it." Johann Gottlieb Fichte, "Deduzierter Plan einer zu Berlin zu errichtenden höhern Lehranstalt, die in gehöriger Verbindung mit einer Akademie der Wissenschaften stehe," in *Gründungstexte: Johann Gottlieb Fichte, Friedrich Daniel Ernst Schleiermacher, Wilhelm von Humboldt*, ed. Rüdiger vom Bruch (Berlin: Humboldt-Universität zu Berlin, 2010), 41. Fichte will propose the strict separation of the sciences and the professions, university and profession, university and schools and technical institutes. But even for professional study, both teaching and learning, the creative principle must be present to avoid "merely repeat[ing] [knowledge] but [to] make something else from it

and with it. In other words, here as elsewhere, the ultimate goal is not knowledge but the art of using knowledge." Fichte, "A Plan, Deduced," 72. If the formative activity of the intellect "is raised into clear consciousness, the learning process will give rise to an art of judiciously putting reason to use. Artfully developing our consciousness of the act of learning any given thing, despite the distraction it entails from actually learning that thing, results in, over and above what we learn, the formation and development of the capacity to learn." Fichte, "A Plan, Deduced," 74–75.

10. Only "if one central principle—the pursuit of knowledge for its own sake—finally gains the upper hand in our higher academic institutions. . . . Such institutions will be both unified and complete, qualities that seek and presuppose each other in a naturally reciprocal relationship. This is in fact the secret of good scientific and scholarly method." Wilhem von Humboldt, "On the Internal Structure of the University in Berlin and Its Relationships to Other Organizations," trans. Chad Wellmon and Paul Reitter, in *The Rise of the Research University: A Sourcebook*, ed. Louis Menand, Paul Reitter, and Chad Wellmon (Chicago: University of Chicago Press, 2018), 111. "A mind trained in this way will grasp science and scholarship on its own, while others with the same diligence and talent but different training will be overwhelmed by practical demands, either at once or before the completion of their education. This will render them uneducable, or else, without the higher drive for knowledge, they will be distracted and lost among the scattered facts they acquire." Humboldt, "Internal Structure," 113.

11. Fichte, "A Plan, Deduced," 71. Fichte's 1807 plan for the university was never adopted and was not even published until 1817, fully five years after his brief stint as rector of the University of Berlin (1811–12).

12. Humboldt, "Internal Structure," 108.

13. "The production of knowledge would go infinitely better without its [the state's] involvement." Humboldt, "Internal Structure," 109.

14. Humboldt, "Internal Structure," 112. "It is primarily the state's obligation to organize its secondary schools so that they effectively feed into the higher academic institutions." Humboldt, "Internal Structure," 112.

15. Humboldt, "Internal Structure," 110.

16. Humboldt, "Internal Structure," 110. See also Lyotard, *Postmodern Condition*, 33.

17. Friedrich Schleiermacher, *Occasional Thoughts on Universities in a German Sense: With an Appendix Regarding a University Soon to Be Established*, trans. Terrence N. Nice and Edwina Lawler (San Francisco: Mellen Research University Press, 1991), 22.

18. Schleiermacher, *Occasional Thoughts on Universities*, 25.

19. It is politically unworkable to institute this separation "in an age when, by the nature of the case, every aristocratic feature must perish." Schleiermacher, *Occasional Thoughts on Universities*, 25; translation modified.

20. It is important that the official be "permeated with the scientific spirit . . . [e]ven without owning this higher spirit." "The state needs even more members of the second set [professionals]. It can very easily perceive that in each branch the principal duties are entrusted to good effect only to those permeated with the scientific spirit." Schleiermacher, *Occasional Thoughts on Universities*, 26.

21. "No, first let the more excellent and the lesser minds together go through the decisive efforts that the university makes to engender a scientific life in each young person. Only when they have all fallen short of their highest aims will the majority naturally place themselves on the subordinate echelon of good and faithful workers." Schleiermacher, *Occasional Thoughts on Universities*, 25.

22. Schleiermacher, *Occasional Thoughts on Universities*, 23.

23. Schleiermacher, *Occasional Thoughts on Universities*, 23.

24. One must mark the precise difference between the propaedeutic functions of the school, the academy, and the university toward that end. The school "must introduce the overall content of what is known in meaningful outlines. . . . [I]t must also put in relief and treat with special diligence that in which the scientific form of unity and of interconnectedness can be clearly demonstrated at the earliest moment and, on the same basis, whatever serves as a general aid to all other knowing." Schleiermacher, *Occasional Thoughts on Universities*, 13–14. The academy, a higher organization (than the school), where the "masters of science . . . form a whole because they feel at one through their lively sense and enthusiasm for knowing, as such, and through their insight into the necessary interconnectedness of all parts of the process of knowing," is the nursery of expertise (14–15). The academy is the nursery of scientific expertise, an institution where the true university spirit feels compelled to draw near to that which disciplinarity negates, that is, the need for an interrelated knowledge endowed with unity and totality "Herein lies the meaning of [the university's] name, since in this place it is not simply the assembling of more information that goes on, even of different information or on a higher level. Rather, the totality of knowledge is to be presented, accounted for; and in this manner the principles and, as it were, the fundament of all knowing are brought into perspective so that each person gains what it takes to become acquainted with every area of learning" (16–17). The university's mission is to "awaken the idea of science in the more noble youths, who are already supplied with many kinds of information, to aid the idea's holding sway over them in the area of knowledge to which each chooses to be especially devoted, so that it will become second nature for them to contemplate everything from the viewpoint of science, to perceive nothing for itself alone but only in terms of the scientific connections most relevant to it, and in a broad, cohesive manner bringing it into a continual relation to the unity and totality of knowledge, so that they may learn to become conscious of the basic laws of science in every thought process" (16). "All teaching at the university ought to be imbued with [philosophy]" (30). Moreover, "the philosophical faculty . . . is the first, and in fact the head of all the others because all members of the university must be rooted in it, no matter to which faculty they belong" (37).

7. Kant's Architectonics

1. Mary Gregory translates the censor's "ländesväterliche Intention" as "paternal purpose." In the Spanish translation used by Thayer, the same phrase is rendered more loosely as "intenciones soberanas" or "sovereign intention."—Trans.

2. Kant, *Conflict*, 11.

3. Kant, *Conflict*, 13.

4. Kant, *Conflict*, 57.

5. Derrida, "Mochlos," 83–112.

6. Kant, *Conflict*, 31.
7. Kant, *Conflict*, 31.
8. Kant, *Conflict*, 37.
9. Kant, *Conflict*, 31–33.
10. Kant, *Conflict*, 9.
11. Kant, *Conflict*, 27
12. Kant, *Conflict*, 27.
13. Kant, *Conflict*, 23.
14. Kant, *Conflict* 25.
15. Kant, *Conflict*, 27, 45, 27.
16. Kant, *Conflict*, 25.
17. Kant, *Conflict*, 27.
18. Kant, *Conflict*, 33.
19. Kant, *Conflict*, 33.
20. Kant, *Conflict*, 39.
21. Kant, *Conflict*, 57.
22. Kant, *Conflict*, 57.
23. Kant, *Conflict*, 45.
24. Kant, *Conflict*, 55.
25. Kant, *Conflict*, 21.
26. Kant, *Conflict*, 43.
27. Kant, *Conflict*, 43.
28. Michel Foucault, "What Is Enlightenment?," trans. Catherine Porter, in *The Foucault Reader*, ed. Paul Rabinow (New York: Pantheon Books, 1984), 32–50.
29. Kant, *Conflict*, 125.

8. Nietzsche

1. At the end of the first part of *On the Genealogy of Morals*, throughout the first book of *Human All Too Human*, in *The Twilight of the Idols*, and in "On Truth and Lying in a Non-Moral Sense."
2. Nietzsche, "On Truth and Lying in a Non-Moral Sense," in *The Birth of Tragedy and Other Writings*, trans. Ronald Speirs, ed. Ronald Speirs and Raymond Geuss (Cambridge: Cambridge University Press, 1999), 146.
3. An alchemy that is never sufficient reason for illusion, like "the flash and spark of drawn swords, the quick radiance of victory in the struggle of the opposites." Friedrich Nietzsche, *Philosophy in the Tragic Age of the Greeks*, trans. Marianne Cowan (Washington, DC: Regnery, 1962), 55.
4. "Consider for a moment how, after Socrates, the mystagogue of science, one school of philosophy follows another, like wave upon wave; how an unimaginable, universal greed for knowledge, stretching across most of the cultured world, and presenting itself as the true task for anyone of higher abilities, led science on to the high seas, from which it could never again be driven completely; and how for the first time, thanks to this universality, a common network of thought was stretched over the whole globe, with prospects of encompassing even the laws of the entire solar system; when one considers all this, along with the astonishingly high pyramid of knowledge we have at present, one cannot do other than regard Socrates as the vortex and turning-point of so-called world history." Friedrich Nietzsche, *The Birth of Tragedy*, in *The Birth of Tragedy and Other Writings*,

trans. Ronald Speirs, ed. Ronald Speirs and Raymond Geuss (Cambridge: Cambridge University Press, 1999), 112.

5. Friedrich Nietzsche, *On the Genealogy of Morality*, trans. Carol Diethe, ed. Keith Ansell-Pearson (Cambridge: Cambridge University Press, 1997), 12.

6. Nietzsche, *Genealogy of Morality*, 12.

7. Nietzsche, "On Truth and Lying," 143.

8. On the "destruction" or "mutation" of the university, compare Nietzsche, *Anti-Education*, 93: "Between now and that time to come may lie the destruction of the gymnasium, maybe even the destruction of the university, or at least a restructuring of these educational institutions so complete that their old charts and tables will look like Bronze Age relics."—Trans.

9. Nietzsche, *Anti-Education*, 89.

10. Nietzsche, *Anti-Education*, 93.

11. Nietzsche, *Anti-Education*, 3.

12. Nietzsche, *Tragic Age of the Greeks*, 43. [Following Nietzsche, Thayer plays on the lexical similarities of the Latin words for taste (*sapor*) and knowledge (*sapere*), which is reflected in the Spanish term *sapiencia* but lost in its English equivalent "wisdom."—Trans.]

13. Compare Thayer's paraphrase to the English-language translation of Nietzsche: "Truth be told, I can only marvel at the towering energy of those who survey the entire path from the depths of the empirical up to the heights of real cultural problems, and then come back down it to traverse the barren lowlands of regulations at their most arid, charts at their most meticulous. I myself am satisfied when, gasping for breath, I have clambered up a relatively high mountain and can enjoy a clear view." Nietzsche, *Anti-Education*, 93.—Trans.

14. Nietzsche, *Anti-Education*, 94.

15. Nietzsche, *Anti-Education*, 93.

16. Nietzsche, *Anti-Education*, 94–95.

17. Nietzsche, *Anti-Education*, 90.

18. Nietzsche, *Anti-Education*, 29.

19. Nietzsche, *Anti-Education*, 29.

20. Nietzsche, *Anti-Education*, 31.

21. Nietzsche, *Anti-Education*, 42.

22. Nietzsche, *Anti-Education*, 34.

23. Nietzsche, *Anti-Education*, 3.

24. Nietzsche, *Anti-Education*, 91.

25. On the question of "notoriety," compare Nietzsche, *Anti-Education*, 17: "In other words, it may seem to these masses that education for the greatest number of people is merely a means to the earthly happiness of the few, and nothing more. Striving for 'universal education' weakens education so much that it can no longer bestow any privileges or be worthy of any respect at all."—Trans.

26. Nietzsche, *Anti-Education*, 51.

27. Nietzsche, *Anti-Education*, 91.

28. Nietzsche, *Anti-Education*, 92.

29. Nietzsche, *Anti-Education*, 21.

30. Nietzsche, *Anti-Education*, 3.

31. Nietzsche, *Anti-Education*, 94.

32. Nietzsche, *Anti-Education*, 92.

33. Compare Thayer's "illuminated vitrine" to Nietzsche's "bell jar." Nietzsche, *Anti-Education*, 25.—Trans.

34. If Descartes reverts to French as mother tongue, "free from prejudice" of the university, the language in which he writes the *Discourse on Method*, manifesto of modernity, that recourse represents a temporary stage since the Cartesian proposition is not the affirmation of phonetic language or the particular empirical riches of the mother tongue but the construction of "the language," the *mathesis universalis*, in which all particularity and difference can be articulated and ultimately subjugated.

35. Nietzsche, *Anti-Education*, 17.

36. Compare Thayer's "what is assumed" and "assumption" to Nietzsche's "self-evident." Nietzsche, *Anti-Education*, 91.—Trans.

37. Nietzsche, *Anti-Education*, 92.

38. Nietzsche, *Anti-Education*, 51.

39. Nietzsche, *Anti-Education*, 92.

40. Nietzsche, *Anti-Education*, 92.

41. Nietzsche, *Anti-Education*, 92.

42. "Restriction" is not identical to the elitist spirit expressed in the slogan "University for the best," a slogan that beginning with Friedrich Nietzsche would lead to the German mandarins. Jürgen Habermas, "Work and *Weltanschauung*: The Heidegger Controversy from a German Perspective," trans. John McCumber, *Critical Inquiry* 15, no. 2 (Winter 1989): 438. This is obvious in Nietzsche's reading of the university as an impoverishing machine.

43. Nietzsche, *Anti-Education*, 14.

44. Nietzsche, "On Truth and Lying," 141.

45. Nietzsche, "On Truth and Lying," 141.

46. Nietzsche, "On Truth and Lying," 146.

47. Nietzsche, "On Truth and Lying," 141.

48. Nietzsche, "On Truth and Lying," 143.

49. Nietzsche, *Anti-Education*, 16.

50. Nietzsche, *Twilight of the Idols*, 189. Toward those same ends, the "research industry" (*Twilight*, 187) allows the state to overlook vernacular poetics—Goethe, Schiller, Lessing, Beethoven, Winckelmann (*Anti-Education*, 30)—and instead privilege philology, stylistics, art history, and linguistics, in other words, those statist and university "interpretations" and "organizations" whereby the poem is objectified as "art," "history," and "language" and the poem's truth is consigned to its disciplinary instituting.

51. Nietzsche, *Anti-Education*, 43.

52. Nietzsche, *Anti-Education*, 48.

53. Nietzsche, *Anti-Education*, 48.

54. Nietzsche, *Anti-Education*, 48.

55. Compare Nietzsche, *Anti-Education*, 16: "As much knowledge and education as possible—leading to the greatest possible production and demand—leading to the greatest happiness: that's the formula."—Trans.

56. Nietzsche, *Anti-Education*, 16.

57. Nietzsche, *Anti-Education*, 55.

58. Nietzsche, *Anti-Education*, 49.

59. Nietzsche, *Anti-Education*, 41.

60. Nietzsche, *Anti-Education*, 33.

61. Nietzsche, *Anti-Education*, 47. The Spanish translation of Nietzsche's text is meaningfully different here.—Trans.

62. Nietzsche, *Anti-Education*, 42.

63. Nietzsche, *Anti-Education*, 42.

64. Compare Nietzsche, *Anti-Education*, 53–54.

65. In this and the following passage, Thayer plays on *formación*, which translates as "education" or "training."—Trans.

66. The state may find a broad education (*ilustración*) of its soldiers (i.e., people) and bureaucrats convenient, because it concretely serves the state in its competition with other states. See Nietzsche, *Anti-Education*, 51–54.

67. Nietzsche and Blair, "'Lecture Notes on Rhetoric,'" 109–10.

68. Nietzsche, *Genealogy of Morality*, 12.

69. See Nietzsche, *Anti-Education*, 33–35.

70. Nietzsche, *Anti-Education*, 22.

71. Nietzsche, *Anti-Education*, 23. In Thayer's quotation of the Spanish-language translation of Nietzsche's text, "higher culture" is rendered as *ilustración superior*.—Trans.

72. Nietzsche, *Anti-Education*, 24.

73. "To take seriously" does not indicate writing exercises whose primary theme is autobiographical. Nor does it suggest learning to write "well" as dictated by journalism, which deems essayistic the rhythm and music of dialect. See Nietzsche, *Anti-Education*, 25.

74. Nietzsche, *Anti-Education*, 29.

75. Nietzsche, *Anti-Education*, 30.

76. Nietzsche, *Twilight*, 190.

77. Nietzsche, *Twilight*, 190.

78. Nietzsche, *Twilight*, 191.

III. The Non-Modern Transition of the Modern University

9. Transition from State to Market

Epigraph: Compare Thayer's paraphrase to Nietzsche, *Gay Science*, 241: "We 'conserve' nothing; neither do we want to return to any past; we are by no means 'liberal'; we are not working for 'progress'; we don't need to plug our ears to the marketplace's sirens of the future."—Trans.

1. Immanuel Kant, *Critique of Pure Reason*, ed. and trans. Paul Guyer and Allen W. Wood (Cambridge: Cambridge University Press, 1998), 141.

2. The text plays on two senses of the term *transición*: one local and historical, the other global and philosophical. The wordplay turns on the familiarity of the text's initial Chilean readership with the periodizing usage of the term to refer to the transition to democracy following the 1988 national plebiscite against extending Pinochet's rule. I have rendered the local, historical usage of the term as "Transition" and the general usage as "transition." The related verb *transitar* is differentially rendered according to context and has been marked throughout.—Trans.

3. Simon Nora and Alan Minc, *The Computerization of Society: A Report to the President of France* (Cambridge, MA: MIT Press, 1981).

4. Lyotard, *The Postmodern Condition*.

5. See Deleuze, *Foucault*.

6. For Leibniz, a world is always a "compossible" series of qualitative differences. As it relates to a world, the *incompossible* is that difference which cannot enter into the series without destroying it. An incompossibility organizes itself in a different compossible series, a different possible world, in competition with the existing *conatus*. Seen through this prism, the primary characteristic of contemporary capitalism is that it engenders compossible series or worlds, mixing them into a transcompossibility where possibles and incompossibles "coexist." In this sense, capitalism is no longer a series, a formula, a frame [*verosimilitud*]; it has grown beyond the series into something beyond the frame [*inverosímil*] of which no discourse can give an account.

7. Hortensia Cuéllar, "Caso México: Una reflexión económico-filosófica," paper presented at the International Colloquium "Nuevo orden económico y desarrollo: Desafíos éticos por el siglo XXI," Universidad de Chile, Santiago, 1995.

8. Cuéllar, "Caso México."

9. See Willy Thayer, "Seminario: Nuevo orden económico y desarrollo. Desafíos éticos para el siglo XXI" (Santiago de Chile: Ministerio de Educación y Democracia Cristiana, 1995).

10. Cuéllar, "Caso México."

11. For the same reason it is also the most horrific—horror being about a change in quality—as Candide describes it in the passage where Voltaire satirizes Leibniz's theory of the "best of all possible worlds" for being unaware that the "best" does not mean the most convenient, good-natured, or habitable but the most varied and, by the same token, therefore a worse, more inconvenient world for a naïf like Candide.

12. Manuel Antonio Garretón, *Hacia una nueva era política: Estudio sobre las democratizaciones* (Santiago: Fondo de Cultura Económica, 1995).

13. Marx, *Capital*, 1:1040.

14. Marx, *Capital*, 1:1040.

15. Marx, *Capital*, 1:1040.

16. Derrida, "The Principle of Reason," 141–42, 143, 143, 143.

17. Derrida, "The Principle of Reason," 142.

18. Derrida, "The Principle of Reason," 142.

19. Derrida, "The Principle of Reason," 143.

20. Derrida, "The Principle of Reason," 143–44.

21. Derrida, "The Principle of Reason," 148. Thayer's *desistir* and *desistencia* refer to Derrida's *désistance*, a term coined in his introduction to Christopher Fynsk's English translation of Philippe Lacoue-Labarthe's *Typography* (1998), in which Derrida reflects on the untranslatability of the term *désistement* that recurs throughout Lacoue-Labarthe's work. The varied translations of Thayer's *desistir* and *desistencia* are informed by Derrida's suggestions—*désistement/désistance* as "a de-constitution rather than a *destitution*," as "the impossibility of consisting," as an "otherwise than being"—while also gesturing toward the terms' untranslatability. Jacques Derrida, "Désistance," trans. Christopher Fynsk, in *Psyche: Inventions of the Other*, vol. 2, ed. Peggy Kamuf and Elizabeth Rottenberg (Stanford, CA: Stanford University Press, 2008), 197, 200, 215.—Trans.

22. Derrida, "The Principle of Reason," 148.

23. Derrida, "The Principle of Reason," 148.

24. Derrida, "The Principle of Reason," 148.

25. Published in *El Mercurio*, March 6, 1979, and signed by Augusto Pinochet Ugarte and Gonzalo Vial Correa, minister of education.

26. José Joaquín Brunner et al., *Los desafíos de la educación chilena frente al siglo XXI: Informe de la Comisión Nacional para la Modernización de la Educación* (Santiago de Chile: Editorial Universitaria, 1994).

27. In Chile freedom of teaching (*libertad de enseñanza*) is a right guaranteed in the 1980 Constitution (Section 11, Article 19). It has been interpreted as giving parents the right to choose what type of education their children receive (e.g., public, private, or parochial) and has been used to justify widespread use of entrance exams, which have produced an overtly stratified school system.—Trans.

28. Juan Andrés Guzmán and Gregorio Riquelme, "CAE: Cómo se creó y opera el crédito que le deja a los bancos ganancias por \$150 mil millones," *Centro de Investigación Periodística (CIPER Chile)*, December 20, 2011, http://www.ciperchile.cl/2011/12/20/cae-como-se-creo-y-opera-el-credito-que-le-deja-a-los-bancos-ganancias-por-150-mil-millones/

29. In English in the original.—Trans.

30. raúl rodríguez freire, *La condición intelectual: Informe para una academia* (Santiago de Chile: Mimesis Ediciones, 2018).

10. The Categorical Crisis of the University

1. As mentioned in the previous section, "transition" here is not understood as the postdictatorship process of redemocractization of Latin American societies but rather, more broadly, the process of "modernization" and the passage from the modern nation-state to the post-state transnational market. In this sense, for us, the Transition is primordially the dictatorship. It was the dictatorship that affected the transition from State to Market, a transition that euphemistically denominates "modernization." Modernization would be a "good saying" that points us in at least five directions at once: (1) the process of enlightenment in the current context of the crisis of the ideological; (2) the consolidation of the economy of planetary production; (3) the technological revolution that would have us transit from a state-industrial market context to the transitional telematic market context (telecommunication and information technology); (4) the displacement of the pedagogical axis from a national, state-historical experience to a transitional informatics decentralization; (5) the urgent need to orient national education in these directions. Modernization therefore does not consist in a process of approximating the modern, but rather the decisive turning away from it.

2. Brunner et al., *Desafíos*.

3. Sol Serrano, *Universidad y nación* (Santiago de Chile: Editoriales Universitarias, 1994).

4. Patricio Marchant, *Escritura y temblor*, ed. Pablo Oyarzún and Willy Thayer (Santiago de Chile: Cuarto Propio, 2000).

5. Julio Ramos, *Divergent Modernities: Culture and Politics in Nineteenth-Century Latin America*, trans. John D. Blanco (Durham, NC: Duke University Press, 2001).

6. Georg Wilhelm Friedrich Hegel, *Lectures on the Philosophy of History: Complete and Unabridged*, trans. Ruben Alvarado (Aalten: WordBridge, 2011).

7. Pierre Bourdieu, *In Other Words: Essays toward a Reflective Sociology*, trans. Matthew Adamson (Stanford, CA: Stanford University Press, 1990).

8. Lyotard, *Postmodern Condition*, 37.

9. Descartes, *Meditations on First Philosophy*.

10. Sergio Rojas, *Fin del texto: Historia, poder y reserva* (Santiago: ARCIS, 1991).

11. See Guattari, *Schizoanalytic Cartographies*.

12. "Property," "autonomy," "centrality," "modes of action," "subordination," "expression": see Deleuze, *Foucault*.

13. Derrida, "Mochlos": "The Western university is a recent *constructum* or artifact, and we already sense that it is *finished*: marked by finitude." (90). "A debate on the topics of teaching, knowledge, and philosophy could at least be posed in terms of responsibility. The instances invoked—State, the sovereign, the people, knowledge, action, truth, the university—held a place in discourse that was guaranteed, decidable, and, in every sense of this word, 'representable'; and a common code could guarantee, at least on faith, a minimum of translatability for any possible discourse in such a context. Could we say as much today? Could we agree to debate together about the responsibility proper to the university? . . . For if a code guaranteed a problematic, whatever the discord of the positions taken or the contradictions of the forces present, then we would feel better in the university" (87).

14. Deleuze, *Foucault*.

15. Rojas, *Fin del texto*.

16. Foucault, "What Is Enlightenment?," 32–50.

17. Friedrich Nietzsche, *Thus Spoke Zarathustra*, ed. Robert Pippin, trans. Adrian del Caro (Cambridge: Cambridge University Press, 2006).

IV. Pinochet's Signature

1. During Chile's dictatorship and to some extent during the democratic restoration, investigative journalism played a role that in "normal" times would fall to judicial investigation.

2. For the historian Gonzalo Vial Correa—at the time of writing, minister of education under right-wing president Sebastián Piñera (2010–14, 2018–22)—the DPSE represented "setting a plan in motion that cannot abide further delay." Gonzalo Vial Correa, *El Mercurio*, March 6, 1979. What the plan envisioned was the "consolidation of Chilean education into one educational system from infancy to adulthood," a consolidation under the personal "guidance" of General Pinochet that had been in preparation since September 11, 1973. "The five previous years have laid the foundations and establish mechanisms without which nothing that the DPSE commands could be accomplished today: the College of Professors, the regionalization of the Ministry of Education, the teaching profession, etc., are a few of the cornerstones mentioned by the President without which we could not move forward. As a matter of fact, many of the ideas soon to be implemented were not yet ready for it. For example, the university's new institutional framework would have been impossible without the work of the rector-delegates to depoliticize and reorganize the universities administratively, economically, and academically." Gonzalo Vial Correa, *El Mercurio*, March 6, 1979. "The university regulation laid out on September 11, 1973, represented the

restoration of the universities in every sense, even though numerous sources of unrest were not eliminated, remained embedded, and today represent potentially negative elements still capable of proselytizing. The country and its universities are thankful for this regulation and to the esteemed rector-delegates, past and present, that higher education has been in large part freed from revolutionary activism and reorganized administratively and financially." Augusto Pinochet, *El Mercurio*, March 6, 1979.

3. Pinochet's constitution considered proscribing for-profit educational establishments.

4. Among these questions, I will highlight the following: (1) that Chile had not created fifty or more new university factories but rather fifty postindustrial companies that are, underneath the juridical and marketing facade of the "university" name, but vehicles of financial accumulation; (2) that the financial aid system is but an indirect means for banks to enrich themselves; (3) that the dictatorship and then the Concertación had created a system of charter schools that, with a few ideological or religious exceptions, seek the greatest quantitative gain at the least qualitative cost. [La Concertación is the centrist coalition of parties that ruled for twenty years (1990–2010) following the restoration of democracy.—Trans.]

5. This turning point in the student movements significantly destabilized the profitability of the CAE (Crédito con Aval del Estado; State Guaranteed Education Loan) and managed to obtain the law for progressive free tuition according to family income that had already been applied to polytechnic education, although not yet university education. The law is financed by the state by subsidizing private capital seeking profit in the education sector, all within the neoliberal interface and its principles of subsidiarity and the pedagogical society (as opposed to the right to education and the pedagogical state).

6. Peggy Kamuf, "Accounterability," *Textual Practice* 21, no. 2 (2007): 255.

7. Naomi Klein, *The Shock Doctrine: The Rise of Disaster Capitalism* (New York: Picador, 2007), 72.

8. Klein, *Shock Doctrine*, 75.

9. Klein, *Shock Doctrine*, 87.

10. Quoted in Klein, *Shock Doctrine*, 89. Peggy Kamuf, "Sobre no tener idea," in *La universidad (im)posible*, ed. Willy Thayer, Elizabeth Collingwood-Selby, Mary Luz Estupiñán Serrano, and raúl rodríguez freire (Santiago: Ediciones Macul, 2018), 19–21.

11. La Alianza (Alliance, formerly Alliance for Chile) was a coalition of right-wing parties from 1989 to 2015 that first came to power with the electoral victory of President Sebastián Piñera in 2010.

12. AFP is the acronym for Admistrador de Fondos de Pensiones (Pension Fund Manager). It is the primary mechanism of Chile's largely private pension system, which was implemented under Pinochet in 1980 by José Piñera, a Chicago-Boy economist and father of president Sebastián Piñera (2010–14, 2018–22).—Trans.

13. In response to the 2011 student movements, controversial reforms to the higher education system were approved in 2016 during the second administration of Michelle Bachelet.—Trans.

14. "Luís Eugenio Díaz charged $100 million for five years of accreditation . . . according to the sources of the prosecutors' investigation which shows just how the system that should have safeguarded quality education failed and how CAE

funds were distributed without any oversight. The scandal of Díaz's contract
with Universidad del Mar raises suspicions about half a dozen other universities. . . . Díaz intervened in favor of Jorge Segovia's Universidad SEK and his link
to Teodoro Ribera, Minister of Justice and owner of the Universidad Autónoma."
Mónica González and Juan Andrés Guzmán, "Las pruebas que confirman la
venta de acreditaciones a universidades privadas," *Centro de Investigación Periodística (CIPER Chile)*, December 10, 2012, http://ciperchile.cl/2012/12/10/.
    15. In English in the original.—Trans.
    16. In English in the original.—Trans.
    17. José Joaquín Brunner and Carlos Peña, eds., *El conflicto de la univers-
idades: Entre lo público y lo privado* (Santiago: Ediciones Universidad Diego
Portales, 2011).
    18. They refer to the scholarship of Walter Rüegg, *A History of the University
in Europe*, vol. 2 (Cambridge: Cambridge University Press, 1996); *A History of
the University in Europe*, vol. 3 (Cambridge: Cambridge University Press, 2004).
See also Hastings Rashdall, *Universities of Europe in the Middle Ages* (New
York: Oxford University Press, 1987).
    19. Brunner and Peña, *Conflicto*, 26.
    20. Ronald Kay, *Del espacio de acá. Señales para una mirada americana* (San-
tiago de Chile: Metales Pesados, 2005), 43.

Afterword to the Second Edition
    1. Santa Cruz refers to the following passage: "Analogously, 'feminist criticism
begins by denouncing the alibis of a philosophy of knowledge that obscures how
an apparatus of hegemonic representation—occidental masculinity—captures
and controls a [class, race, gender, species?] monopoly of absolute truth based on
the false pretense of the transparency of its codes, the neutrality of its knowledge,
its indifference to any difference." Richard, "Saberes clasificados," 31. Through
its critique of heterosexual androcentrism, feminist theory makes visible the masculinity of university knowledge that poses as asexual, universal, disembodied.
Feminist critique subverts one of the most mystified foundations of university
knowledge as a presumably pure, "neutral knowledge, the product of a dry intelligence, without history, capable . . . of [objectively] reading the truth of any text,
from any time, at any time." Marchant, *Árboles y madres*, 115.
    2. Federico Galende, Pablo Oyarzún, Guadalupe Santa Cruz, and Willy Thayer,
"Conversación en torno al texto," in Willy Thayer, *La crisis no moderna de la
universidad moderna: Epílogo al conflicto de las facultades* (Santiago: Cuarto
Propio, 1996), 237–38.
    3. Galende et al., "Conversación en torno al texto," 222.
    4. Minor insofar as they do not reach gender or unity; that disappear in
representation.
    5. See Alejandra Castillo's *Ars Disyecta* (Santiago: Palinodía, 2014); and
Matrix, el género de la filosofía (Santiago: Macul, 2019).
    6. Jacques Derrida, *Geschlect III*, ed. Geoffrey Bennington, Katie Chenoweth,
and Rodrigo Therezo, trans. Katie Chenoweth and Rodrigo Therezo (Chicago:
University of Chicago Press, 2020); Teresa de Lauretis, *Technologies of Gender*
(London: Macmillan, 1989); De Lauretis, *Alice Doesn't: Feminism, Semiotics,
Cinema* (Bloomington: Indiana University Press, 1984); Judith Butler and Joan

W. Scott, eds., *Feminists Theorize the Political* (London: Routledge, 1992); Donna Haraway, *Simians, Cyborgs and Women: The Reinvention of Nature* (New York: Taylor and Francis, 1991); Haraway, "The Promises of Monsters: A Regenerative Politics for Inappropriate/d Others," in *The Haraway Reader* (New York: Routledge, 2004); Rosi Braidottti, *Nomadic Subjects: Embodiment and Sexual Difference in Contemporary Feminist Theory*, 2nd ed. (New York: Columbia University Press, 2011); Deleuze and Guattari, *A Thousand Plateaus*.

7. See Thayer, *La crisis no moderna de la universidad moderna* (Santiago: Cuarto Propio, 1996), 11.

BIBLIOGRAPHY

Adorno, Theodor, and Max Horkheimer. *Dialectic of Enlightenment: Philosophical Fragments*. Edited by Gunzelin Schmid Noerr. Translated by Edmund Jephcott. Stanford, CA: Stanford University Press, 2002.

Agamben, Giorgio. *The Man Without Content*. Translated by Georgia Albert. Stanford, CA: Stanford University Press, 1999.

Ajens, Andrés. *Con dado in-escrito*. Córdoba: Verbena Ediciones, 2009.

———. *Más íntimas mistura*. Santiago, Chile: Intemperie Ediciones, 1998.

———. *Poetry after the Invention of America: Don't Light the Flower*. Translated by Michelle Gil-Montero. New York: Palgrave Macmillan, 2011.

Althusser, Louis. *On the Reproduction of Capitalism: Ideology and Ideological State Apparatuses*. Translated by G. M. Goshgarian. New York: Verso, 2014.

Alvárez de Morales, Antonio. *La ilustración y la reforma de la universidad en la España del siglo XVIII*. Madrid: Ediciones Pegaso, 1985.

Aristotle. "De Interpretatione (On Interpretation)." Translated by E. M. Edghill. In *The Basic Works of Aristotle*, edited by Richard McKeon, 40–64. New York: Random House, 1941.

———. *Metaphysics*. Translated and edited by C. D. C. Reeve. Indianapolis: Hackett, 2016.

Barthes, Roland. "Lecture in Inauguration of the Chair of Literary Semiology, Collège de France, January 7, 1977." Translated by Richard Howard. *October* 8 (Spring 1979): 3–16.

Becerra López, José Luis. *La organización de los estudios en la Nueva España*. Mexico City: Universidad Nacional Autónoma de México, 1963.

Benjamin, Walter. "The Work of Art in the Age of Its Technological Reproducibility (Second Version)." Translated by Edmund Jephcott and Harry Zohn. In *The Work of Art in the Age of Its Technological Reproducibility, and Other Writings on Media*, edited by Michael W. Jennings, Brigid Doherty, and Thomas Y. Levin, 19–55. Cambridge, MA: Harvard University Press, 2008.

Blanchot, Maurice. *The Infinite Conversation*. Translated by Susan Hanson. Minneapolis: University of Minnesota Press,1993.

Borges, Jorge Luis. "John Wilkins' Analytic Language." In *Selected Non-Fictions*, translated by Esther Allen, Suzanne Jill Levine, Eliot Weinberger, edited by Eliot Weinberger, 229–33. New York: Viking Penguin, 1999.

Bourdieu, Pierre. *In Other Words: Essays toward a Reflective Sociology*. Translated by Matthew Adamson. Stanford, CA: Stanford University Press, 1990.

Braidottti, Rosi. *Nomadic Subjects: Embodiment and Sexual Difference in Contemporary Feminist Theory*. 2nd ed. New York: Columbia University Press, 2011.

Brunner, José Joaquín, et al., *Los desafíos de la educación chilena frente al siglo XXI: Informe de la Comisión Nacional para la Modernización de la Educación*. Santiago: Editorial Universitaria, 1994.

Brunner, José Joaquín, and Carlos Peña, eds. *El conflicto de la universidades: Entre lo público y lo privado*. Santiago: Ediciones Universidad Diego Portales, 2011.

Butler, Judith, and Joan W. Scott, eds. *Feminists Theorize the Political*. London: Routledge, 1992.

Canudo, Ricciotto. "Manifesto of the Seven Arts.'" Translated by Steven Philip Kramer. *Literature/Film Quarterly* 3, no. 3 (1975): 252–54.

Castillo, Alejandra. *Ars disyecta*. Santiago: Palinodía, 2014.

———. *Matrix, el género de la filosofía*. Santiago: Macul, 2019.

Chocano Mena, Magdalena. *La fortaleza docta*. Barcelona: Bellaterra, 2000.

Cuéllar, Hortensia. "Caso México: Una reflexión económico-filosófica." Paper presented at the International Colloquium "Nuevo orden económico y desarrollo: Desafíos éticos por el siglo XXI," Universidad de Chile, Santiago, 1995.

De Lauretis, Teresa. *Alice Doesn't: Feminism, Semiotics, Cinema*. Bloomington: Indiana University Press, 1984.

———. *Technologies of Gender*. London: Macmillan, 1989.

Deleuze, Gilles. *The Fold: Leibniz and the Baroque*. Translated by Tom Conley. London: Athlone Press, 1993.

———. *Negotiations 1972–1990*. Translated by Martin Joughin. New York: Columbia University Press, 1995.

———. "A New Cartographer (*Discipline and Punish*)." In *Foucault*, edited and translated by Seán Hand, 23–46. Minneapolis: University of Minnesota Press, 1986.

Deleuze, Gilles, and Félix Guattari. *A Thousand Plateaus: Capitalism and Schizophrenia*. Translated by Brian Massumi. Minneapolis: University of Minnesota Press, 1987.

Derrida, Jacques. *Eyes of the University: Right to Philosophy 2*. Translated by Jan Plug et al. Stanford, CA: Stanford University Press, 2004.

———. *Geschlect III*. Edited by Geoffrey Bennington, Katie Chenoweth, and Rodrigo Therezo. Translated by Katie Chenoweth and Rodrigo Therezo. Chicago: University of Chicago Press, 2020.

———. "If There Is Cause to Translate I: Philosophy in Its National Language (Toward a "*licterature en françois*"). Translated by Sylvia Söderlind. In *Eyes of the University: Right to Philosophy 2*, 1–19. Stanford, CA: Stanford University Press, 2004.

———. "Mochlos, or, The Conflict of the Faculties." Translated by Richard Rand and Amy Wygant. In *Eyes of the University: Right to Philosophy 2*, 83–112. Stanford, CA: Stanford University Press, 2004.

———. *Of Grammatology*. Translated by Gayatri Chakravorty Spivak. Baltimore: Johns Hopkins University Press, 1997.

———. "Onto-theology of National-Humanism (Prolegomena to a Hypothesis)." *Oxford Literary Review* 14, no. 1 (1992): 3–23.

———. "The Principle of Reason: The University in the Eyes of Its Pupils." Translated by Catherine M. Porter and Edward P. Morris. In *Eyes of the University: Right to Philosophy 2*, 129–55. Stanford, CA: Stanford University Press, 2004.

————. "Tympan." In *Margins of Philosophy*, edited and translated by Alan Bass, ix–xxix. Chicago: University of Chicago Press, 1982.

————. "Where a Teaching Body Begins and How it Ends." Translated by Jan Plug. In *Who's Afraid of Philosophy? Right to Philosophy 1*, 67–98. Stanford, CA: Stanford University Press, 2002.

Descartes, René. *Discourse on Method*. Translated by Donald Cress. In *Philosophical Essays and Correspondence*, edited by Roger Ariew, 46–82. New York: Hackett, 2000.

————. "For [Arnauld], 29 July 1648." In *The Correspondence*, translated by John Cottingham, Robert Stoothoff, Dugald Murdoch, and Anthony Kenny, 356–59. Vol. 3 of *The Philosophical Writings of Descartes*. New York: Cambridge University Press, 1991.

————. *Meditations on First Philosophy*. Translated by Donald Cress. In *Philosophical Essays and Correspondence*, edited by Roger Ariew, 97–141. New York: Hackett, 2000.

————. "Objections by Some Learned Men to the Preceding Meditations, with Replies by the Author." Translated by Donald Cress. In *Philosophical Essays and Correspondence*, edited by Roger Ariew, 142–206. New York: Hackett, 2000.

————. *Principles of Philosophy*. Translated by Elizabeth S. Haldane, G. R. T. Ross, Marjorie Grene, and Roger Ariew. In *Philosophical Essays and Correspondence*, edited by Roger Ariew, 222–72. New York: Hackett, 2000.

————. *Rules for the Direction of the Mind*. Translated by Marjorie Grene and Roger Ariew. In *Philosophical Essays and Correspondence*, edited by Roger Ariew, 2–28. New York: Hackett, 2000.

————. *The Search after Truth by the Light of Nature*. Translated by Elizabeth S. Haldane, G. R. T. Ross, Marjorie Grene, and Roger Ariew. In *Philosophical Essays and Correspondence*, edited by Roger Ariew, 315–24. New York: Hackett, 2000.

————. "To Mersenne, On the Eternal Truths (April 15, May 6, and May 27, 1630)." Translated by Donald Cress. In *Philosophical Essays and Correspondence*, edited by Roger Ariew, 28–30. New York: Hackett, 2000.

————. "To Mersenne, 15 April 1630." In *The Correspondence*, translated by John Cottingham, Robert Stoothoff, Dugald Murdoch, and Anthony Kenny, 20–25. Vol. 3 of *The Philosophical Writings of Descartes*. New York: Cambridge University Press, 1991.

————. "To Mersenne, 27 May 1630." In *The Correspondence*, translated by John Cottingham, Robert Stoothoff, Dugald Murdoch, and Anthony Kenny, 25–26. Vol. 3 of *The Philosophical Writings of Descartes*. New York: Cambridge University Press, 1991.

Durkheim, Émile. *Sociology and Education*. Translated by Sherwood Fox. Glencoe, IL: Free Press, 1956.

Fallon, Daniel. *The German University: A Heroic Ideal in Conflict with the Modern World*. Denver: Colorado Associated University Press, 1980.

Feyerabend, Paul. *Against Method*. 4th ed. New York: Verso, 2010.

Fichte, Johann Gottlieb. "A Plan, Deduced from First Principles, for an Institution of Higher Learning to Be Established in Berlin, Connected to and Subordinate to an Academy of Sciences." Translated by Chad Wellmon and Paul Reitter. In *The*

Rise of the Research University: A Sourcebook, edited by Louis Menand, Paul Reitter, and Chad Wellmon, 67–83. Chicago: University of Chicago Press, 2018.

Fichte, Johann Gottlieb. "Deduzierter Plan einer zu Berlin zu errichtenden höhern Lehranstalt, die in gehöriger Verbindung mit einer Akademie der Wissenschaften stehe." In *Gründungstexte: Johann Gottlieb Fichte, Friedrich Daniel Ernst Schleiermacher, Wilhelm von Humboldt*, edited by Rüdiger vom Bruch, 9–122. Berlin: Humboldt-Universität zu Berlin, 2010.

———. "A Plan, Deduced from First Principles, for an Institution of Higher Learning to Be Established in Berlin, Connected to and Subordinate to an Academy of Sciences." Translated by Chad Wellmon and Paul Reitter. In *The Rise of the Research University: A Sourcebook*, edited by Louis Menand, Paul Reitter, and Chad Wellmon, 67–83. Chicago: University of Chicago Press, 2018.

Foucault, Michel. *The History of Sexuality: Volume 1, An Introduction*. Translated by Robert Hurley. New York: Pantheon Books, 1978.

———. "Truth and Juridical Forms." Translated by Lawrence Williams and Catherine Merlen. *Social Identities* 2, no. 3 (1996): 327–42.

———. "What Is Critique?" Translated by Kevin Paul Geiman. In *What Is Enlightenment? Eighteenth-Century Answers and Twentieth-Century Questions*, edited by James Schmidt, 382–98. Berkeley: University of California Press, 1996.

———. "What Is Enlightenment?" Translated by Catherine Porter. In *The Foucault Reader*, edited by Paul Rabinow, 32–50. New York: Pantheon, 1984.

Freud, Sigmund. *Beyond the Pleasure Principle*. Translated by C. J. M. Hubback. London: International Psycho-Analytical Press, 1922.

Galende, Federico, Pablo Oyarzún, Guadalupe Santa Cruz, and Willy Thayer. "Conversación en torno al texto." In *La crisis no moderna de la universidad moderna: Epílogo al conflicto de las facultades*, by Willy Thayer, 211–39 . Santiago: Cuarto Propio, 1996.

Garretón, Manuel Antonio. *Hacia una nueva era política: Estudio sobre las democratizaciones*. Santiago: Fondo de Cultura Económica, 1995.

Gil de Zárate, Antonio. *De la instrucción pública en España*. Vol. 3. Madrid: Colegio de Sordo-Mudos, 1855.

Gilson, Étienne. *La philosophie au moyen age*. Vol. 1. Paris: Payot, 1922.

González, Mónica, and Juan Andrés Guzmán. "Las pruebas que confirman la venta de acreditaciones a universidades privadas." *Centro de Investigación Periodística (CIPER Chile)*, December 10, 2012. http://ciperchile.cl/2012/12/10/.

Gramsci, Antonio. *Selections from the Prison Notebooks*. Translated and edited by Quintin Hoare and Geoffrey Nowell Smith. New York: International Publishers, 1971.

Gruzinsky, Serge. *La guerra de las imágenes: De Colón a Blade Runner*. Mexico City: Fondo de Cultura Económica, 1994.

Guattari, Félix. *Schizoanalytic Cartographies*. Translated by Andrew Goffey. New York: Continuum, 2012.

Guzmán, Juan Andrés, and Gregorio Riquelme, "CAE: Cómo se creó y opera el crédito que le deja a los bancos ganancias por $150 mil millones." *Centro de Investigación Periodística (CIPER Chile)*, December 20, 2011. http://www.ciperchile.cl/2011/12/20/cae-como-se-creo-y-opera-el-credito-que-le-deja-a-los-bancos-ganancias-por-150-mil-millones/

Habermas, Jürgen. *Knowledge and Human Interests*. Translated by Jeremy J. Shapiro. Boston: Beacon Press, 1971.

———. "Modernity vs. Postmodernity." *New German Critique*, no 22, special issue on Modernism edited by Seyla Ben-Habib (Winter 1981): 3–14.

———. "Work and Weltanschauung: The Heidegger Controversy from a German Perspective." Translated by John McCumber. *Critical Inquiry* 15, no. 2 (Winter 1989): 431–56.

Haraway, Donna. "The Promises of Monsters: A Regenerative Politics for Inappropriate/d Others." In *The Haraway Reader*, 63–124. New York: Routledge, 2004.

———. *Simians, Cyborgs and Women: The Reinvention of Nature*. New York: Taylor and Francis, 1991.

Hegel, Georg Wilhelm Friedrich. *The Difference between Fichte's and Schelling's System of Philosophy*. Translated by H. S. Harris and Walter Cerf. Albany: State University of New York Press, 1977.

———. *Lectures on the Philosophy of History: Complete and Unabridged*. Translated by Ruben Alvarado. Aalten: WordBridge, 2011.

Heidegger, Martin. *Kant and the Problem of Metaphysics*. 5th ed. Translated by Richard Taft. Indianapolis: Indiana University Press, 1997.

———. "Overcoming Metaphysics." In *The End of Philosophy*, translated by Joan Stambaugh, 84–110. New York: Harper and Row, 1973.

———. *The Principle of Reason*. Translated by Reginald Lilly. Indianapolis: Indiana University Press, 1991.

———. *Schelling's Treatise on the Essence of Human Freedom*. Translated by Joan Stambaugh. Athens: Ohio University Press, 1985.

———. *What Is Called Thinking?* Translated by J. Glenn Gray. New York: Harper and Row, 1968.

Hobbes, Thomas. *Leviathan*. Edited by J. C. A. Gaskin. New York: Oxford University Press, 1998.

Humboldt, Wilhem von. "On the Internal Structure of the University in Berlin and Its Relationships to Other Organizations." Translated by Chad Wellmon and Paul Reitter. In *The Rise of the Research University: A Sourcebook*, edited by Louis Menand, Paul Reitter, and Chad Wellmon, 108–16. Chicago: University of Chicago Press, 2018.

Kafka, Franz. "An Old Manuscript." Translated by Willa Muir and Edwin Muir. In *Complete Stories and Parables*, 416–17. New York: Schocken, 1983.

Kamuf, Peggy. "Accounterability." *Textual Practice* 21, no. 2 (2007): 251–66.

———. "Sobre no tener idea." *La universidad (im)posible*, edited by Willy Thayer, Elizabeth Collingwood-Selby, Mary Luz Estupñán Serrano, and raúl rodríguez freire, 14–24. Santiago: Ediciones Macul, 2018.

Kant, Immanuel. *The Conflict of the Faculties:* Der Streit der Fakultäten. Translated by Mary J. Gregor. New York: Abaris, 1979.

———. *Critique of Pure Reason*. Edited and translated by Paul Guyer and Allen W. Wood. Cambridge: Cambridge University Press, 1998.

Karmy, Rodrigo. "*Políticas de al en(x)carnación: Elementos para una genealogía teológica de la biopolítica*." PhD diss., Universidad de Chile, 2010.

Kay, Ronald. *Del espacio de acá. Señales para una mirada americana*. Santiago de Chile: Ediciones Metales Pesados, 2005.

Klein, Naomi. *The Shock Doctrine: The Rise of Disaster Capitalism*. New York: Picador, 2007.

Kuhn, Thomas. *The Structure of Scientific Revolutions*. 3rd ed. Chicago: University of Chicago Press, 1996.

Las Casas, Bartolomé de. *History of the Indies*. Translated by Andrée Collard. New York: Harper and Row, 1971.

Leibniz, Gottfried Wilhelm. *Monadology: A New Translation and Guide*. Translated and edited by Lloyd Strickland. Edinburgh: Edinburgh University Press, 2015.

Lévi-Strauss, Claude. *The Raw and the Cooked: Mythologiques, vol. 1*. Translated by Doreen Weightman and John Weightman. Chicago: University of Chicago Press, 1983.

Lewes, George Henry. *The Life of Goethe*. 2nd ed. London: Smith Edler, 1864.

Lyotard, Jean-François. *The Postmodern Condition: A Report on Knowledge*. Minneapolis: University of Minnesota Press, 1984.

———. *Why Philosophize?* Translated by Corinne Enaudeau. New York: Polity Press, 2013.

Mackey, William F. "Mother Tongues, Other Tongues, and Link Languages: What They Mean in a Changing World." *Prospects* 22, no. 1 (1992): 41–52.

Marchant, Patricio. *Escritura y temblor*. Edited by Pablo Oyarzún and Willy Thayer. Santiago: Cuarto Propio, 2000.

———. *Sobre árboles y madres*. Buenos Aires: La Cebra, 2009.

Marx, Karl. *Capital: A Critique of Political Economy*. Vol. 1. Edited by Ernst Mandel. Translated by Ben Fowkes. New York: Penguin, 1976.

———. *A Contribution to a Critique of Political Economy*. Translated by N. I. Stone. Chicago: Charles H. Kerr, 1904.

Marx, Karl, and Frederick Engels. *Manifesto of the Communist Party*. In *Marx and Engels Collected Works*, vol. 6. London: Lawrence and Wishart, 2010.

Mayz Vallenilla, Ernesto. *El ocaso de las universidades*. Caracas: Monte Ávila, 1991.

McLuhan, Marshall. *Understanding Media: The Extensions of Man*. Berkeley, CA: Gingko Press, 2013.

McLuhan, Marshall, and Quintin Fiore. *The Medium Is the Massage*. Edited by Jerome Agel. New York: Penguin, 1967.

Menard, André. "Universidad y brujería (entre las salamancas y la crisis (no) moderna . . .)." In *La universidad (im)posible*, edited by Willy Thayer, Elizabeth Collingwood-Selby, Mary Luz Estupiñán Serrano, and raúl rodríguez freire, 72–83. Santiago: Ediciones Macul, 2018.

Nietzsche, Friedrich. *Anti-Education: On the Future of Our Educational Institutions*. Translated by Damion Searles. Edited by Paul Reitter and Chad Wellmon. New York: New York Review of Books, 2016.

———. *The Birth of Tragedy*. In *The Birth of Tragedy and Other Writings*, translated by Ronald Speirs, edited by Ronald Speirs and Raymond Geuss, 1–116. Cambridge: Cambridge University Press, 1999.

———. *The Gay Science*. Translated by Josefine Nauckhoff and Adrian del Caro. Edited by Bernard Williams. Cambridge: Cambridge University Press, 2001.

———. *Human, All Too Human: A Book for Free Spirits*. Translated by R. J. Hollingdale. Edited by Richard Schacht. New York: Cambridge University Press, 1996.

————. *On the Genealogy of Morality*. Translated by Carol Diethe. Edited by Keith Ansell-Pearson. Cambridge: Cambridge University Press, 1997.

————. "On Truth and Lying in a Non-Moral Sense." In *The Birth of Tragedy and Other Writings*, translated by Ronald Speirs, edited by Ronald Speirs and Raymond Geuss, 139–53. Cambridge: Cambridge University Press, 1999.

————. *Philosophy in the Tragic Age of the Greeks*. Translated by Marianne Cowan. Washington, DC: Regnery, 1962.

————. *Thus Spoke Zarathustra*. Translated by Adrian del Caro. Edited by Robert Pippin. Cambridge: Cambridge University Press, 2006.

————. *Twilight of the Idols*. In *The Anti-Christ, Ecce Homo, Twilight of the Idols, and Other Writings*, translated by Judith Norman, edited by Aaron Ridley and Judith Norman, 153–230. Cambridge: Cambridge University Press, 2005.

————. *Unpublished Fragments from the Period of Thus Spoke Zarathustra (Summer 1882–Winter 1885/84)*, translated by Paul S. Loeb and David F. Tinsley. In *The Complete Works of Friedrich Nietzsche*, vol. 14, edited by Alan D. Schrift and Duncan Large. Stanford, CA: Stanford University Press, 2019.

————. *Unpublished Fragments (Spring 1885–Spring 1886)*, translated by Adrian del Caro. In *The Complete Works of Friedrich Nietzsche*, vol. 16, edited by Alan D. Schrift and Duncan Large. Stanford, CA: Stanford University Press, 2020.

Nietzsche, Friedrich, and Carole Blair, "Nietzsche's 'Lecture Notes on Rhetoric': A Translation." *Philosophy and Rhetoric* 16, no. 2 (1983): 94–129.

Nora, Simon, and Alan Minc. *The Computerization of Society: A Report to the President of France*. Cambridge, MA: MIT Press, 1981.

Oyarzún, Pablo. "Universidad y creatividad." *Anales de la Universidad de Chile*, series 6, no.1 (1995): 141–63.

Oyarzún, Pablo, and Adriana Valdés. "Fragmentos de una conversación acerca de la universidad." *Revista Lo* 1 (November 1992).

Parsons, Talcott, and Gerald M. Platt. "Considerations on the American Academic System." *Minerva* 6, no. 4 (Summer 1968): 497–523.

Peset, Mariano. *Obra dispersa: La universidad de México*. Mexico City: Universidad Autónoma Metropolitana, 2001.

Philosophies de l'université: L'idéalisme allemand et la question de l'université. Textes de Schelling, Fichte, Schleiermacher, Humboldt, Hegel. Translated by Gérard Coffin, Jean-François Courtine, and Luc Ferry. Edited by Luc Ferry, Jean-Paul Pesron, and Alain Renaut. Paris: Payot, 1979.

Plato. *Republic*. Translated by G. M. A. Grube and C. D. C. Reeve. In *Plato: Complete Works*, edited by John M. Cooper and D. S. Hutchinson, 971–1224. Indianapolis: Hackett, 1997.

Porto-Bompiani, González. *Diccionario literario de obras y personas de todos los tiempos y países*. Barcelona: Montaner y Simón, 1967.

Rama, Ángel. *The Lettered City*. Translated by John Charles Chasteen. Durham, NC: Duke University Press, 1984.

Ramos, Julio. *Divergent Modernities: Culture and Politics in Nineteenth-Century Latin America*. Translated by John D. Blanco. Durham, NC: Duke University Press, 2001.

Rashdall, Hastings. *Universities of Europe in the Middle Ages*. New York: Oxford University Press, 1987.

Richard, Nelly. "Saberes clasificados y desórdenes culturales." In *La invención y la herencia*, 26–34. Santiago: LOM-ARCIS, 1995.

Ringer, Fritz K. *The Decline of the German Mandarins: The German Academic Community, 1890–1933*. Cambridge, MA: Harvard University Press, 1969.

rodríguez freire, raúl. *La condición intelectual: Informe para una academia*. Santiago: Mimesis Ediciones, 2018.

Rojas, Sergio. *Fin del texto: Historia, poder y reserva*. Santiago: ARCIS, 1991.

Rüegg, Walter. *A History of the University in Europe*. Vol. 2. Cambridge: Cambridge University Press, 1996.

———. *A History of the University in Europe*. Vol. 3. Cambridge: Cambridge University Press, 2004.

Schleiermacher, Friedrich Daniel Ernst. "Gelegentliche Gedanken über Universitäten im deutschem Sinn: Nebst einem Anhang über eine neu zu errichtende (1808)." In *Gründungstexte. Johann Gottlieb Fichte, Friedrich Daniel Ernst Schleiermacher, Wilhelm von Humboldt*, edited by Rüdiger vonm Bruch and Engelbert Habekost, 123–228. Berlin: Humboldt-Universität zu Berlin, 2010.

———. *Occasional Thoughts on Universities in a German Sense: With an Appendix regarding a University Soon to Be Established*. Translated by Terrence N. Nice and Edwina Lawler. San Francisco: Mellen Research University Press, 1991.

Schopenhauer, Arthur. *On Philosophy at the Universities/*. In *Parerga and Paralipomena: Short Philosophical Essays*, vol. 1, translated by E. F. J. Payne. Oxford: Clarendon Press, 1974.

Seneca. *Selected Philosophical Letters*. Edited and translated by Brad Inwood. New York: Oxford University Press, 2007.

Serrano, Sol. *Universidad y nación*. Santiago: Editoriales Universitarias, 1994.

Shelley, Mary. *Frankenstein*. New York: Open Road Integrated Media, 2006. ProQuest.

Spinoza, Benedictus de. *Ethics*. Translated by George Eliot. Edited by Clare Carlisle. Princeton, NJ: Princeton University Press, 2019.

Thayer, Willy. *La crisis no moderna de la universidad moderna: Epílogo al conflicto de la facultades*. Santiago: Cuarto Propio, 1996.

———. "Revolt/Performance: The Performative Pause." *South Atlantic Quarterly* 122, no. 4 (2023): 849–854.

———. "Seminario: Nuevo orden económico y desarrollo: Desafíos éticos para el siglo XXI." Santiago: Ministerio de Educación y Democracia Cristiana, 1995.

Thayer, Willy, Elizabeth Collingwood-Selby, Mary Luz Estupiñán Serrano, and raúl rodríguez freire, eds. *La universidad (im)posible*. Santiago: Ediciones Macul, 2018.

Vargas, Paola. "Educación superior intercultural en disputa." *Polis* 38 (2014). http://journals.openedition.org/polis/10136.

Vattimo, Gianni. *The Transparent Society*. Translated by David Webb. Baltimore, MD: Johns Hopkins University Press, 1990.

Zapater, Horacio. *La búsqueda de la paz en la Guerra de Arauco: Padre Luis de Valdivia*. Santiago: Editorial Andrés Bello, 1992.

Zavala, Silvio Arturo. *Las instituciones jurídicas en la conquista de América*. Mexico City: Editorial Porrúa, 1988.

CREDITS

Excerpt from Thomas Hobbes, *Leviathan*, ed. J. C. A. Gaskin (New York: Oxford University Press, 1998). Used by permission.

Excerpt from Peggy Kamuf, "Sobre no tener idea," in *La universidad (im)posible*, edited by Willy Thayer, Elizabeth Collingwood-Selby, Mary Luz Estupiñán Serrano, and raúl rodríguez freire (Santiago: Ediciones Macul, 2018). Used by permission.

Excerpt from Patricio Marchant, "Sobre la creación de un centro de estudios de todas las formas de escritura que escapan al discurso Universitario," 1983. Used by permission.

Excerpt from Patricio Marchant, "Sobre la necesidad de fundar un departamento de filosofía en (la Universidad de) Chile," in *Escritura y temblor*, edited by Pablo Oyarzún and Willy Thayer (Santiago: Editorial Cuarto Propio, 2000). Used by permission.

Excerpt from André Menard. "Universidad y brujería (entre las salamancas y la crisis (no) moderna . . .)," in *La universidad (im)posible*, edited by Willy Thayer, Elizabeth Collingwood-Selby, Mary Luz Estupiñán Serrano, and raúl rodríguez freire (Santiago: Ediciones Macul, 2018). Used by permission.

Excerpt from Friedrich Nietzsche, *The Gay Science*, translated by Josefine Nauckhoff and Adrian del Caro, edited by Bernard Williams (Cambridge: Cambridge University Press, 2001), and "Twilight of the Idols," in *The Anti-Christ, Ecce Homo, Twilight of the Idols, and Other Writings*, translated by Judith Norman, edited by Aaron Ridley and Judith Norman (Cambridge: Cambridge University Press, 2005). Used by permission.

Excerpt from Arthur Schopenhauer, *On Philosophy at the Universities, in Parerga and Paralipomena: Short Philosophical Essays*, vol. 1, trans. E. F. J. Payne (Oxford: Clarendon Press, 1974). Used by permission.

Excerpt from Willy Thayer, Elizabeth Collingwood-Selby, Mary Luz Estupiñán Serrano, and raúl rodríguez freire, eds., *La universidad (im)posible* (Santiago: Ediciones Macul, 2018). Used by permission.

INDEX

action/meaning difference, end of, 110–12
actuality (*actualidad*), 39, 40, 41, 87, 93
affect, 33–34, 93–95
Alianza por Chile, 127
Allende, Salvádor, xi
alterity, 100. *See also* difference
Althusser, Louis, 25, 74, 139
Amorós, Celia, 137
Anales de la Universidad de Chile, 115
anarchy, 96
animation, 30–31
anthropological finitude, critique of, 61
anthropology, 140
architectonics, 83–86
Aristotle, 21–22, 50, 51–52, 58, 155n5
arts, 80, 96
assessment, enlightened university style of, 91–92
assimilationism, 14
assumed, the: structure of, 95–97
autonomy, 62–64, 74, 85–86, 86, 87, 96, 118, 155n5

Babel, myth of, 51, 52, 58
Bachelet, Michele, 112, 169n14
barbarism, subordination of, 56–57
Barbarossa, Frederick, 57–58
Barthes, Roland, xiii
Battle of Aspern, 77
Beethoven, Ludwig von, 30
Bello, Andrés, 50, 117
Benjamin, Walter, xii, 30
Beyer, Harald, 130
Beyme, K. F., 77–78
Bible, translation of, 156n12
Boggs, Abbie, xiii
Borges, Jorge Luis, 23
Boric, Gabriel, x
Bousquet, Marc, xiii
Brunner, José Joaquín, 107, 127, 132–33

Bruno, Giordano, 10
Burckhardt, Jacob, 93
bureaucracy, 38

campus, as metropolis, 29
canon, 43, 85; canon formation, 14–15, 16, 43; performative impact of, 53; univocity of, 56
Canudo, Ricciotto, 30
capitalism, ix–xii, xiv, 29, 31, 49, 107–10, 112–13, 120, 129,130, 135; accumulation, xiv, xv, 8, 13, 21, 49, 126; globalization and, 25–26
Cartesianism, 50, 61–75, 78, 80, 164n34
Castille, 58
Castillo, Alejandra, xii
censorship, 24, 28–31, 83, 153n15
Chicago School, ix, 124, 125–26, 169n13
Chile: 1980 constitution of, x, 167n27; 1989 amendment to constitution, 124; 2011 student uprising in, 134; 2019 insurrection, xi; Basic Law on Universities, 112; Brunner-Frei reforms, 112; censorship in, 24; climate change in, 129; Concertación governments in, 126–27, 169n4; constitution of, 141n12; coup in, x, 124, 141n9; democratic history of, 128; dictatorship in, 109–10, 112, 126–27, 167n1, 168n1; education in, ix, 8, 112, 124, 168n2, 169n4, 169n14 (*see also* Chilean universities); freedom of teaching in, 124, 167n27; General Law of Universities, 124; Guaranteed Student Loan (Crédito con Aval de Estado), 112; insurrection of 2019, viii, x; investigative journalism in, 168n1; marketized pension system in, ix–x; megaprojects in, x; Ministry of Education in,

Chile (*continued*)
134–35; neoliberal accreditation
system in, 130–31; neoliberal
university interface of, 129–31;
postdictatorship, viii–ix, 109–10,
141n9; predictatorship democracy
in, 113; right to education in, 124;
as social laboratory of neoliberalism,
ix, xiii; student movements in, ix–x,
169n5, 169n13, 169n14; theory in,
xii; transition from dictatorship to
Concertación, 126–27; transition
from state to market, 105–14, 167n1;
Transition in, 113–14, 131–32,
141n9; transition to democracy, viii,
x, 109–10, 112, 141n9, 165n2
Chilean universities, 123–35;
accommodation of dictatorship's
university design to democracy,
126–27, 169n4; financialization of,
8; neoliberalism and, 124, 128–31;
privatization of, 124. *See also specific
universities*
"Chile Project," 125–26
Chinese Encyclopedia, 23
Christianity, 57–58
city, ruin of, 64–66
civil service, 75
cogito, 72–73
Collingwood-Selby, Elizabeth, xii
Collodi, Carlo, 30–31
colonialism, 49, 56–57, 58
colonization, xv, 18, 19, 58, 110. *See
also* imperialism
Commission for the Study of Higher
Education, 127
Committee of Expert Consultants, 127
communicability, 51
communications, 24–25, 26
communion, 51
"community of thinking," 111
Comte, Auguste, 7, 13, 49, 75
Concertación, 126–27
context, as university, 3–4
Copernican revolution, viii
Copernicus, Nicolaus, 11
cosmopolitanism, 25, 108
Council of Trent, 156n12
Council of Vienne, 57
creative intelligence, 159n9

crisis, viii; category of, 107; non-
modern, 21; performance of, viii
critical philosophy, 39
critical university studies, xii–xiii
critique, viii, 39, 40, 66, 84, 118, 129;
critical performance, 39–41, 44;
language of, 38–39
curriculum, 95, 98

Darío, Rubén, 50
Dasein, xiv
death, 28, 95
Debord, Guy, 23
decolonial university project, 147n35
deindustrialization, ix
Deleuze, Gilles, xii, 107
democracy, viii, x, 108–10, 112, 113,
120, 128, 141n9, 165n2
Derrida, Jacques, xii, 111–12, 139, 140,
166n21
Descartes, René, viii, 10, 11, 13, 19,
50, 61–75, 78, 79; *Correspondence*,
66; *The Discourse on Method*, 64,
67, 69, 164n34; "First Meditation,"
62–63, 64, 66, 68–73, 74; "Letter
to Picot," 65; *mathesis universalis*,
xiii; *Meditations on First Philosophy*,
62–63, 64, 66, 68–74; *Objections
and Replies*, 71; *The Principles
of Philosophy*, 64; razing of old
university and, 63–64, 68; replacing
old with new, 63–64, 65, 68; *Rules
for the Direction of the Mind*, 67;
"Second Meditation," 71, 72–73. *See
also* Cartesianism
D'Estaing, Valéry Giscard, 107
dialects, 62, 156n12
Díaz, Luis Eugenio, 130
Díaz Cuevas, Gonzalo, xi
dictatorship, 109–10, 112, 126–28,
167n1, 168n1
difference, 99, 101, 110–11
digital images, 30, 31
discipline(s), 95; collapse of disciplinary
organization, 19–21; gathering of, 10
discourse, 119; crisis of, 36; educational,
134–35
disempowerment, 36–37
dissent, 88
diversion, 101

diversity, 13, 17, 23
doctrine, 15, 84–85, 86, 88
dogmatism, 16
doubt, 66, 67, 68; as condition of
    modern university, 62; "hyperbolic,"
    119; "methodical," 65, 69–70, 74;
    performance of, 72

economic justice, 107
écriture, xiii
education, 101–2, 119, 120, 129; in
    Chile, 112; educational discourse,
    134–35; educational modernization,
    117–18; funding for, 112; "higher,"
    96 (*see also* university/universities);
    "implantation model," 27;
    professional, 26–27; right to, 124;
    scientific, 26–27
efficiency, 102
electric mediation, university and, 23–24
El Mercurio, 124
emancipation, 33–35, 119
enclosure, professional, 81
Enlightenment, 7, 23, 75, 87, 92, 95,
    121; constriction or restraint of, 96;
    expansion and, 96, 98; language(s)
    and, 101; Nietzsche and, 92–101;
    rejection of, 92; specialization and,
    96, 98; state as Enlightenment subject,
    97–101; two drives from, 96, 98
Epicureanism, 9
erasing (*effacer*), 62, 68
eternal return, 101
ethics, 99
Eurocentrism, 49
exclusion, 7, 137–38
experience, 28–29, 94, 105–6, 113
extraction, 129–30

facticity (*facticidad*), xiv, 17, 40, 99,
    108, 109, 121, 148n43
faculties: conflict of, 40–41, 43, 49,
    83–88, 110–11, 128–29, 139–40,
    145n11; faculty of genealogy, 89–
    102; faculty of philosophy, 15–17,
    39–41, 43–53, 80, 86–87, 89–102,
    140, 148n37; higher, 83, 85–88, 110–
    11, 145n11, 148n37; lower, 16–17,
    41, 66, 80, 88, 110–11, 128, 139,
    145n11, 148

feminism, x, 27, 135, 137–38, 140
Ferguson, Roderick, xiii
Feyerabend, Paul, 26–27
Fichte, Johann Gottlieb, 36, 77, 78, 79,
    159n9
film, 30–31
finance, 110–14
finance capital, x, 8, 49, 109, 110–13,
    124, 126, 130
financial accumulation, 8, 20, 21, 169,
financialization, ix, x, 8, 35, 49, 109,
    110–11, 126, 142, 152n5
forgetting, 90–91
Foucault, Michel, 27, 107, 113, 153n1,
    154n1
fragmentation, 19
François I, 62
Franz II, 77
freedom, crisis of, 49
Frei Ruiz-Tagle, Eduardo, 127
French, 61–62, 164n34
Freud, Sigmund, 15, 39
Friedman, Milton, ix, 125, 126
Friedrich Wilhelm II of Prussia, 83,
    153n15
Friedrich Wilhelm III of Prussia,
    77–78
Fukuyama, Francis, 108, 120

Galeano, Eduardo, 126
Galen, viii
Galende, Federico, xii, 137
Galileo, 10, 11
Gance, Abel, 30
gathering, 98, 99; faculty of philosophy
    as principle of, 15–17, 39–41;
    university as gathering of the strange,
    11–15, 39–41
genders, 139
genealogy, 9, 90–91, 96, 98–99, 101–
    2; faculty of, 89–102; genealogical
    critique, 101; geniality of, 99; of idea
    of the university, ix; reflection and,
    101–2
general interest, local interests dissolved
    into, 98
General Law of Universities, 124
German idealism, philosophical
    university of, 78–79
German universities, 77–81, 131

Germany: idea of university in, 74 (*see also* German universities); "spiritual resistance" to Napoleonic politics, 49–50
globalization, 24–26
Global South, theory from, xii
Goethe, Johann Wolfgang von, 77
good, the: as category that gathers, 8–9
government, 84–86, 85
Grande, Sandy, xiii
Grau, Olga, xii
Gregory XI, Pope, 57
Guattari, Félix, 25, 120

Habermas, Jürgen, 96
happiness, 131
Harney, Stefano, xiii
Hayek, Friedrich von, ix
health, 129
Hegel, Georg Wilhelm Friedrich, 13, 49, 78, 92
Heidegger, Martin, xii, xiv, 84, 139, 140, 144n4, 148n43
heterogeneity, 13, 56, 57, 94
heteronomy, 63–64, 74
hierarchies, 80–81
higher education, ix, x, 97, 112, 168n2, 169n4, 169n14. *See also* university/ universities
higher faculties, 83, 85–88, 110–11, 145n11, 148n37
history, 37; end of, 110; faculty of philosophy and, 41; philosophy of, 33–35
Hobbes, Thomas, 55
Homer, 101
homogenization, 29–30
humanism, 140
humanities, 140
Humboldt, Wilhelm von, 7, 13, 23, 27, 50, 78, 79, 160n10
Hume, David, 33
Husserl, Edmund, 17

idea, ontology of the, 52
identity, vs. alterity, 101
identity formations, deconstruction of, xii
ideology/ideologies, 49, 108–9, 119, 120

imperialism, ix, 31, 34, 49, 50, 99
implant, prospective fiction of, 26–27
"implantation model," 27
inactuality (*inactualidad*), vii–viii, 40
inclusion, 14
incompossible, the, 12, 13, 107, 166n6
indifference, 62–63
Indigenous cultures, 147n35, 155n2
Indigenous knowledge, 50
Indigenous languages, 57, 155n2
Indigenous peoples, x, 30
Indigenous universities, 147n35
informatics, 21–23, 28–31
information, 7, 14, 37–38
informationalization of society, 23, 29
Innocent III, Pope, 57
international colloquium "The Possible University" [La universidad posible], 18–19
interpretation, enlightened university style of, 91–92
interstate competition, 99–100

Jerome, Saint, 156n12
Jesuits, 155n2
John XXI, Pope, 57
journalism, 98, 168n1
judgment, 13, 15, 40, 61, 71, 86, 86–88, 102, 105, 135
Juli Mission at Lake Titicaca, 155n2

Kafka, Franz, 48
Kamuf, Peggy, 124–26
Kant, Immanuel, viii, 7, 12, 33, 39–41, 43, 44, 78, 80, 83–86, 101, 105, 119, 153n15; *The Conflict of the Faculties*, 36, 49–50, 139; division of labor between "higher" and "lower" faculties, 110–11, 145n11, 148n37; faculty of philosophy as principle of gathering and, 15–17; Kantian university, ix, 50, 101, 102; *Religion within the Limits of Mere Reason*, 153n15; as university professor, 83
Karmy, Rodrigo, xii
Keynesian economics, 125
kitsch, 34, 44
Klein, Naomi, 125–26
knowledge(s), 6–7, 79, 107, 120, 135, 145n11, 148n37; autonomy of, 87;

canonical, 129; centralization of, 7; commercialization of, 7–8; conditions of, 15–16; in-corporating "other," 96; critique of, 87–88; as disparate, 17; displaced by research, 15–16; exclusion of, 137–38; gathering of, 43; "higher," 44; Indigenous, 50; instituted, 43; instrumental application of, 78; of knowledge, 13, 17, 43, 44, 80; metaknowledges, 17; of nonknowledge, 17, 80; nonuniversity, 14; philosophy of, 27; production and reproduction of, 129; relationship between providers and users, 7; segmentation of, 19; specialization of, 19–20; speculative vs. applied, 66, 78; subjectivity and, 67–68; technical division of, 43; theory of, 67; totality of, 12–13; unity of, 17; use value of, 8; "zero degree" of, 63

Kraniauskas, John, xv

labor, division of, 6, 110–11
Lacan, Jacques, 19
Lacoue-Labarthe, Philippe, 166n21
Lagos, Ricardo, 112
Lalande, André, 21
language(s), 58, 93–94, 154n12; academic, 94; dialects, 62, 156n12; dissemination of, 51; Enlightenment and, 101; materiality of, xv; *mathesis universalis*, xiii, 62, 73, 164n34; mother tongue, 93–94; national, 75; other, 95; philosophy and, 43; regional, 62, 75, 156n12; "savage," 56–57; truth and, 51–52; unfamiliar, 95. *See also specific languages*
Larra, Mariano José de, 50
Las Casas, Bartolomé de, 50, 57
Latin, 61–62, 69, 105
Latin American philosophy, x–xi
Latin American Spanish, 50
Lavoisier, Antoine, 11
law, 86, 102; autonomy of, 88; faculty of philosophy, 56
leadership, 75
learning, 159n9
Left, the, 83, 88

Leibniz, Gottfried Wilhelm, 12, 13, 58, 107, 108, 155n5, 166n6
Letelier, Orlando, 50, 126
liberalism, telematic, 22–23
Llull, Ramon, 57
lower faculties, 16–17, 41, 66, 80, 88, 110–11, 128, 139, 145n11, 148
Lyotard, Jean-François, vii, 24, 28, 107, 118

Mapuche, x
Marchant, Patricio, 2, 77
market, 50; financialization of, ix, x, 35, 109, 126, 152n5; market fundamentalism, x
Martí, José, 50
Marx, Karl, xii, 13, 19, 25–26, 50, 110–11
maternal rootedness, 96
mathesis universalis, xiii, 62, 73, 164n34
mayo feminista, 135, 138
meaning: secularization of, 44; "zero degree" of, 68–73
media, 30–31
medicine, 56
medieval university, 10, 23, 41, 50, 55–59; autonomy and heteronomy in, 58–59; empirical impact of, 57–58; four faculties of, 19; governance of, 155n5; as pedagogical apparatus, 56
Melamed, Jodi, xiii
memory, 102
Menard, André, 147n35
mestizaje, 58
metanarrative, progressive, 74–75
metaphysics, 39, 68
metauniversity, 13
metonymy, 138–39
Meyerhoff, Eli, xiii
Minc, Alain, 107
modernism, 129, 135
modernity, 6–7, 13, 19, 61, 118–20; capitalist, ix; crisis of, 119; Enlightenment, 94; erasing (*effacer*) and, 62; experience and, 105–6; negation of, xv; Transition and, 116–18; transition and, 105–7
modernization, 14, 116–18, 129, 135, 167n1
modern politics, collapse of, 48–49

modern university, 41, 50, 61–75, 135;
    architectonics of, 49–50; categorical
    institution of, 128–29; conflict of
    the faculties and, 128–29; crisis of,
    48–50; dislodge from "subject" to
    "object" position, 36–37; doubt
    as condition of, 62; faculties of,
    19; Franco-Cartesian-Napoleonic-
    Comtean, 61–76; German, 78;
    non-modern crisis and, 135;
    "transcendental architectonics" of,
    36; transition and collapse of, 110;
    untimeliness of, vii–xi
monad, 58, 155n5
Mönckeberg, María Olivia, 124, 126–27
monetarist policy, ix
monstrosities, 10–11, 14–15
Moten, Fred, xiii
mother tongue, 93–94
Moulián, Tomás, viii

Napoleon Bonaparte, 7, 50, 77, 78
Napoleonic politics, 49–50
Napoleonic state-technical university,
    13
National Accreditation Commission
    (Comisión Nacional de Acreditación;
    CNA), 130
national identity, professionalization
    and, 99–100
nationalism, 78
national university, collapse of, 49
nature, 88
Nazism, 13, 14
Nebrija, Antonio de, 58
neoclassical economic theory, ix
neoliberalism, ix, x, xiii, 8, 13, 108–9;
    Chilean universities and, 124, 128–31,
    147n35; degradation of the right to
    the university, 21; global hegemony
    of, ix; neoliberal universities, 129,
    147n35
neurology, 15
Newfield, Chris, xiii
Nietzsche, Friedrich, xii, 9, 12, 13, 19,
    50, 61, 89–102, 105, 130; addressees
    of his lectures, 92–93; Anti-
    Education: On the Future of Our
    Educational Institutions, 80, 90–102,
    131; on destruction or mutation of

    the university, 91; Enlightenment and,
    93, 94, 95, 96–101; Gay Science, 61,
    89; genealogy and reflection, 101–2;
    Genealogy of Morals, 99; Nietzschean
    university, ix, 96, 101; opposition
    to modern statist university, 102;
    rejection of Enlightenment by, 92;
    style and, 91–92; Twilight of the
    Idols, 89
Noble, David F., xiii
nonknowledge, knowledges of, 80
non-modern crisis, xv, 120, 135
non-modern university, 37; big bang of,
    17; entrepreneurial, 49
nonuniversity, 98
Nora, Simon, 107

Occidentalism, 140
orality, 53
oral pedagogy, Aristotelian "fable" of,
    23
organic structure, concept of, 21–22
organized labor, class war against, ix
origins, 101, 102; forgetting of, 90–91.
    See also genealogy
orthótes (correct orientation of the
    gaze), 56, 154n1
Oyarzún, Pablo, xii, xiv, 137

painting, 30, 31
papacy, 59
Parsons, Talcott, 35
particular, the, 53
pastoral, the, 55–56, 154n1
Paul III, Pope, 156n12
Peace of Tilsit, 77
Peña, Carlos, 132–33
Pérez, Francisca, xii
periodization, 141n9
philology, 101
philosopher-king, idea of, 53
philosophical universality, 49
philosophy, 78; aesthetics of
    philosophical discourse, xiii; crisis
    of, 36, 49; disciplinary constitution
    of, 43; disciplines of, 43; faculty of,
    15–17, 16–17, 39–41, 41, 43–53,
    80, 86–87, 89–102, 101, 102, 140,
    148n37; as habitat of the universal,
    49; of history, 33–35; history of, 43;

of knowledge, 27; language(s) and, 43; practice of, 44; professionalized, 44; teaching of, 44–45; "useful" vs. speculative, 65; writing and, 43
photography, 30
Piñera, José, 169n13
Piñera, Sebastián, 112, 168n2, 169n13
Pinochet, Augusto, x, 112, 126, 127, 169n3, 169n13; 1988 plebiscite, 165n2; consolidation of Chilean education under, 168n2; Constitution of, 169n3; dictatorship of, viii, ix, 124, 126; higher education reforms enacted by, ix; Presidential Directives on Education, 112, 124
Pixar, 30–31
Plato, 8, 15, 44, 50, 51, 53; cave allegory, 28, 55; *The Republic*, 51; *Seventh Letter*, 51
Platonism, 28, 51–52, 55–56, 154n1
Platt, Gerald M., 35
plurality, 23
poetry, 12, 96
polis, the, 51
political economy, deregulation of, 112–13
politics, 49–50, 107, 119, 120
Pontifical Catholic University (PUC), 126
positivism, 44, 78
postmodern, the, vii, xv
postponement, 101, 102
poststructuralism, xii, xiii
power, 85–88, 86, 95, 107, 120, 129, 148n37
Presidential Directive on Education (Directiva Presidencial sobre Educación; DPSE), 112, 124
production, 31
professionalism, 35, 44, 78, 79, 81, 96, 159n9
professionalization, 26–27, 94, 95, 96, 97, 98, 99–100
professors, 83–85. *See also* teaching
progress, ideology of, 119; crisis of, 49; universality of, 74; weakening of, 33–34, 35
prophecy, 93
provincial, the: converted into the national, 99

provincialism, abandonment of, 98
Prussia, 77
psychoanalysis, xi, 15, 39

racialization, processes of, xii
ranking, 40
reading, distance and, 94
Readings, Bill, xii–xiii
Reagan, Ronald, ix
reception, 14–15
Reed, Conor Tomás, xiii
reflection, 17, 66, 83, 85–88, 101, 102, 118
reflexivity, 87–88
regionalization, 19
Rembrandt van Rijn, 30
representation, 113, 120
research, 38, 79; applied, 3, 17, 73–74, 110–11; basic, 3, 67, 73–74, 110–11; knowledge displaced by, 15–16; writing and, 12
Richard, Nelly, viii, xii
Right, the, 83, 88
Rivas, Felipe, xii
rodríguez freire, raúl, xii, 114
Roman Empire, Christian, 56
Romanticism, 90, 91

Sabati, Sheeva, xiii
Santa Cruz, Guadalupe, 137–38, 139, 140
Santiago, Chile, underground avant-garde art scene of 1980s, xii
Sarmiento, Domingo Faustino, 50
Schelling, Friedrich Wilhelm Joseph, 36, 78
Schleiermacher, Friedrich, 13, 36, 77–81, 161n24
Schmalz, Theodor Anton Heinrich, 77
scholasticism, 56
Schopenhauer, Arthur, 44–45
Schulz, Theodore, 125–26
science(s), 6–7, 78, 79, 119, 159n9; as extralinguistic, 51; scientific community, 88; scientific education, 26–27; scientific method, 67. *See also* social sciences
screens, 23–24
Seneca, 8
sexualities, 139

Shakespeare, William, 30
Sixtus V, Pope, 156n12
social justice, 107
social mobilization, ix–x
social sciences, xiii, 44, 127, 128
sociology, 33, 37, 109,
Socrates, 28, 52, 95
solitude, 79
Sophocles, 101
Sorbonne, 156n12
sovereignty, 39–40, 43, 108, 113, 126,
    127, 128
Spanish, 50
Spanish American University, 50
speaking universitarily, 38–39
specialists, practice of, 44
specialization, 81, 95, 96
spectacle, 23
speculative principle, corrosion of,
    34–35
Stalinism, 13
state, the, 78, 80, 88, 113; collapse of,
    49; as an effect of philosophy, 78; as
    Enlightenment subject, 97–101; as
    instigator of transcendental ideals,
    97; mediation of, 96; modern, 109;
    state apparatus, 74–75; the university
    and, 79, 84–85, 90, 97–101; truth
    and, 79
State Guaranteed Education Loan
    (Crédito con Aval del Estado; CAE),
    169n5
state technical universities, 74
statist universities, Nietzsche's
    opposition to, 102
strange, the: university as gathering of,
    11–15
structural adjustment programs, ix
student debt, ix
student movements, ix–x, x
studium generale, 57
style, 91–92; Nietzsche and, 91–92;
    Thayer's emphasis on, xiii–xiv
subalterns, 137–38, 140, 147n35
subjection, university as source of, 5–6
subjectivity: knowledge and, 67–68;
    liberation of, 65; ruin of city in, 64–
    66; standardization of, 112
substance, 52, 58
systematization, 19

teaching, 84–85, 101–2, 159n9;
    freedom of, 124; restriction of, 24;
    standardization of, 85
technical professional labor, 38
technology, 7, 30–31, 88. See also
    telematics; specific technologies
telematics, 21–23, 28–30, 49, 50, 113;
    ascendance of, 24; telematic liberal
    pluralism, 23
teleology, 99, 155n5
television, 23
temporality, 93–95
terminology, xiv–xv
Thales, 52
Thatcher, Margaret, ix
Thayer, Willy, x, xii–xiii, 138, 139;
    citational practice of, x–xi; emphasis
    on style, xiii–xiv; Technologies of
    Critique, xv; writings of, xi–xii
theology, 56, 99
theory: in Chile, xii; death of, xii;
    geopolitics of theory production, xii;
    of knowledge, 67
thought: autonomy of, 118; internal
    forum of, 118
thrownness, xiv
Todorov, Tzvetan, 144n2
totalitarianism, 5, 22–23, 98
totality, metanarrative of, 10
transcendentia, 55–60, 56, 57, 74
transculturation, xiv
transhumance, 52
transitio, 105
Transition, 106–7, 109–10, 112–14, 116,
    128, 131–32, 142n18, 165n2, 167n1;
    in Chile, 113–14, 131–32, 141n9;
    corollary to, 112–14; modernity and,
    116–18; modernization and, 116–18;
    paradox at work in, 128; from state
    to market, 105–14; University of Chile
    and, 116–18
transition(s), 117, 119, 165n2;
    Cartesian, 61–62; to democracy, 109–
    10, 112, 141n9, 165n2, 167n1; from
    dictatorship to Concertación, 126–27,
    128–29; following calamities, 109;
    from Latin university and universality
    to modern national university and
    universality, 61–62; modernity and,
    61–62, 105–7; as modernization,

167n1; as mutation in the mode of meaning making, 113; neoliberal transition of Chilean university brought on by 1973 coup, 124; from the old to the new, 61; of paradigms effected by the dictatorship, 132; Pinochetista, 126–27; postfascist, 109; postwar, 109; from state to market, 105–14. *See also* Transition
"transitology," 109–10
translation, xiv–xv, 50, 156n12
transparency, 36–37, 51
transportation, 24–25
truth, 72–73, 78, 88, 97, 98, 99, 113, 135; as extralinguistic/as supralinguistic, 51–52; ground of, 53; idea of, 51; spirit and, 78; the state and, 79; technical domestication by disciplinary specializations, 87

unfamiliarity, 95
unhappiness, 131
unity, metanarrative of, 10
universal, the, 53, 89–90; access to, 52; translinguistical, 55
universalism, professional, 94
universality, 14, 51; Christian, 57; crisis of, 49–50; French, 78; genealogical dissolution of, 50; genealogy of, 98; manufacture of, 89–90; metaphysical, 64; metaphysical conception of, 50; philosophical, 49; as planetary movement of capital, 50; of *transcendentia*, 56; university and, 4–5, 55–56, 57–58, 98–99
universe, as clock, 65, 66
Universidad del Mar, 130
Universidad Metropolitana de Ciencias de la Educación (Metropolitan University for Educational Sciences; UMCE), 124
universitas, 9–10, 13, 56, 64, 65, 66, 74
University of Berlin, 36, 49–50, 74, 77–82
University of Bologna, 57–58
University of Chicago, ix, 124, 125–26, 169n13
University of Chile, 121; absence of foundational thinking about, 117–18; call for papers at, 115–18

University of Halle, 77
University of Jena, 77
University of Oxford, 57
University of Paris, 57
University of Salamanca, 57
university regime, universality of, 10
university representation, crisis of, 36
university/universities, 6, 13, 23, 41, 50, 55–59, 78, 96, 101, 135, 161n24; accommodation of dictatorship's university design to democracy, 169n4; architectonics of, 36–37, 49–50, 83–88, 120; autonomy and, 43, 58–59 (*see also* autonomy); as baroque, 13; boundaries of, 19–20; breakup of unity of, 17–19; capitalism and, 129; Cartesian-Napoleonic, ix, 50, 61–75, 101, 102; categorial crisis of, 115–36; categorical crisis of, 115–21; categorical institution of, 128–29; as center, 7–8; Chilean, 8, 123–35 (*see also specific universities*); class, 50; collapse of, 48–50; Comtean, 75; colonial constitution of, 56; as conflict, 11; conflict of the faculties and, 17, 128–29; context as, 3–4; as context, 4–7; creole, 50; crisis of, 17, 48–50; decline of, 7; defense of, 79; destruction of, 91; as disciplinary panopticon, 7; dislodged from "subject" to "object" position, 36–37; displacement of, 23; doubt as condition of, 62; electric mediation and, 23–24; empirical impact of, 57–58; Enlightenment, 23; faculties of, 19, 128–29 (*see also specific faculties*); feminism and, 140; financial facticity of, 40; financialization of, xiii, 8, 49, 110–11, 132; four faculties of, 19; French, 61–75, 78; French Enlightenment idea of, 75; as gathering of the strange, 11–15; genealogy of, ix, 40; German, 77–81, 131; German philosophical thinking on, 78; governance of, 155n5; how to speak nonuniversitarily about, 38–39; humanist-technical, 13–14; idea of, ix, 6, 7–8, 13, 23, 79; as ideological state apparatus, 23; imperialist, 34; Indigenous, 147n35; informatics as,

university/universities (*continued*)
21–23; Kantian-Humboldtian, ix, 50,
101, 102; language of critique and,
38–39; Latin American, 50; medieval,
10–11, 19, 23, 55–60, 155n5 (*see also*
medieval university); medieval vs.
modern, 10–11; metauniversity, 13; as
metropole, 4, 29; missionary character
of, 57; missionary structure of, 55–
60; modern, vii–xi, 10–11, 19, 36–37,
41, 48–50, 61–75, 78, 110, 128–29,
135 (*see also* modern university);
modernization of, 131; neoliberal,
129–30, 147n35; Nietzschean, ix,
96, 101; non-modern, 17, 37, 49;
non-modern crisis and, 135; organic
unity and gathering principle of, 8–11;
as pedagogical apparatus, 56; as
pedagogical mediation between state
and people, 23–24; philosophical,
13–14, 78; philosophical project and,
50–53; positive-humanist, 14; as
principle of spiritual emancipation,
23; professional, 78; as professional
panopticon, 5; profession and, 79; as
progress of an instrumental utopia,
50; in prospective fiction of the
implant, 26–27; razing of old, 63–64;
replacing old with new, 63–64, 65;
secularization of, 41, 50; as source of
subjection, 5–6; Spanish American, 50;
speaking of, 38–39; the state and, 79,
84–85, 90, 97–101, 102; as a subject,
3–4; technical, 17; technological, 49;
telematic transnational, 49; teleological
and theological, 50; temporal
separation from the present, 110;

theory of, 37–38; of the *transcendens*,
55; "transcendental architectonics"
of, 36; transition and collapse of, 110;
transition from medieval to modern,
41; transition from state to market, ix,
105–14; universality and, 4–5, 48–53,
55–56, 57–58, 98–99; university city,
29; university governmentality, 43;
university machine, 56; untimeliness
of, vii–xi
univocity, 51, 55, 56
untimeliness, viii–ix, 95
unworlding, 108
upper faculties. *See* higher faculties

Valderrama, Miguel, xii
Vallenilla, Mayz, 58
verosímil, 144n2
verosimilitud, 12–13, 144n2
Vial Correa, Gonzalo, 168n2
Villalobos-Ruminott, Sergio, xii
Villers-Cotterêts, royal decree of, 62
Voltaire, 166n6

weariness, 33
Williams, Jeffrey, xiii
wireless communications, 26
women, 137–38; excluded from
university contract, 140; women's
rights, x (*see also* feminism)
worker subjectivity, standardization of,
112
writing, 12, 14–15, 39, 40, 43, 52–53,
53, 72–73, 86, 111, 131, 139–40. *See
also écriture*

Yang, K. Wayne (la paperson), xiii